TAPESTRIES

Weaving Life's Journey

Betty K. Staley

Tapestries, copyright © 1997 Hawthorn Press, Stroud
Published by Hawthorn Press, Hawthorn House, 1 Lansdown Lane,
Stroud, Gloucestershire, GL5 1BJ, UK
Tel:(01453) 757040 Fax:(01453) 751138

Cover design by Ivon Oates
Design and typesetting by Lynda Smith and Frances Fineran
Printed in the UK by Redwood Books, Wiltshire

Acknowledgements
Linda Bergh for her kind permission to quote 'To My Papa' from *She
Would draw Flowers.*
Stan Padilla for his kind permission to quote 'Song of the Sky Loom'
from *Chants and Prayers.*
Kay Skonieczny for her kind permission to quote from her late husband's
Mission Statement.

British Library Cataloguing in Publication Data applied for

ISBN 1 869 890 15 9

Lullaby for Benjamin at 3 a.m.

You will not sleep, you will not sleep
Though the world sleeps around you

The clock on the mantel, its two hands
Folded, its tiny gears snoring in ticks

The piano with its one eyelid closed
And beneath it, the songs fading gradually

The lightbulb's filament, resting under the dark
Dome, still trembling from the passage of electricity

The door's hinges hold steel pins in their brass embrace
And the tumblers secure in the locks

The snapdragons doze in the crystal vase
Dreaming of the black labyrinth of soil

The slumbering roots of the potted palm
Clutching earth in their tiny fists

In the pen's cartridge blue ink stirs, then settles
Back to count the furrows it made on the paper's white field

And in my arms your breathing deepens, fanned
By the butterfly wings of your lungs

Soothed by your heart and its dominions of blood
You sleep, you sleep, you sleep.

George S. Kane

Table of Contents

SECTION I: TIME, GROWTH AND HUMAN RELATIONSHIPS

SECTION II: THE PHASES OF ADULT LIFE

I dedicate this book to my grandchildren, Benjamin Stuart Kane, Adam Sutcliffe Kane and Louise Forbes Kane. May they lead full and meaningful lives.

Foreword

Linda Bergh

When Betty Staley first told me about the genesis of *Tapestries,* she spoke of her conversations with women and men in Latvia (formerly part of the USSR): how she felt hearing their personal journeys, and how she was moved to document these life experiences. As she listened to their life stories she realized that they illustrated the seven-year life phases and revealed universal patterns: a human tapestry which went beyond cultural, racial, gender and ethnic boundaries. To see the book that has evolved from the gathering of her stories and perceptions is to witness the emergence of a treasure.

For now we see through a glass darkly, but then face to face.
Corinthians I 13:12

How do we come to see ourselves face to face? How often in our lives do we look through a glass darkly, wishing we could see more clearly?

Betty Staley's *Tapestries* helps us see more clearly by offering us a view into the cycles and patterns of adult life. When I was in graduate school in the mid-sixties, the whole concept of adult development was non-existent. Our studies of child development were based on the assumption that when one became an adult, that was it – adult until death. And so I, and presumably others, approached adulthood and entered 'life' believing everything would remain constant – fixed. We viewed our parents and the entire older generation from this perspective.

I experienced a breath of fresh air in the 1970s when I was introduced to Rudolf Steiner's approach to biography work. It was a powerful tool for 'seeing through the glass'. I recall having many *a-ha's* about my life; I felt a growing empathy and understanding for adults, seeing them as developing, not stagnant, beings with constant challenges, crises of soul, and opportunities for development and new awareness. Shortly thereafter Gail Sheehy's *Passages* brought the concept of adult stages further into mainstream thinking.

Tapestries takes the study of human development one huge step further. Through including us, stage by stage, in the life journeys of twelve individuals from many countries around the world, Betty Staley enhances our understanding of life's phases. What shines through clearly is that underneath the threads of individual uniqueness and even cultural difference, the warp of the loom – the underlying and inherited factors our lives begin from – brings with it a similarity of issues we face in each stage of our adulthood.

So what does this book offer us as readers? Let me first share a bit of my personal story. I am 54 years old. For the last twenty years I have been a teacher, a teacher trainer and a therapist. In November 1996 I was in an accident in which my only child, Kirsten, aged 17, and her close friend were killed instantly. I was seriously injured. In August 1995 my husband had died suddenly. In the last four years, both my parents and my husband's parents passed on. The tapestry of my life has been forever altered by these outer events. I strive to open myself to the new threads connecting me with the spiritual world where my beloved ones dwell, as well as to new meaning and connections woven within the world in the light of these changes. At this moment, I have surrendered knowing who I am. At the same time, I know clearly that the fabric of love is stronger than the threads of grief, and in this I find strength to face the unknown future without my beloved companions present in earthly form. Many ask how I can go on. Perhaps part of the answer is found in this book. The inner courage to face an unfathomable present comes from the strength and consciousness built through each stage of development. The on-going search for 'Self' is deepened by life's challenges if we can open to it. This book brings hope about our human condition, and our development through life.

I read this text while freshly confused by the greatest mystery of my life – the loss of my family, and my physical injuries from the accident. I was standing outside of my life in a kind of limbo. While reading *Tapestries*, I experienced humility and peace: humility from reading about the lives of others who had gone through loss and moved on in their lives; peace from the knowledge that destiny carries us, giving us always the choice of how we will respond. If we make 'a mistake', and later meet it with new awareness, we can then 'see through the glass more clearly – even face to face.' From loss, from mistakes, from courageous acts, we grow and become more the person we seek to be, altering our tapestry, weaving that which we once could not imagine.

The stories of the twelve people interviewed in *Tapestries* bring the human journey to life. I found myself entering into each story, then back into my own, then into the qualities of the particular stage of life. As I began to interface with the book, I could not help myself from wondering: how did 'I' respond to that issue? What was 'I' doing at that age? What did 'I' learn from a similar crisis? So, reflection – looking through my glass – became an integral part of reading this book. The true life stories found in this work, without the glitz and glamour of a Hollywood screen play, touch us deeply. The individuals cannot get airlifted out of their dilemma, or take a break from their pain or loss. And so I found myself joining with them. I sensed each person's courage in both practical day to day living as well as in facing the more elusive life destiny questions.

In *Tapestries,* Betty Staley is following and strengthening the thread she began in her contribution to an earlier book *Ariadne's Awakening,* which focused on the power and challenges of relationships. This new work brings color and vitality to this issue, so central to our lives. For example, it is different entering marriage at twenty than at thirty or forty. But why? This book helps us understand the reason. I followed each person's story through each seven-year cycle – one person who married a much older man, another who was divorced with young children, another who made a career choice that brought her into a relationship. I found myself building with Betty Staley twelve separate 'novels', wondering what would happen next... I felt sadness at their larger life picture and my own. It was not just abstract, theoretical information but living destinies – sometimes in war, sometimes behind the Iron curtain, sometimes in Black America.

In *Tapestries,* the author is courageous in sharing her life's wisdom and opinions in a helpful though not dogmatic fashion, for example in the issues confronting young mothers struggling with the pull of career and mothering. Betty Staley has enormous empathy for such situations assisting the reader to journey through all the possible options. In the 90s with a heightened focus on careers for women, it is helpful for the author to confirm that motherhood too can be a career.

The author also brings insight into the issue of ageing. Many people view their lives as increasingly meaningless, particularly in the older years. *Tapestries* sees adult development in terms of ripening rather than withering. To many elders, and their families, it appears that the door is closing – at a time when the door can be open. Instead of life as a giving up, a dying while still alive, there can be beauty in the very art of living.

This book helps us stay awake to the purpose and meaning of all of life, including ageing. Let us, as Betty Staley suggests, 'meet the fear of ageing with capacities for deep and meaningful life and love'. We have a choice in the way we see those around us and in the way we ourselves age and mature. What a different world this would be if our lives are lived, in the words of the author, 'fuller and fuller', while we 'move with anticipation to the next phase.'

In Betty Staley's *Tapestries,* we witness respect for the uniqueness of each person's journey beginning in infancy through to the stages of later life. Wonder and awe for the human journey come through in shining colors. Through conscious living and dying, we can deepen and enrich the colors of the cloth. Thank you, Betty, for sharing with us this tapestry, for helping see through the glass more clearly, and awakening in us awareness of the sacredness of this journey on earth.

Prologue

May the warp be the white light of morning,
May the weft be the red light of evening,
May the fringes be the falling rain.
May the border be the standing rainbow.
Thus weave for us a garment of brightness.

Song of the Sky Loom (Tewa)
Native American [1]

Late twentieth-century life is complex, fast-paced, and constantly changing. A new consciousness is calling on us to re-examine all our past assumptions and ask ourselves who we are, how we should relate to one another and the world around us; what, in other words, it means to be a human being.

According to differing views and theories, the human being can be seen simply as an animal, or as a mere cog in the economic machinery of production; or as a machine whose biological systems operate like plumbing parts or chemical factories, and whose brain operates like a computer. All of these views are *partially* true, but none of them give us a full picture.

The way we see ourselves also affects how we are. If we think people are merely animals (though animals in their own environment, in harmony with nature, are beautiful, noble creatures), we are likely to start fighting each other for survival. If we believe ourselves to be machines or cogs in the economic machinery of production, we become interchangeable parts without relationship to our communities, feeling ourselves at the mercy of forces beyond our control, experiencing ourselves as nobodies, nothing. Our accomplishments can appear to be just the result of some form of external programming. Such a view denies our true humanity, undermining our freedom and our place in the universe so that we lose sight of our higher nature and our capacity for taking responsibility for our own actions.

When Rachel Carson wrote *Silent Spring,* she described a world in which pesticides were destroying the environment, replacing a world that sustains life and beauty with one of silence and death. If we were to continue in the way we have been going, she said, the earth would be destroyed. Her warning, and the awakening of many people in response, has given rise to a new awareness of the fragile condition of our planet and the urgent need to make major changes in the way we think and live.

But besides the earth, our own human nature is in danger. An inhumane, mechanical or 'mere animal' view of the human being undermines the human spirit, which then either gives up in resignation or fights back to destroy the world that devalues it. Hardly surprising, then, that we are living in a time of terrible violence and destruction. We have come to a point in human evolution when we have the capacity to destroy the planet, other human beings, and ourselves on a grand scale. We have the freedom and the means to do so.

Pondering these things led me over and over again to questions about how we live our lives, how we understand the human journey, how we live in relationships, and how we build communities that acknowledge the higher nature of the human being and the magnificent earth on which we live. Henry David Thoreau said that we can only change society by starting with the individual. As I thought about this, I started to wonder how we might better understand the nature of human life. How are we shaped by our family, our environment, our physical constitution, as well as what we bring from our individual past? How do we take hold of our particular personalities and situations and change them to allow the human spirit to shine through? What is the activating force behind such change? How can we consciously work to strengthen it out of our own activity? How do these changes occur during different periods of life? What is the relationship of our 'I' to the spiritual world?

Looking at our lives from outside, in a more objective way than we usually do, can help us gain a clearer sense of the overall landscape of influences that shape and mould us, the dynamics which create new possibilities or hold us back, the strength or weakness of our individuality. In this book I chose to focus on the network of personality characteristics, relationships and identities we have in life, how they change in time, and how we can participate in self-transformation to awaken insight and bring balance to our lives as well as blessings to others.

An image, for me, of the complexity of human life is that of tapestry weaving. In each of our lives the warp is formed of those strands which are 'given': what we bring with us and what we are born into. As we examine the warp we can see that some threads are tight, others are loose, some are smooth, others may be rough. The warp bears the imprint of the one who threaded it on the loom. This underlying foundation is the basis upon which we can build an imagination of what our weaving will be like. Then we take the shuttle in our hands – each shuttle has threads of different colors and textures – and begin to weave the tapestry of our lives. How we fashion it depends on how we respond to and interact with what we experience and encounter, how we shape it through our free will. Each of our lives is different, no two tapestries are the same.

Images of spinning threads, preparing the loom, and weaving, have long held symbolic importance in myths, folk songs, and poetry. Athena, the Greek Goddess, springing full grown from the forehead of Zeus, was both the goddess of weaving and of wisdom. In Crete, Ariadne unwound the ball of thread (representing thinking) so that Theseus could follow it and find his way out of the labyrinth (image of the human brain). In the Norse myths, the *Eddas,* three women known as the Norns, sit by a well. One spins the thread of a person's life, the second measures it, the third snips the thread as each life comes to its destined end. In Latvia the weaving of belts is a major part of the cultural heritage, and in one area of Latvia, Lielvarda, the belt does not have repetitive patterns but consecutive sections, each of which reveals a new design. These designs are not merely decorative but symbolic representations of the relationship to sun, moon, stars, the natural world and the human being's place within it.

In Native American tradition the Navajos learned the art of weaving from the Pueblo people who were taught it by Spider Woman, who lives atop Spider Rock in Canyon de Chelly. Spider Woman was taught weaving by a spider. Navajo weavers would leave a hole in the center of each blanket, so acknowledging their debt to Spider Woman in the form of a spirit outlet in the design – a thin line passing from the hole at the center of the blanket to the edge. This spirit outlet was also thought to prevent blanket sickness, for if Spider Woman were not acknowledged, she would spin cobwebs in the brain. Might not some of the illnesses we suffer today be partly due to our failure to acknowledge our spiritual debts?

Ettie Hillesum in her diary, *An Interrupted Life*,[2] written at Westerbork concentration camp, employs the spiderweb image to moving effect:

> When a spider spins his web, does it not cast the main threads ahead of itself, and then follow along them from behind? The main part of my life stretches like a long journey before me and already reaches another world... as if I had been through it already and was now helping to build a new and different society... I just hope it can be the same for you and all my friends... for we have so much still to experience and so much work to do. And so I call upon you; stay at your inner post and please do not feel sorry for me, there is no reason to do so...

So tapestry weaving, in which the warp and the weft combine to reveal pattern and meaning, can express something about our life journey. We are born into a physical body with its magnificent design of skeletal structure, muscles, organs, hormones, senses, and nervous system. We are received into a family with complex inter-relationships of sisters, brothers, mother and father. Our soul unfolds as we live in the world and meet other people. Our lives are embedded in a process of time, so that we undergo change from one phase to another, experience soul struggles. By the fact of being born to a particular set of parents in a particular place, certain things are given to us such as our gender, nationality, race and physical constitution. Out of the interaction between our higher self, or individuality, and our physical body, our temperament arises, expressing itself in our gesture toward life. As we come into adolescence we develop soul attitudes with which we focus our attention and relate to the inner and outer world. As we develop through life stages our 'I' has the possibility to transform our personality.

As children we lived actively in the moment, without reflection; we were unaware of different inner attitudes to the world. As we mature we learn about similarities and differences, about receiving and giving joy. We get hurt; we hurt others. We make mistakes and learn from them. Some mistakes we make over and over, and slowly we begin to see that there are patterns in our own behavior, personality characteristics which give us an experience of the world that is different from other people's. As we grow into adulthood we become aware of aspects of ourselves we would like to change, and also how hard it is to do so. As we pass through the various life phases we are given opportunities to decide how we will shape our lives.

Who does the weaving? What is this 'I' that sees and learns and transforms? It is our individual human spirit. Out of this spirit we can decide how we will work to transform our temperament and our soul attitude, and broaden our viewpoint to encompass wider possibilities. Our true selves can shine through more and more effectively until the spirit illumines our lives. This human spirit is the highest expression of our human self. Born out of the spiritual world our 'I' delves into earthly life, takes hold of the warp and weaves the **tapestries** of our lives which it then offers up to the divine world at our death.

The main inspiration for my work has been the significant contribution which Rudolf Steiner (Austrian philosopher and spiritual researcher, 1861-1925) has made to the understanding of human development. I am also grateful to other researchers who have enlightened us by their understanding of specific aspects of human life.

SECTION I

TIME, GROWTH AND HUMAN RELATIONSHIPS

I

The Human Being in the World of Matter, Soul and Spirit

One cold November evening in Riga, Latvia, during a sabbatical year, I was having a cup of tea with the grandmother of our host family. After living in her home for six weeks I had come to know and love her. I asked her to tell me about her life. As I sat and listened to her (through translation provided by her daughter) I was deeply moved by the insights she had arrived at. During the rest of the year, and after I returned to the United States, I asked all sorts of people in different situations to tell me about themselves.

Many people I questioned had tried to make sense of their lives. In some cases they had been strongly influenced and affected by outer events such as war or political tyranny; in others by illness. But regardless of outer circumstances, they had sought an inner attitude, a response to the changes they experienced. It took some people many years to arrive at insight; others received an almost immediate inrush of recognition and understanding.

Some people conduct their search for identity and meaning by looking for outer happiness. Others define the meaning in their lives by their achievements, by a feeling of being needed, or by an understanding of their relationship to the spiritual world. But in both cases I found that as people moved through time, through the cycles and rhythms of their lives, new capacities awakened that were expressed in wisdom, courage, and insight. Their comments are based on real situations rather than abstract principles. I have woven these biographical accounts into the end of every chapter about each particular seven-year-period.

The uniqueness of every human being continually reveals itself if we have eyes to see and ears to hear. The presence of the divine awakens in us the search for meaning, the affirmation that we are more than we seem.

E.E. Cummings says it so well:

> i thank You God for most this amazing day,
> day: for the leaping greenly spirits of trees
> and a blue true dream of sky; and for everything
> which is natural which is infinite which is yes
>
> (i who have died am alive again today,
> and this is the sun's birthday; this is the birth
> day of life and of love and wings: and of the gay
> great happening illimitably earth)
>
> how should tasting touching hearing seeing
> breathing any – lifted from the no
> of all nothing – human merely being
> doubt unimaginable You?
>
> (now the ears of my ears awake and
> now the eyes of my eyes are opened)[1]

We live in three worlds – the physical world of matter; the world of soul – desires, motives, feelings, hopes, and ideals; and the world of spirit – all that is divine, timeless, spaceless, and eternal. We can measure what goes on in the first world, we can feel what goes on in the second, and we can have intuitions about what goes on in the third. But we usually treat everything as hypothesis which is not part of the measurable physical, material world, unless we have experienced the reality of our own soul or spiritual experiences.

We might, in the morning, glance briefly out of the window and say, 'It's a beautiful day!' However, if we look more closely and see *how* the day is beautiful – the flowering of the trumpet vine blossoms, the gnarled branches of the oak tree shining in the morning sun, the clarity of light, the sweetness of the air, the birds darting in and out among the scented vines, and our neighbor who is already up puttering in the garden, our experience is much richer. Then we have a picture filled with detailed sense perceptions. The scene touches our hearts and we are filled with gratitude. Having looked more closely, our experience is differentiated rather than vague, and we are more closely connected with the scene than we were at first.

In the same way we could either just speak in broad, general terms about the human being as a very complicated and mysterious organism; or go deeper and try to understand how spiritual, soul and earthly forces actually interweave and work together in particular and specific ways.

Living in the physical world

We live in a physical body composed of matter, shaped and formed through nine months in utero. After being permeated with life in complete interconnection with our mother in the womb, we achieve a first kind of independence at birth. A lifetime later the physical form will be laid aside, 'ashes to ashes and dust to dust' to rejoin the mineral world.

In the physical body are the elements found elsewhere in physical nature, among them carbon, hydrogen, oxygen, and nitrogen. While the human being is alive the activity of all of these elements is available to serve the highest human thoughts, feelings, and endeavors. When death comes, these elements are given over to the earth just like any other part of the mineral kingdom. The physical form then disintegrates. The human being is therefore part mineral.

Life forces stream into the physical body at conception and leave when the body dies. This formative activity shapes the mineral substances, and structures the physical body as we know it. These life or formative forces comprise a dynamic interrelated field of activity where everything is in living, interweaving motion. They bring life to what is otherwise dead. Just as the human being's physical body is related to the dead, lifeless, mineral kingdom, these formative forces which work in the human body are also active in the living, growing plant kingdom. The human being is therefore part plant. These formative forces express themselves in natural rhythms, including the rhythm of living and dying.

In addition to physical substance and life forces, we also have the experiences of our senses: heat and cold, pain and pleasure, hunger and thirst, desire and satiation. We experience drives to eat, to procreate, to create shelter, and to defend our property or territory. Animals also have this world of sensation and drives. In this way we are partly animal. The field of sensations, of inner reactions to the outer world, is connected to our physical body, but it is also something more, is also connected with the soul.

Living in the soul world

The soul plays a very special role in human life, mediating between the physical body and the spirit; we experience it in our conscious waking life in our senses and feelings. The soul world has three different aspects – those which are more connected with feelings, with thinking, and with will. Our feelings are largely dependent on what comes from our surroundings, but when the 'I' penetrates our drives and desires, we begin to understand ourselves by becoming aware of our feelings, not by being at the mercy of them. Then the whole world of concepts, feelings and will impulses opens up for us. We experience joy, wonder, love, and beauty.

There is a part of the soul not dependent on outer impressions, where we become aware of our spiritual nature. This aspect of the human being is immersed in the divine, in which the soul can perceive its own existence. Human beings gain a knowledge of themselves in their inner world through the spirit-soul, just as through the body-soul they gain a knowledge of themselves in the outer world. When the 'I' grasps itself as independent being, we begin to see the relationship of our soul to the world of spirit. Inner 'I' activity begins by perceiving the 'I', in other words, with self-contemplation.

The soul is always in tension between its lower and higher aspects. Depending on how strong this tension is, problems can develop within our soul life. For example, if we become too aware of hunger we experience pain, which is an expression of consciousness encroaching into a sphere where we are usually unconscious. Or if our unconscious drives are too strong, they can overpower our consciousness, so that we end up just reacting to life, 'going through the motions' in a dull way without thinking. If soul forces are too strongly linked with physical forces, we can be driven by animalistic behavior. On the other hand, if the soul separates too prematurely from the physical body – which may for example occur in a child introduced to sexuality at a young age – development is accelerated and childhood quickly left behind. Such development should wait until the physical organs are mature. A healthy soul life depends on an equilibrium between the poles of consciousness and unconsciousness.

When the 'I', through thinking, shines its activity on the knowledge acquired from the physical world, this lights up in our soul life. The 'I' takes in impressions of objects and works with what is retained from these impressions in memory. Through the activity of thinking we awaken to the realities of the world. No longer content with having things just happen, we question their meaning and bring form and order to life. As we distinguish between truth and untruth, we strive to become independent thinkers.

The upper pole of thinking activity brings order and objective certainty, while the lower pole creates randomness and even chaos. The soul lives in tension between the abundant willful life forces working from below and thoughtful objective activity working from above. When the vitality of life forces meets with the 'cooler', more thoughtful qualities, infusing them with strength and enthusiasm without overwhelming them, independent thought can arise. The best way to nurture this balance is through the arts and through an attitude of reverence. An artistic approach to education develops intellectual forces at the right time, by bringing thinking and will together in balanced, harmonised feeling life.

One-sidedness in our thinking can cause emotional problems. Too early stimulation of the intellectual capacities between seven and fourteen, without a social impulse, creates abstract thinking disconnected from life. How often have we met brilliant children rather like 'walking heads', with poor social skills. They seem dried up and stuck in their intellects, unable to spontaneously share in the excitement of life. Their thinking may be encyclopedic but it lacks imagination. This disturbance may also become apparent in children whose parents and teachers pushed computers in the early years.

Other people, in contrast, resist any attempt to harness and discipline the vitality and strength of their life forces. They relish spontaneity and resist order, flitting enthusiastically from one thing to the other at the mercy of the inclinations of the moment. They cannot bring the strands of their life together.

Another example of one-sidedness is when thinking and social forces find no connection. A person may have abstract notions of how things should be, but lack any kind of reverence or religious feeling toward life. It is possible to have 'high ideals' but chaotic, destructive will. Such a split, almost invariably originating in childhood, may render a person capable of performing acts of cold terror. Such people lack reverence for other human beings, treating them as if they were objects.

Alternately, if life forces are too over-powering and chaotic, and thinking forces too weak, our thoughts may wander in vague mystical meanderings, without clarity or precision. It is necessary to develop and challenge thinking forces in adolescence in a way that awakens self-discipline and order. A young person afloat on a nebulous cloud of mysticism may at first resent such demands, but they are very necessary to establish balance. Without them there is a danger that such a person will be vulnerable to manipulation by powerful figures who can take advantage of his* weakness and lack of clear judgment.

Although most of us are not as extreme as these examples, we all experience such tensions. We can become too cool in our thinking or too hot in our will impulses, either of which can divert us from the task at hand. More often, we swing from one pole to the other, as we try to learn to manage our time and energy. One moment we may carefully deliberate over a decision, and the next moment drop all our plans in order to visit a friend. The 'I' is hard at work trying to bring balance.

When we examine the soul we see two other divergent tendencies which create tension. At the upper pole the spirit longs to loosen itself from matter, its gesture is toward true individuality and the spirit world. At the lower pole, heredity and tradition exert their pull on us, hindering our freedom to arrive at independent truth. This tension can be balanced and harmonized by the 'I' working to enable the individual to permeate the physical world with spirit. Spiritual ideals that can be brought down into physical form, into practical ways of working, strengthen the connection between soul and spirit.

* I will alternate the masculine and feminine forms from chapter to chapter

Unbalanced, one-sided spiritual ideals can make people fanatics who lose contact with earthly life and label as heretics all those who do not agree with them. A person of balanced spiritual ideals could not justify attacking another human being because he did not embrace the 'truth'. Many historical examples demonstrate the cruelty and blindness of such fanaticism, usually in the name of a high religious ideal (as in the Inquisition, some of the Holy Wars or some extreme fundamentalist sects).

People with strong spiritual tendencies often have trouble coming down to earth. They wander around looking for a way to 'land'. After a time this sense of homelessness creates a crisis. Artistic activities, though, can help them find a relationship to earthly life. Working with groups is also important so that they find a way to reach out to other people and live with them.

Some people feel trapped by heredity and tradition, imitating what is in front of them rather than finding their own spiritual identity. Although they yearn to find their individual spirit, they experience themselves as limited. They may feel hopeless, imprisoned on the earth, and try to break free in a violent way through drugs or suicide. They cannot find strong enough bonds with their fellows to hold them here.

All of us encounter influences that distract us from our true being. On one hand we are reaching for the stars where everything will be heavenly, and on the other we feel the loneliness and despair of our separate individuality. We have to experience this separation in order to choose freely to reunite with the spirit. Otherwise we have no freedom, and no impetus for self-development. This is the challenge of the times in which we live.

Gisela and George O'Neil in their book *The Human Life*,[2] connected the changing relationship of the soul and the 'I' with the image of a horse. We are merged with the horse, in centaur-form, in the feeling aspect of the soul, in which the forces of youth and vitality predominate. The knight clad in shining armor, with sword and spear, expresses the thinking aspect of the soul, a distinct human form, yet still dependent on the horse. But the spiritual aspect of the soul is characterized in the image of 'man and his horse separated'. The experience is one of losing our steed and then finding it again. The new horse, one hopes, will be 'a winged horse', a symbol of spiritualized intelligence (intelligence illuminated by the 'I'), which can creatively carry the rider through all trials.

The working of the 'I'

The 'I' is of the same divine essence and nature as the divine, but it is not the same as the divine. If we wish to make a comparison, we may say that the drop of water has the same relationship to the sea as the 'I' has to the divine.

Rudolf Steiner

Beyond the physical body, the formative forces and the soul, there exists as we have already seen, a uniquely human quality of individuality which has been described by many great religious teachers, philosophers, mystics and scientists. It has been given many names: the higher self, the higher ego, the divine spark, the Holy Spirit, the Christ, the inner light. In this book I call it the 'I'. Through its activity we can transcend purely soul experience and sensation. Our 'I' activity arises from a source beyond space and time, endows us with a sense of permanency and continuity while all else around and within us is constantly changing. 'I' activity works particularly within the rhythm of remembering and forgetting. We gain awareness of an object in the present through soul activity, but the 'I' allows us to recall a mental image when the object is no longer before us, to visualize it inwardly.

We can observe how the 'I' gradually penetrates the soul and body as a child grows up. It lights up in the baby's smile of recognition, in the use of the word 'I', in children's awareness of themselves as having a separate physical existence from the rest of the animated world around them. It lights up in a child's development of memory. Think of the nursery rhymes or songs children learn because the words are carried by rhythm. When this later passes over into conscious memory (such as being able to speak the poem or song without the rhythm or without the rest of the group) we see the 'I' has been at work.

During the second seven-year period, the 'I' lights up in the nine-year change when children step back from their earlier unity with the world and realize they have a separate life of feelings that are private. This pulling back from feeling one with the world is a separation that creates more independence. Up until now the child lived strictly in the present, dependent on the here and now. After this change, he is more able to produce images inwardly without an external object to stimulate them, to retain inner imagery from stories, and to compare images which only exist within an inner world. For example, when children compare the creation myths from the Egyptian and the Greek cultures, they are working only with images that live within their feeling-filled thoughts.

The 'I' is active in bringing about cause and effect thinking at around the age of 12, when the child becomes able not only to hold images side by side, but also to make a causal connection between two events. 'If I do this, then that happens every time.' It is a connection that is understood even when the objects are not present (although their presence was necessary to start the process going). This provides the basis for the formation of abstract concepts.

The 'I' is active throughout the period when adolescents become aware of themselves in relationship to other people. Around the age of 17, the 'I' shines through the soul as teenagers sense the working of the divine in their life. By about the age of 21 the 'I' fully enters the human being, and he experiences a change of consciousness.

Throughout life the 'I' works to permeate the body and soul with spiritual forces. Whenever a child recognizes, however vaguely or unconsciously, that he has a connection to the spiritual world, this is a reflection of the light of the 'I' permeating physical and soul life. During the first twenty-one years the soul is built up from outside, from what has been brought through the parents, the family, the school, the environment. From the age of 21 the 'I' shines more consciously, penetrating first the feelings and then thinking. It works upon the soul, transforming it and giving it individual shape and substance.

During the middle period of life, from 35-42 years, the 'I' illumines the 'I' itself. Once people grasp this and recognize the 'I' within themselves, then they are able to perceive its working in the outer world as well, are able to see the footprints of the spirit at work in the world. During these years the soul is most closely connected with the spirit. When we conquer the lower nature of our own feeling life, when we purify and transform it through the spiritualizing force of the 'I', by means of active work on the soul, we are creating a new aspect of our own nature. We master our soul life. We do not actually have to be conscious of this process to participate in it. Probably every human being living in the present age is doing this to some extent. We may call it by different names – such as 'the working of the conscience', doing 'God's will', or living by a moral code. We may experience times of desperation and helplessness which are suddenly dispelled and illumined, as though by the warmth of the sun filling our hearts. This is the working of the spiritual world through our 'I'. The more consciously we can work with these thoughts, though, the more we participate in our own self-transformation.

Living in the spirit

The 'I' can go beyond mastering the soul and move into another stage. The more we work on this aspect of ourselves (refining and purifying our desires, passions, joys, sorrows) the stronger the seed of our spiritual consciousness grows. We can then begin to look back to our childhood years and examine what strong feelings we still carry from those times. What prejudices? What assumptions? What fears? What have we learned since then? In what ways are our desires still too excessive, our reactions too extreme? How can we bring moderation into our feeling life? How do we use our spiritual consciousness and thinking to ennoble our feelings and actions? It is not a matter of denying our emotional needs but of transforming them so that the old desires no longer exert the same power. A cleansing of the emotional life brings about equanimity in the soul.

To the degree to which we activate our spiritual forces, the 'I' penetrates and transforms our habits, customs, temperament, soul mood, character, and mental outlook. Two kinds of activities are particularly effective in this transformation – religious impulses, and the appreciation of and/or participation in artistic activity. Religious impulses are powerful because they connect us directly with the unchanging eternal world. Working through repetition, they have a deep transformative effect, changing our unconscious habits into conscious attitudes. This is a very slow process.

Artistic experience works differently. When we have an experience of pure color and tone, or observe and contemplate the spiritual foundations of a work of art, the effect penetrates right down into our formative life forces. When we work artistically we develop inner flexibility and creativity, which helps us in the great act of reshaping ourselves.

When we try to live as moral human beings, we are also bringing spiritual forces into our lives. As we mature, our spiritual nature helps to transform our earthly nature. But beyond these changes a much more subtle change occurs. We actually begin to spiritualize our physical bodies. Very developed personalities such as saints or initiates attain this to a high degree, but most of us awaken only a few aspects of our higher self during our lifetimes.

II
The Alchemy of Relationships

Your children are not your children.
They are the sons and daughters of Life's longing for itself.
They come through you but not from you,
And though they are with you, yet they belong not to you.
You may give them your love but not your thoughts.
For they have their own thoughts.
You may house their bodies but not their souls,
For their souls dwell in the house of tomorrow, which you cannot
visit, not even in your dreams.

Kahlil Gibran [1]

1. We are born into a family

From the moment we are born we are never really alone. In the complex network of relationships that weave through our lives, our parents form the strongest bond we have to the earth. Through them we have the gift of life, gender, physical characteristics, predisposition to illnesses, family, community and nationality. We also have many personality and temperament characteristics such as strength of intellect, talents, and artistic gifts. Through their capacities and attitudes our parents strongly influence our patterns of thought, our interests, attitudes, passions, physical talents, and ambitions. Our parents provide us with the blueprint of life, a primary pattern which includes their relationship to the world of nature and to society, the home atmosphere they create for us and the way they relate to each of their children and to each other.

If they succeed in their task, they provide a cocoon within which we find love and shelter, acceptance and limitations, a sense of wholeness and purpose. When we leave home they send us on our way with the map that charts our unique journey through life. What a gift our parents give us! All those years of nurturing, of sacrifice, of protecting and guiding, of embodying that element of love which expresses the highest of human endeavors. But then we must leave them and as the fairy tales say, 'go out into the world to seek our fortune'.

Our parents provide us with the prime example of what a relationship is. For the rest of our lives we measure our own experiences against the relationships we observed in our parents' home. Some of us admire their values and the atmosphere they created. The way they related to each other becomes a picture for us of the way husband and wife, parent and child should be, and we may try to emulate them. How often we may say to ourselves 'Of course you iron underwear, put ketchup on your eggs, clean the house on Saturday mornings...' We bring 'Of course you do...' with us into our adult life. 'Of course parents should not show their angry feelings in front of children.' Or, alternatively, 'Of course parents argue in front of children so they can see that arguing is part of life.'

Even if we don't consciously think these thoughts, we can't help being influenced by them. They are the first images of family life and parent relationship we absorb. Unconsciously, we may burden our spouses with our own father- or mother-image; but they too have their images of the way 'it's supposed to be'.

Being a parent is one of the most powerful mysteries of life: overwhelming joy and responsibility intertwined. Are any of us ever prepared for this experience? How can we explain the feeling of awe during pregnancy?

April

Staying up late to read James Wright
your swollen belly touching my hip
I feel the baby moving inside you.

Does it know my body is beside yours
or that the rain clings
to the budding branch of the sycamore
outside our window?

George Kane [2]

When we first glimpse the newborn child we cannot help but be moved by this great miracle of life. The combination of joy and responsibility never goes away. As we realize what models we are for the child and how our actions are imitated, it is hard not to feel burdened. When we realize how much they look to us for help and guidance, we can only feel humble. Yet as we glimpse the beautiful shining eyes of our children, tenderness and joy fill our hearts. From now on we live with a sense of responsibility and wonder. As the child grows from toddler to school age to adolescence, we continue to live within the tension of these feelings.

I recently visited a friend whose daughter had celebrated her Bar Mitzvah. Rose had written her own prayer book which was distributed to her family and friends, who shared this special event with her. Included in the book were poems written by mother and daughter celebrating this threshold experience. They express the tenderness and beauty that often exists unspoken between parent and child:

In Answer To My Daughter's Question

Well, my dear, it's like this:
When it pleased Great Spirit
to know itself ever more,
It divided itself first in two –
the Yin and the Yang.
From these It created all the billions of things
that make the Great Dance.

It also pleased Great Spirit to make of itself
millions of tiny mirrors,
in which to see Itself.

It may surprise you to know
that these mirrors were filled with grief,

For they were pulled so far away
from their beloved Creator,
to serve as mirrors properly.

They stayed away so long
   that they forgot they
   were made from Great Spirit.

And so, of course, they even forgot
   why they were so very lonely.
Then I look into your
   wide,
   blue
   eyes,
And the tears come.
For here we are.
At long last – and as always,
   Oh, Beloved.
Here
   we
   are.

Linda Pritzker [3]

My Mother

   I love my mother,
With all of my heart,
I love her.
She watches over me with such tenderness.
She is one of the most
   wise, healing, talented people I know.

   If my mother were to die,
Part of me would die with her.
Not my whole self,
I would live on,
But in me there would be an unfillable gap.
I would be devastated.
And as my father used to say,
   'Linda, you're wonderful!'

Rosemary Pritzker [4]

We may not look back to our childhood with happy feelings. Perhaps we have been damaged by the relationships at home and want to keep as safe a distance from our parents as possible. We may spend much of our lives trying to undo the unrealistic or unfair expectations and the dysfunctional dynamics that influenced our own behavior, trying to find our own true personalities within the distortions and dependencies that developed. The attempt to become conscious of our family dynamics sheds light on what has been hidden in the shadows for years. We can become aware of behaviour patterns that may have had a compelling effect upon members of our family through generation after generation. But even in the most difficult relationships with parents, there is, hopefully, at least something we can find that awakens gratitude, understanding, and forgiveness.

Most of us select some aspects of our parents' relationship and our upbringing, and incorporate these into our own lives where they seem appropriate. We may start out doing things the way our parents did, but as we become more independent we find our own ways. Or we may rebel to start with and only later concede that they had some good ideas. We can choose to cultivate those attitudes we admire in our parents if we wish. Sometimes we need to get some distance from our parents to see their fine qualities, their acts of courage, or how generous and forgiving they were to others. So many of their virtues are lost in the clutter of our childhood experiences. Some aspects of them we may want to reject. Do we argue with them? Do we refuse to visit them? We may well find aspects of our parents' outlook, prejudices and values creeping into our own feelings and thoughts from time to time. This is when we need to examine ourselves. 'Is this really what I think? How I want to behave? Is this *my* code of values? We become clearer about how we don't want to be like our parents, as we gradually define how we really want to be. The complexity of the parent-child relationship meets us at every turn. Our parents give us the framework, the structure within which we will build our identity. The rest is up to us.

In the US and the UK, family bonds are loosening, and most young people now move out of the home after high school. The idea is to 'get away' and be on your own, become independent. Most of us don't live in the home environment we grew up in – in fact we probably live hundreds, if not thousands of miles away from it. People's relationship to their parents has become weaker. There is very little in our culture – aside from such gestures as Mother's Day or Father's Day (which are suspect because they have become so commercialized), and the Ten Commandments (which seem pretty antiquated) – that openly supports and values parents. Do we run away from these relationships and not attempt to resolve the difficulties? Are we too preoccupied with our own independent lives? Is it too much of a bother to maintain close relationships? It is difficult to find models in public images, in movies or on television to help us understand and acknowledge this central relationship in our lives.

Perhaps we also devalue the meaning of our own roles as parents because we are so determined to be 'modern'. We often don't want to be regarded primarily as 'mom' or 'dad', but as independent people living full lives aside from our parental roles. Full-time motherhood, for example, goes against the newest paradigm. People who derive great satisfaction from being parents may feel defensive or old-fashioned because they are not 'liberated' from their traditional roles. Yet a more conscious approach to parenting might yet become 'fashionable' again, as people begin to realize what effect a loss of parental nurturing may be having.

In *Habits of the Heart*, Robert Bellah[5] and his team of sociologists examined American life and came to the conclusion that the price of independence and individuality has been terrible loneliness and alienation, resulting in a loss of community. When society starts once more to realize the importance of parental roles, and pays more than lip service to them, we may see greater provision of such support-programs as parental leave, tax credits for parents being at home full-time while their children are young, and social services that emphasize parent education.

In central and eastern Europe, in contrast, a greater percentage of people still continue to live either in their childhood home with one or both parents, or in the town where they grew up. The family home is often passed on to the children and the chances are that one of them will continue to live there, whereas in the US the family home is usually sold when the parents move into a retirement home or after their deaths.

In some countries young people are expected to live with their parents until they marry and move into their own home. A young Italian woman, Paola Buonadonna, described her flight from the customary home relationship in Italy as one of panic. She needed to prove herself and 'I wanted my life to begin'. She is satisfied with the decision even though there are difficult times, but her parents feel they must have done something wrong to drive her out, and have taken to blaming each other.

'Every time I go back for a holiday I find my friends, who all still live at home, more confused and disappointed. As their need for autonomy increases they devise different strategies for survival. The women tend to lock themselves into steady relationship. Their partners control every crumb of the slice of life that they wrested from the scrutiny of protective parents. The men enjoy the fictitious freedom of their own car or motorbike...'

She finds this arrangement at home suffocates the birth of individuality, 'the triumphs and bruises of adult existence'.[6]

Not everyone looks upon the search for individuality as something positive. When my husband and I brought a group of high school students to the former Soviet Union in 1988, we took part in conversations with psychologists and young adults in several cities. In Kishinov, Moldova, some psychologists commented on how unsatisfactory they thought it was for young people to leave their parents' home, as happens in the West, and the US in particular. They could not see any value in it, only problems. They felt the drive towards independence and individuality threatened the family unit. Then one of the sixteen year-old American boys spoke out passionately: 'It is as if your parents give you your skeleton, but you have to go into life and fill it out with muscles yourself.' After his speech (which surprised all of us), a woman of about 25 timidly raised her hand. She said, 'I have always admired the way young people in your country can leave home and go on their own. I wanted to leave Moldova to study in Moscow, and my parents would not let me do it.' Another woman described how difficult it was to continue living in her parents' flat while she was married with a child. 'It is very hard for us to become the mistresses of our own homes and families as long as we continue living with our parents.' Although they respected their parents, these women in Moldova also longed for opportunities to be more independent.

This theme of sharing living quarters was echoed in many conversations we had in Latvia, Lithuania, and Russia. 'We waited twelve years to get our own flat, and it feels wonderful for me to feel this is 'our' place. We get along much better with my parents now that we each have our own space,' said a woman in Lithuania whose family of four had lived in one room during all those years. Other people find it natural and desirable to live together with their parents, and do not feel they lose their independence. In the Caucasus mountain town of Telavi, Georgia, we had several conversations on this topic. Here there was no housing shortage and many people lived in very comfortable, individual stone houses. However, several generations living together was still the norm. One woman said, 'My husband and I were living with my parents. When my father died, my mother told me, "This is your house now". She was very good about letting me rearrange furniture and add new pieces. I cannot imagine my mother not living with us. She does the baking and laundry so I can work. We all have our ways of contributing. Sometimes we have arguments, but this is just part of life. It's nothing to run away from.'

One Polish friend told me that when she was twenty-three she felt she would die if she continued living with her parents. She escaped the situation by going to another country and working there with handicapped children. In such a situation young men and women may marry partly, at least, so they can change their relationship with their parents. Although shortage of housing means that they often continue to live with parents, they are granted more freedom and rights as married people. These 'escape marriages' often end in divorce, but a divorced woman still has a more independent status than one who has never married.

Whether we feel suffocated or supported by our parents, whether they are our close friends or our adversaries, or whether we maintain a pleasant but casual relationship with them, we have to find a way to define the relationship. We may be highly regarded professionals in our fields, but we are still our parents' daughters and sons.

The spiritual research of Rudolf Steiner led him to describe how we choose our parents, how we find a way to come from the spiritual world to the people we need to be our parents. Complex dynamic forces are at work to bring about such a connection. This view might help us to look at our relationship with our parents in a new way.

Is our father an authority figure, the symbol of power or protection? Is he Pop or Dad, someone to turn to when we are in need? Is he accessible? Is he a stranger to us? Does he understand us? When was the last time we saw him? Was he in our lives at all? Do we understand him? When was the last time we sat down to have a real conversation with him? Do we know how he felt about changes he went through in his life?

Especially in the US where the women's liberation movement has also stimulated men to examine their behavior, men are now learning that feelings are as important as achievements. Roles are changing, and it is confusing. How are our boys being prepared for this task? How are they being helped to transform the models most of them have grown up with? And, as many of my women friends say, 'Where are the strong men today?' But what is strength?

Our mothers have had a particularly challenging time living through the second half of the 20th century. They have experienced the changing role of women in society, and have been confused about whether being a housewife was to be admired or not. Many of us now about 50 were used to having our mothers at home when we were children. These mothers found the women's liberation movement perhaps a little extreme. They had to watch their daughters deny the value of motherhood (at least in the way they had defined it for most of their own adult life). They may have shaken their heads as we attempted to become liberated, tried to find happiness in a new role.

However, mine is also a confused generation. We still had a sense that it was important to be a mother, that family was a priority. Yet we also wanted careers. We wanted independence – sort of. We wanted all that women's liberation could bring, but not to lose what we liked about the old ways. So we tried all kinds of things: We celebrated motherhood, *and* downplayed its importance; we tried to put our careers first, or motherhood first. We tried it all, and it's still not resolved. The big difference is that today there are role-models: women who have had a career, a family, a role in the community, independent friendships, and a strong sense of individuality. It isn't easy, and it isn't troublefree, but what is clear is that there are choices available to us today. This means we have to be more conscious about our decisions and what the repercussions will be on the lives of all around us. We are constantly having to choose what's important *now*. We've come a long way from the ways of our grandparents.

As I look at the generation of my daughters, my step-daughters and daughter-in-law, I have great admiration. They have seen all the muddle we went through. They and their friends have experienced mothers who were too focused on their own lives to pay adequate attention to their children's needs, they have experienced the chaos of divorce and the rootlessness of a generation which hardly knows what a family is. They have experienced the courage and commitment of single parents trying to survive. They know more about the importance of independence and self-fulfilment. Some of them have been dragged through court custody fights; some have experienced the abandonment of never knowing a parent or grandparent. Some of them are scared to commit to a relationship because they have first-hand knowledge of their own vulnerability. They are armed with more information, more of a sense of reality than past generations. Not fed 'happily-ever-after' images of marriage, they have seen more of the dark side of life – through films and video as well as from life experience – by the time they are 21 than all past generations. They know about stress, support groups, counselling, mid-life crises, divorce statistics, and the difficulties of being single parents. Yet they still enter relationships with hope. They are fighting for improved legislation for child-care and health benefits, for maternity leave, birthing centers, help for nursing mothers, and the involvement of fathers in family life. They see how much more has to be done for the honoring of motherhood and fatherhood and the nurturing of children. I think this is a smart generation, and I hope they will grow wise. Life is not easier for young women today, but it surely is different from past generations.

Consider what 29 year-old Judith Schwartz, author of *The Mother Puzzle, A New Generation Reckons with Motherhood*,[7] writes.

> As the female members of our generation – those of us born at the end of the baby boom and just after, a generation that's hard to define elegantly – we're understandably a confused bunch. Society is sending us so many signals (be successful, have babies, be independent, look like a fashion model) that none of us knows where to begin – or when to take a break. We're the first generation of women who have grown up with the expectation of educational and professional achievement. While we've been raised to identify with our mothers domestically, it's our *fathers* whom we identify with professionally. So when motherhood threatens to transfer our focus from the workplace to the home, our sense of identity gets thrown out of whack. Who are we? Who have we *been?* When our view of our mate shifts from partner in life to partner in parenthood, what happens to the bond? Compared to cohorts of women before us, we have different expectations of our relationships, our doctors, our careers, our capacity to control our bodies and our lives. We're not necessarily in a *bad* place, merely a disorienting one.

We cannot talk about parents without discussing family structure. The greatest disruption for children in the first part of this century was the death of a parent. Divorce was not common. Bearing children out of wedlock was also rare. Both were frowned upon. The generation after World War II was the most stable generation in terms of family structure. Parental deaths for children below eighteen came down sharply. Divorce was still uncommon. But then in the 1960s the divorce rate suddenly soared: from fewer than ten divorces in 1,000 married couples, the rate increased to 23 per 1,000 by 1979 (levelling off to about 21 divorces per 1,000 in 1991). Out-of-wedlock births went from five percent in 1960 to 27 per cent in 1990. About one out of every four women who had a child in 1990 was not married. Each year a million children in the US experience divorce or separation and about the same number are born out of wedlock.

In the early seventies it was thought that all family structures were equally good, that single parent families and step-parent families brought out strength in children, that flexibility and getting to know a greater number of people would be to the benefit of children, that although they might be experiencing painful separation during divorce, they would soon recover and bounce back. Unfortunately this has turned out not to be true.

Children from disrupted families (single-parent families and step-parent families) suffer because they are more likely to experience poverty or economic insecurity. They lack a stable set of authority figures against which they can rebel and find their boundaries; their parent is more likely to be preoccupied with trying to earn a living and dealing with stress (of being a single parent or the complexity of a step-parent household); there is less time and support for their school work; their emotional needs are more confused and unsatisfied, with the result that they carry emotional problems with them into adulthood, have more difficulty trusting and making bonds with older people, are more likely to get involved in crime and truancy, and carry feelings of loneliness and lack of belonging far beyond the period of adolescence in which these are normal.

In short, although two-parent families may not be perfect they offer children stability, better economic security, a wider variety of different strengths and weaknesses to relate to, shared care and concern. Although some young people may complain that their fathers were preoccupied with work and hardly connected with them, the stress of not having a father or losing contact with him is much greater in the long run. The shape of American society is being changed by the fact that family life is being disrupted for large numbers of children. Emotionally unstable young people cannot put their powers and talents to the service of society, but drift aimlessly, lacking the will to get on with their lives. This problem cuts across class divisions and appears in suburbs as well as in inner cities, on farms as well as in small towns. Of course there are situations in which the family dynamics are so unhealthy that the children are better off when a divorce takes place. In general, parents may benefit from having more choices and possibilities of freedom and new relationships, but children are suffering.

Such a view is not popular with the large numbers of single parents or step-parents in our society. Yet it is time we took a hard look at what is happening. The change in family structure is not an isolated phenomenon, but a major force determining the future of our lives. How are we going to stop the cycle of damage that is now being passed on through the generations? Can we turn it around? Can schools handle the emotionally damaged children who are yearning for solidity and stability, who are disruptive in the classroom, who feel abandoned and ignored, or stressed by their parents' burdens and helpless to deal with such things. These questions test our own sense of commitment, of responsibility toward our children and to society. How do we take care of our own needs and protect and care for our children? What is the role of sacrifice? What does it mean to be a parent?

Parents are links to the past, guardians of the present, and preparers of the future. And our future is in great danger.

The place of the child in the family

> *Praise be to the destiny of first children. They walk in the wake of creation. The image of God the Father is imprinted on their forehead.*
>
> *Praise be, too, to the task of second children. They keep our life alive; they fill it with joy and beauty and help us to overcome the heaviness of all existence. In their hearts Christ's image is engraved.*
>
> *Praise be further to the visions of third children. They prepare our future. They seek for new patterns of existence; they consume themselves for the sake of others. Their hands bear the sign of the Holy Spirit.*
>
> König [8]

Our brothers and sisters are as central a part of our identity as being the son or daughter of a particular set of parents. Our siblings are the representatives of the larger world of society. What we learn with them teaches us social skills, how to defend ourselves, how to share, how to find a space for ourselves. Through our older siblings we gain a sense of what's ahead of us, and from our younger ones we see what we have already passed through. We are constantly redefining ourselves within this sibling network. Our universe is widely expanded through their interests, their friends, and their paths in life.

Much research has been done to determine the way in which character traits and mental make-up are influenced by birth order. Such patterns seem to be more connected with emotional life and personality than with intelligence and ability. The family constellation shapes people's social behaviour, how they react to other people, how they make friends or don't, how they live in community with others, how they choose their partners and relate to goals in their life. The central element here is that our place in the family strongly influences *the way we make human contact.*

Does the individual move out to meet her environment (extrovert) or withdraw from it (introvert)? Naturally, we all have both introverted and extroverted aspects in our personalities. When we are engaged in thinking about a problem we become more introvert, and more extrovert when we are active in the world and use our will. In the realm of feelings some of us tend to move inwards while others go outwards. Each of us expresses a gesture towards the world. When we move outward we live in great sympathy with our surroundings, when we withdraw we have less contact. How we make contact is influenced, among other things, by the position we occupy within our family. Each child has a different task in life. It is not a matter of better or worse, but of understanding the reality which the person in each position experiences, which in turn fosters different capacities – all of which are needed in society.

The confusion within families today – divorce, second and third marriages, half-brothers and sisters, step-brothers and sisters, also creates confusion in the destiny of the child in the family. The picture becomes more complicated, and children are likely to be subject both to aspects of their birth order and aspects of the new order brought about by the rearranged family.

Let us start by looking at the special role of the only child.

The only child

The only child grows up in a world of adults. Protected from the give and take of siblings, the child becomes much more emotionally dependent on her parents than is the case for children who are buffered to some degree by being one of several. A great deal of attention is focused on the only child who tends to consider this appropriate (although in later years this attention can feel like a burden). The parents invest everything in their one child, and their expectations are often unrealistic. Only children often expect to be acknowledged and have a special place in life. They are frustrated and disappointed when they are just considered to be 'one of many'. If the parent(s) have had the insight to form close relationships with other families, the only child has the opportunity to learn to get along with others.

The only child is self-contained, taking part in activities often without *really* taking part. On one hand, only children look at other children and want to be included; but when they are, they don't always want to go along with the rules the group has made. They are used to being alone and making their own rules or doing whatever they want. While some only children make great efforts and achieve great things, others expect everything to 'fall into their laps' because of their special status in life. Often uncertain of how to act socially, only children may oscillate between wanting too much or too little contact. They take themselves very seriously, often feeling insecure among the teasing and romping of their peers.

The eldest child

The eldest child is also an only child at first. During this time, eldest children develop a strong relationship to the parents. Usually their personality takes one of two directions – either very shy and fearful, clinging to the parents and dependent upon them, or strongly independent, self-directed, self-sufficient, and often undemonstrative. The eldest child stands as a bridge between the adult world and the siblings who come later. Identifying with the adult world, she becomes the leader, the authority, and the model for younger sisters and brothers. Of course, much depends on how many years pass before the second child appears, and on how parents define the eldest child's role. Eldest children can be aggressive, ambitious, high-achieving, and concerned about doing their duty, and often show more drive and perseverance. Because they look at life seriously, feeling that they carry the burdens and weight of the world, they may leave the carefree world of childhood behind them earlier than second children do.

When a brother or sister arrives, the eldest child has to learn to share her home. The way the first child accepts the newcomer depends on 'the difference of age, on the attitude of the parents, on the general conditions in the home and last but not least, on the temperament and the personality of the child himself'.[9] The first child has been Queen of the palace and now has to defend her place; and thus becomes a defender – of faith, tradition, the family, the past. 'There where law and order, tradition and continuity are needed, the first child has his place.'[10] The first child can build a bridge between the younger ones and the parents, or erect a barrier isolating the younger children from the parents. The first child is the maker of the family, for it is through her that the parents learn. Into the structure created by the parents and the first child, the other children come. The way has been paved. If the parents felt they were too lax with the first child, they will be stricter with the others. If they feel they were too nervous and uptight with their eldest, they will relax with the other children. The eldest child's experience and responses to the parents shapes the atmosphere for the younger children.

Although the first child has an 'only-child' experience for a while, her contact with the world is very different. The first child has a clear purpose, a determined sense of responsibility and accountability. As with all positions in a family, this one is not trouble-free. The eldest child lives in a tension between wanting to be rebellious and carefree and feeling the need to do her duty.

The experience of the eldest child will be influenced by the pattern of siblings. Let us look at a few of these. If there are two sisters, the older one may develop her masculine characteristics more strongly, dominating and overshadowing her younger sister. Or she may, instead, become the more feminine one. Or strive to become independent and follow her own star, having very little to do with her siblings. If the eldest sister is followed by a brother, this is likely to strengthen her feminine aspect. She may become more motherly, helping and supporting her brother. If there are three sisters, the first will often develop a 'queenly' character and get her younger sisters to wait on her. But if a little brother is born into a family of one, two, or three girls, the position of the eldest is balanced by a stronger focus on the new little fellow.

In a family where the eldest child is a boy, a different dynamic occurs. Where the first brother is followed by a younger brother or brothers, a struggle to maintain the position as leader and guide often takes place. The eldest may develop a special skill or hobby to show his strength. If, instead, one or several sisters follow, this may have a balancing effect on him. But he can also behave as a king with his servants – either a good-humored king or a bossy dictator. If the older brother has one younger sister, he often takes on the role of teacher to his female companion. An older boy with one younger brother may treat the latter as his servant or attendant. But some first sons, especially very sensitive ones, feel very threatened by the second and become discouraged and insecure, especially when the younger brother surpasses the older and shines in the competition – even though the eldest has tried to sabotage him behind the scenes. Eldest brothers may then feel weakened by the struggle, lose their self-reliance, refuse to accept responsibility, and become shiftless, while their younger brothers take on the role of upholding the honor of the family.

Much of the self-image of the eldest child is a reflection of her relations with the parents. Some parents delegate a great deal of responsibility to the eldest, who gets used to wielding this authority. But when the younger ones protest about this, the parents may start to treat the eldest as a child once more. She can, as a result, feel betrayed, be angry at the parents, perhaps seek revenge on the younger siblings. If parents are sensitive to this situation they can find a way to acknowledge the special status of the eldest while still maintaining their parental position. It is not unusual for the eldest child to counsel or criticise the parents on their child-rearing practices. All too often the eldest feels the younger ones 'get away with everything'.

Because eldest children feel so responsible for everything they do, they often feel the burden of responsibility others place on them. Although they may sometimes resent this, they also feel the need to prove they are worthy of the confidence placed in them and work harder and longer hours than others do. They won't leave a job half done. As adults, their priorities can become confused so that they overcommit to their job and neglect their family. (In their minds they may feel they are doing their part by providing monetarily for the family.)

During the middle years, from 35 on, first-born men and women may suddenly decide they are tired of being so responsible, they've had enough of others' counting on them, they are bored by the routine. At that moment they may choose to do the unexpected, to act rashly. In such cases they yearn to throw away all responsibilities and be reckless. Some only go as far as to fantasize; others may run off with a younger man or woman, buy a snazzy sports car, disappear for a wild night on the town, or do anything else out of character. However, the ecstatic feeling of having 'done it' may quickly dissolve into guilt at having disappointed other people and themselves. At the same time they enjoyed the experience and are frustrated that spontaneity comes at such a heavy price.

Torn between 'You can count on me', and 'I want to do something exciting for once', the first-born adult can suffer mid-life crisis in a more exaggerated form than other siblings.

The second child

From the beginning, the second child has to share the parents with an older sibling. Unlike the first child who identifies so closely with the parents and wants their approval, the second child is often more easy-going, friendly, and cheerful. Usually second children see life as an opportunity to have fun and experience the wonder and beauty of existence. But they also have their special difficulties. They are always having to try to stake a claim on what has already been conquered by someone else. It is not unusual for them to develop serious illnesses or difficulties in response to the challenge of this kind of situation. They may also take refuge in their powers of fantasy and have special spiritual powers. 'To be a second child mostly means to walk along a rope between heaven and earth; to maintain the balance between the above and below'.[11]

Two common patterns emerge – the second child can become rebellious, stubborn, seemingly independent, able to withstand punishment (almost a martyr), and determined to find a different interest and area so as not to compete with the older brother or sister; or be placid and easy to take care of, soft, and dreamy. Underneath either of these two stances is a strong awareness of the eldest child, whom the second child tries either to emulate or distance herself from by being something quite different. If the eldest sibling is too successful, the second may feel unable to compete, and then become difficult, insecure, and troublesome, giving up all attempt to catch up.

The second child is often a dreamer, a poet, a seeker. Rarely a fighter, she is less concerned with worldly matters. Not driven as much to succeed, second children do not feel the need to strive or to fulfil their duty, but instead to enjoy the world. Usually their sense of humor is stronger than that of first children, who tend to become upset or supersensitive more easily. This makes second children tougher – they are less sensitive to adult scolding or the need to be accepted. Because they live more in realms of fantasy, though, than first children, they often create an unreal world in which the older sibling seems to takes on larger-than-life importance. They invest their older siblings with qualities they feel that they themselves can never attain.

If a second child is a son following an older sister, his feminine characteristics can become exaggerated. In the beginning his sister may be protective towards him and so he learns to rely on her, not needing to prove himself. When she leaves home his masculine, more competitive characteristics are likely to start developing. As he gets older and if the distance in age is not too great, he may take on some of the characteristics of the eldest son, becoming protective of her. He may assume the position of the 'man' of the family, while his older sister becomes dependent on him. In this case the boy combines aspects of the first and second son. A similar pattern emerges if a first-born son dies and the second-born son becomes the eldest. In these situations he carries a tension between his original and his acquired self.

If the second child is a girl following an older brother, she may become the 'eternal sister', the companion, the good friend and helper. She mostly remains in the background, working behind the scenes, helping others gain recognition. She can be a very strong personality, but she shows her strength by pulling strings from behind and guiding those around her. She makes it possible for others to succeed and receive acknowledgment. Such second-born sisters have a special place in all communities. They are devoted, sometimes tyrannical companions. If their older brothers make a mess of their lives, the sister feels apologetic and embarrassed, but also protective, and may try to take on some of the expectations the older brother is not fulfilling. But this causes her tension and contradictory feelings. She wants to be carefree and fun-loving, but her brother has left her with a burden – so she may swing between being an excellent organizer and having a sense of ambivalence about accepting responsibility she feels is not really hers.

Although younger sisters may fight with their older brothers during some of their childhood, they also look up to them. They may become friends of their brothers' friends, especially as they enter adolescence and can be admired by these male friends. But older brothers can often be rather harsh on their younger sisters in their desire to protect them. The younger sister will then have a struggle for independence on her hands – not only from her parents but from her surrogate parent, her older brother, as well.

If the second sister follows an older sister, quite a different situation arises. She often becomes stiff and cool. If she tries to compete with her older sister or find her own area to excel in, she drives herself night and day to do well. One older sister, quite secure in her position in the family, was impatient with the hysterics of her younger sister who made such a fuss over everything, who wanted to be recognized but never believed she was good enough. Another younger sister tried to commit suicide because she felt she could not become as beautiful as her older sister. Some second sisters become like brothers to escape being competitors in the feminine realm. They become tomboys, the sons their fathers had wanted. This gives them a clearly defined role and eases their sense of inferiority. Many second sisters have a strong spiritual quality (as do second sons), and choose occupations in which they can devote themselves to others by being nurses, teachers, social workers, or doctors.

The third child

The third child is usually regarded as an outsider, a 'Johnny come lately'. The older two siblings often bury their differences with each other to join forces against the third. They have learned to get along with each other, and plot ways of causing misery to the third child. The third child therefore often grows up feeling 'odd man out', inferior, not easily mixing with others, over self-conscious and perhaps difficult to get on with. The family was in existence long before she arrived. The older children can talk about experiences that happened before she was born, and often in answer to 'Was I there?' comes the response, 'No, you weren't here yet'. The third child feels 'I missed all this'. The parents also often have less time to spend with her.

Third children have to find an area that is special to them. In response to this sort of situation they often strive hard and sometimes become visionaries or leaders. If third children have pluck, they will fight their way into the circle of the older ones. They will try all kinds of ways to be respected and included even if it means being a clown or demeaning themselves. They want to get some attention for themselves. If they are weak personalities, instead of fighting against such difficult odds they will sulk. They will accept the image of themselves as the 'little one' and set low standards for themselves until they come into maturity; at which point they may discover to their surprise that they have outstanding abilities they were unaware of.

If quite a few years have passed between the birth of the second and third child, a feeling of anticipation and specialness may surround the new birth. But the new child is also separated from the older two by the age-difference, which intensifies her feeling of being apart, cut off and inferior. As the older siblings go about their daily lives (often involved with school and older friends), the third child feels the gulf and decides the others are barely aware of her existence. The third child is always aspiring to be included, but never quite making it, which can result in a feeling of distrust towards all other people and a feeling of rejection. Third children carry a sense that they never received what was due them, that they were neglected and even rejected. The score can never be evened. In response to this feeling, they may adopt one of two attitudes. They can withdraw into self-pity or they can gather strength and try to conquer by force. They try to catch up, often reaching too high and wanting to achieve results too quickly because they sense time is passing. They can exhaust themselves in these attempts, and are seldom satisfied with their achievements. While the first-born children are concerned with the past, the third children often look towards the future. 'In character and social bearing, the third child is at least as problematical as the only child.' [12]

Patterns of behavior depend on the arrangements of brothers and sisters. Three or four children present more possible configurations than two. In a family with two or three girls followed by a boy, for instance, the boy (third or fourth child) has the qualities of his family position, but also the elite role of being the long-awaited son. Rather than push him away, his older sisters will be protective. He is not a rival to them, but someone special. He gets used to being doted upon and does not have to fight his way up. He will be allowed and expected to have different interests and different goals from his siblings. If the third child is, instead, the third brother or third sister, competition will be fierce and he or she will often suffer from the struggle. If two brothers are followed by a sister, she may be the odd one out and often ignored; she may not even have the involvement of being considered a rival to the brothers, who are busy competing among themselves, but as more of a nuisance they wish would go away. When there is a combination of girl, boy, girl; or boy, girl, boy; or girl, boy, boy; or boy, girl, girl, the situation is different in each case. But general characteristics of the third child still apply.

Destinies of later children, 4th, 5th, 6th, and so on, are not as clear as the first three. 4th (and 7th) tend to have qualities of the first; the 5th (and 8th) have qualities of the second; and the 6th (and 9th) have qualities of the third. Children of different position need each other. Each is necessary for the building of humanity.

König says each position can be summed up in the following statements.

The first-born attempts to conquer the world.

The second-born tries to live in harmony with the world.

The third-born is inclined to escape the direct meeting with the world.

The only child stands on the threshold, neither in nor out.

As a first child, he defends the past, as a second, he lives with the present, and he prepares the future as the third... All three are needed in the great web of human life.' [13]

2. Friends

Your friend is your needs answered.

When your friend speaks his mind, you fear not the 'nay' in your own mind, nor do you withhold the 'ay.' And when he is silent your heart ceases not to listen to his heart; for without words in friendship, all thoughts, all desires, all expectations are born and shared, with a joy that is unacclaimed.

When you part from your friend, you grieve not; for that which you love most in him may be clearer in his absence, as the mountain to the climber is clearer from the plain.

And let the best be for your friend. If he must know the ebb of your tide, let him know its flood also. For what is your friend that you should seek with him hours to kill? Seek him always with hours to live.

And in the sweetness of friendship let there be laughter, and sharing of pleasures. For in the dew of little things the heart finds its morning and is refreshed. [14]

Each of us stands at the center of our own world. Our friendships spread out from us in ever widening concentric circles, ranging from our closest confidantes to casual daily acquaintances. These relationships create the network of human ties in which we stand.

As children we tentatively move out from under the protective shield of our parents into the neighborhood. Through other children we meet the influences of other parents and other homes. Some of our friendships are based on being the same age, enjoying playing the same games, and just 'hanging out'. Through these relationships we learn to give and take, to stand up for ourselves, to make up after a fight, to conspire and to share. We learn to be a member of society.

Some friendships are stronger than others, and these may last a long time, or at least their influence may. We share our secrets with these friends. We find out that we are different. Slowly through our friendships we come to realize that each of us has a special identity.

As we go to school the circle of our relationships widens even more. Now we meet people who live further from our immediate neighborhood. They may be very different from the people who live on our street, so they bring something new into our experience. Our school friends bring new ideas, new ways of relating and doing things. Together we explore the world of childhood. We experience what it is like to be in groups. We learn to relate to power, experience being included or left out. A wider choice of friends becomes available to us. We begin to find out that we like certain kinds of people, but not others.

As we move into puberty, the circles become even wider, but a new *quality* also makes itself felt. Our feelings are deepened: new emotions dawn as we begin to experience physical attraction and stirrings of the soul. Deep ties develop which feel as if they will last forever. Different kinds of relationships may emerge through long intimate conversations with an older person, a special respect for a teacher, or a 'crush' on an unattainable hero. Excitement and adventure accompany the making of our new connections. Meanwhile our relationship to our parents goes through strain and stress as we pull further away on some days and want to be closer on others. As we make different kinds of relationships, we become more selective, continually refining our image of who we are and what kind of people we want to be with. Our ideals become clearer.

As we reach adulthood our relationships – our family, our friends, the people we work with – tend to stabilize. The ripples widen on the waters of our life-experience as we move from being concerned only about ourselves to becoming truly interested in other people. Friendships continue to bring great richness into our lives.

Relationships exist and change in time, undergoing metamorphosis. Certainly the relationship to our parents is likely to be the longest of our lives. We have a different relationship to each of our brothers and sisters, uncles, aunts, cousins, and grandparents. Of these relationships there may be one or two that are special. We feel closer to some of these people than to our parents at times – a cousin who shared our interests but also acted as a mentor, an aunt who provided a haven in her home for us to feel peace and contentment, an uncle with whom we could have deep conversations. These relationships also change over the years. There are periods of closeness and periods of distance. But those relationships remain there, ready to be picked up again. The family bonds that unite us are different from friendship bonds. We don't choose them consciously. They are part of the 'given', the tapestry warp. And they are a thread with our past – with our ancestors, with our inheritance. Whether they are a thread with our future remains a question. Relationships with our friends are different.

Some friendships last only for a particular period – such as a close childhood friendship that seems to be very strong for a while and then fades away as we grow older. When I was in 7th and 8th grade I was friends with Anita Gilardi. Every Sunday I bicycled over to her house. There I was absorbed into her large Italian family: some members were in the kitchen making pasta, others were playing bocci-ball out on the lawn, the younger children were chasing each other around the garden, the teenagers were talking in the back bedroom. Then we all gathered at dinnertime for a wonderful feast of eating and talking. I never experienced such warmth as on those Sundays. But after two years Anita and I lost interest in each other and the friendship faded. Yet the experience remained vivid. This friendship gave me a feeling for what it means when a large family gathers, alive with the enjoyment of each other. Beyond the tears, the smiles, the arguments, the forgiveness, something special lived and thrived. Can this kind of group-feeling come about without being rooted in family? We *can* experience a new kind of 'family' – one we choose rather than inherit, but it takes extra effort and commitment to build something new. It is also very rewarding.

Some relationships are active in youth, then fade and are renewed again in later life. I was very close friends with Dara from seventh grade through eleventh grade. After that I moved and we kept in touch rather erratically. In the last ten years we have renewed the friendship. There is a special element to this relationship: each of us knows aspects of the other that no one else in our present circles can understand. She can tell me what I was like at a younger age, and I can tell her. We can remember making up stories with imaginary characters, discussing our first loves, and developing interests that lasted for years. I had a special affection for her mother (who has since died). Dara is one of the few people alive today who knew and experienced my parents with me as a family. These are important aspects of our friendship, but they are not enough in themselves. What has drawn us back together is that in addition to our familiarity with each other from the past, we also enjoy and admire each other now. We still learn from each other, and we are concerned about each other. There is a comfort and familiarity in the relationship that is different from others.

I feel the same way when we visit a friend of my husband. Jim and David played together from the time they were three years old. They have many common values and interests that keep the friendship alive even though it isn't close the way it used to be. When we visit David, I feel a special connection to a part of my husband's past. He understands Jim and knows him from long before I came into his life. Yet it is a free, undemanding relationship. Friendship doesn't have such strong expectations as family relationships do.

Some friendships are strongly focused on our common work and may end when we change jobs. It's not unusual for friends of this sort to try to keep the relationship going after one of them has left the job, but most often it doesn't work. Such a relationship is frequently based on the common experience of being in a particular group at the same time. Work-related friends offer support for each other. They make the day more pleasant, perhaps feel solidarity with each other against their employers or discover new ways of doing their job. But although they may have spoken together about intimate details of their lives, there often isn't enough depth to the relationship for it to last in different circumstances.

Some friendships develop because we are neighbors. We are in touch with each others' day-to-day lives. We help each other out, chat, go for walks, have some meals together. We care about each other's children, often providing a friendly place for them to visit or take refuge. If they are childless (or we are) there may be a special relationship that develops between adult and child – an invitation for milk and cookies, an opportunity to learn how to garden or change a flat tyre. As neighbors we often join together to improve our neighborhood, to organize the putting in of sewers, cleaning up trash, ensuring safety, and dealing with traffic. We borrow tools or eggs. Our friendship gives our neighborhood (or our apartment house) a warm, secure feeling

Other relationships develop because our children are friends. Sharing a rainy afternoon with someone who has children of similar ages helps us see a little beyond our own family preoccupations. As the children get older we participate in school events together, take our children to each other's houses, have tea or coffee while they play, gossip about acquaintances we have in common, share some of our problems. We strengthen each other during this particular time in our lives. However, as the children make more choices in their friendships and pull apart from old relationships, we adults usually pull apart too. We no longer have enough in common to continue the relationship.

In all these situations there are also special relationships that don't fade away but grow stronger as time goes on. These carry on through many years, undergoing cycles of change and growth. They affect us deeply, and we change because of them.

The key element in friendship is that we don't inherit friends the way we do our family. We freely choose to begin and end these relationships. Something from the distant past may be drawing us together, but the decision to stay together is one that we make out of our own free will. Our friendships have different levels of intimacy. With one friend we may share fears or unhappiness only in fairly general, conversational ways, while with another we bare our souls and tell all the details of what is frightening us or causing despair.

There are other relationships which are neither inherited nor exactly chosen. For example teachers. In the teacher-student relationship we expect the teacher to act responsibly, hopefully inspiring a young person to learn; the student is expected to listen, to learn, to converse with, and to respect the teacher. But in some such relationships the teacher's influence on the young person becomes more powerful and enduring. The teacher may also be influenced by the student – perhaps developing a warm appreciation of her individuality, perhaps through new ideas which the student contributes, or a stinging comment that startles the teacher to new awareness. Some of the strongest relationships of my life have been with teachers (and later with students). It is probably not surprising therefore that I became a teacher too.

Friendships are special relationships, providing a stage for the acting out of human drama and the cultivation of love. Although the degree of intensity varies, the room for growth is always there. Friendships can come and go, but deep friendship invested with emotional involvement, with its pain and joy, influences us profoundly.

Women's friendships have in the past often centered around household tasks such as washing clothes or caring for children. Such relationships have provided support, an outlet for expressions of frustration, and companionship. Women's relationships, however, have usually taken second place to their marriage. Friendships for single women take on a particularly important role, providing the companionship and support that is otherwise given by a partner. In more recent times women's friendships have come to be valued in their own right, not just as a second-best substitute for man-woman relationships.

Men's friendships are often centered on their work – on the farm, in the office, or on the battlefield – where they can experience strong bonds of support in the face of danger. They may nurture their relationships in the corner pub, the gym, the athletic field, the hiking trail or fishing spot. Their value has often consisted in mutual support against an enemy, of accomplishing a task together, nurturing each other, and in the satisfaction comradeship brings.

Woman-man friendships are more complicated. Some people feel there can never be a true platonic relationship between a man and woman because the tension of a romantic/sexual element is always potentially there. This is not necessarily so. A flirtatious element *can* be part of the friendship in a harmless, enjoyable way without it ever becoming anything more. Some people find they enjoy man-woman friendships the most because of the complementary balance of different elements that is possible. The success of a true friendship between man and woman is also affected by the response to it of one's spouse and vice versa. Delicacy, sensitivity and special understanding are necessary for a close man-woman friendship to thrive.

Where societies are authoritarian, even tyrannical, friendship becomes a means of survival. Once trusted, a friend becomes a lifeline. In many discussions with friends and acquaintances in the former Soviet Union, this theme continually surfaced. When you have a friend in such circumstances, you trust that person with your life. You know what a risk the wrong friend can be. Such friends might well become closer than family members. And where economic stresses are particularly difficult, a network of friends makes it possible to get the food necessary for a family to survive. One friend may have an opportunity to get hold of a basket of apples while the other reciprocates with sausages. They think about each other's needs. In such situations, instead of operating with money, barter and skill-sharing becomes the means of exchange. When we had car problems in Lithuania, our hostess called up a mechanic to help us. She told us, 'I give him English lessons. He helps us when we need it. There will be no exchange of money'. This man took a day off work to go with my husband to a special mechanic who knew more about our particular car (The special mechanic was in *this* man's network of friends). In these situations the interlocking network of friendships forms an alternative system within society. Over and over again I was told in the former Soviet Union: 'When you trust a friend, you are friends for life. If need be, you die for your friend.'

Friendship as the basis of the new family

Friendships are the key to new kinds of families. So different from our hereditary families, our friendships are a reflection of our interests, our needs, our soul struggles, our values, and our self-chosen identity. Through our friends we extend our awareness of life's struggles and joys, of beauty and of love. Making friends who are different from ourselves carries us beyond our familiar way of approaching life's questions, to a more specifically 'human' experience. We weave intimate, interconnecting threads. Friendship is a celebration of love. Our friends love us because we are who we are – they don't have to but they want to. How wonderful! How filled with blessings that makes us feel!

Having friends spread around the country or in different parts of the world gives us a completely different relationship to space and time. It is as if those particular places light up on a map and change the way we read the news. The faraway land is no longer a collection of statistics of population and land area, but the home of Natasha, Keniche, Maria Louisa, or Hassan. Such friendship may not have the same daily involvement and intensity, but it changes our relationship to the world.

3. Man and woman

The question of masculine and feminine

In the second section of this book I will describe the changes that the special relationships of lovers, spouses and life partners go through, but here let us explore the question of gender differences. How do we work with the similarities and differences between males and females? When I was growing up in the forties and fifties, we got the message that boys and girls were different. We dressed differently. We behaved differently. Then in the sixties, we heard: 'We're all the same.' Unisex fashions were in vogue. We tried to pretend there weren't any big differences, beyond the obvious ones. That wasn't satisfactory either. But research is now uncovering more differences than had been previously assumed, including those between male and female brain structure and even blood-composition.

Part of the difficulty is that we have confused being equal before the law with being the same. When it comes to being paid equally for the same job, having an equal chance at promotion – all the areas which touch on the political, economic, and social life – it is right that no distinction should be made between male and female.

But there are real differences, of both biological and soul nature, between men and women. We have also been influenced differently by our societies and cultures. We should be focusing our attention on understanding the differences rather than on arguing about rights and supremacy. The ancient Chinese use the yin-yang symbol, a circle with two forms fitting into each other. One is dark, the other light. Yin is female and has a small circle of yang within it; yang is male and likewise contains a small circle of yin. Each is its own, yet each has the other in it. This is a picture common to various cultures. Jung's psychology of animus and anima also relates to such an understanding. Steiner, too, sees this as a central aspect of soul development.

We have one set of characteristics determined by our physical gender, and another set of opposite characteristics which live in the soul (often hidden). The female or feminine characteristics are receptive, intuitive, sensitive, and tend to *harmonize* with nature. The male or masculine characteristics are more active, rational, objective, more related to *mastering* nature. Women and men have both aspects: men have more outward masculine characteristics, but their soul bodies, which influence feelings and soul-experience, are feminine. Some men are more in touch with these soul characteristics than others; some try to deny them because of the gender-expectations and norms of society, are frightened of what lies in the shadows, in the depths of their soul. Although women relate to others through their more obvious female characteristics, their souls also have masculine qualities. Women, though, find it easier to be in touch with these qualities, because contemporary society tends to uphold them as necessary for success.

The important point is that we have access to both masculine and feminine characteristics in ourselves. There is great wisdom in these complementary qualities: each is appropriate in different situations, and in many situations both are called for. For example, there are situations we grasp intuitively (using our feminine characteristics), but then have to justify our view logically (using our masculine characteristics). There are times we have to master an aspect of nature, but we can do it in a sensitive way, using feminine qualities, by considering the ecology and interrelationships of the natural world. It is the active use of both sets of characteristics that will lead to the wisest decisions. All over the world today we see the results of human beings pursuing short-sighted 'objective' goals, which have allowed us to master nature by misusing our energy resources, destroying the fragile balance of the planet. It is clear this cannot go on – that we need a greater balance of masculine and feminine.

For six years, a French professor called Elisabeth Badinter opened her philosophy seminar by asking her class – of mostly male students – questions to do with male identity. Although she didn't arrive at concrete answers, she brought the experiences together in the book *XY: De l'Identité masculine*.

She says: '...because women have had to redefine themselves in the last three decades it is time for men to do the same. The traditional male is being replaced by someone more in touch with his female, as well as his male side.'

Drawing on Scandinavian and American studies, Badinter discusses the old fashioned 'hard man', the present-day 'soft man' – a sort of post-feminist human dish-rag – and the 'gentle man' who combines strength and sensibility, who has become a male without destroying his feminine side. Badinter prefers the phrase 'reconciled man' to 'gentle-man' as better suggesting joining of separate elements, the steps that must be taken... She advocates 'a new androgyny that does not mean the male is unmanned or feminized, but that he will go beyond gender to partake of both as needed.' [15]

Carol Gilligan in her book *In a Different Voice, Psychological Theory and Women's Development*,[16] highlights differences between the psychological development of men and women. She draws our attention to the fact that most studies of human development have been based on males. The need to separate from the parent is not generally as strong for girls, who model themselves on the mother, usually the primary care giver. The boy experiences himself as separate from his mother and strives to find his own identity. This basic difference between the needs and experiences of young boys and girls, influences their feelings about themselves and their social relationships. It is one more ingredient to add to all the others that shape us.

4. The mystery of relationships

The inner sun of my destiny
Rises over the night,
Lighting my heart with certitude.
It touches with its rays those who are near to me,
And slowly the blessed circle expands
To embrace at last all men and all creation.

Trives [17]

One of the great mysteries of human life is the fact that we meet and enter into relationships with certain people. Are these meetings accidental, predetermined, random? How did I take the steps that led me here? If I hadn't enrolled in that class would I ever have met you? There is great wonder and wisdom in such questions. People meet and form relationships in most varied places and circumstances – in the park, on an airplane, taking shelter during a storm, in the library, in the army, on top of the Eiffel Tower, in the grocery store, in car accidents, and every other place you can imagine. Why do they develop? Why do we feel drawn to one person and not another? Sometimes we feel something (someone?) from the spiritual world has led us to the very moment when we could meet this person, and now we cannot imagine life without him or her.

In the eight volumes on *Karmic Relationships*[18], Rudolf Steiner explores the laws of karma and destiny that express themselves in human life. For anyone interested in such questions these books are of great interest. He shows that these relationships are not chance meetings but are deeply connected to our past lives. He characterizes the different kinds of meetings we have with people – the ones where we feel immediate familiarity, sometimes great sympathy; other times great antipathy, in which we constantly get on the wrong side of each other. Almost always such strong attractions, both positive and negative, come out of past-life relationships, from the deeds and connections of our distant past. Sometimes we need to compensate for wrongdoings we have committed, and now are given the opportunity to do so. Other times we have worked very closely together in the past and enthusiastically continue such a relationship.

We aren't usually aware of relationships from previous lives, but sometimes we have intuitions. We dream about these people. We feel we know them in a different way. Other people we meet are very interesting to us, but the interest remains on a more intellectual or aesthetic level, and we seldom dream about them. Steiner speaks of how our destiny brings us to a necessary meeting point with certain people. But what we do from that moment on, how we relate and carry the relationship forward, lies within our own freedom. If we consider the possibility of the working of karma in our relationships we may come to an intuitive understanding of the dynamics at work in our relationships.

When I was a child I had a recurring dream. I lived in a village with small houses, made of wooden blocks painted to look like a German village, certainly nothing like the houses of my city neighborhood. The houses were arranged in a circle. This village felt warm and secure. It was 'my' village, no one else's.

Whenever I met a person who turned out to be significant in my life, I dreamed this dream, and this person came to dwell in one of the houses. This dream continued into my adulthood. Now I can see that the dream was a picture of the relationships that formed the 'building blocks' of my destiny.

5. The individual and the group

Not only are we members of groups from the moment of our birth, but our development as individuals depends on this. The individual and the group may seem to be polarities at first. Freud held that the group, represented by society, frustrated and oppressed the desires of the individual, causing serious psychological problems.

But that is the paradox of the reality which the human being inhabits. There is always tension between what the individual wants and what the group wants. As long as we stay on the level of desires there is going to be opposition and competition. But if we could consider that it is only within the context of such tension that the human being can transform and develop spiritually, then we might find the dynamics of relationships more interesting and even helpful. When we meet and relate to another person, we find the limits of ourselves. We may step into someone else's space, not truly respecting her, or step too far back and ignore the other's needs. There are times we need to step back into ourselves to touch base, take stock, face ourselves. At other times we need to reach out more, be interested in the other person, serve that person's needs. There are also moments when we feel there are no boundaries between us, that we're 'one'. Relationships are the testing ground of our continuing development.

Love and growth are two related but distinct aspects we can find in relationships. We may think that the most important thing in life is to find the right person to love. If only we can find the right partner, we believe, then everything will be fine. But once the beloved is found, challenges arise to test that love, to demand our growth. Or we may decide that developing our human potential is what is most important. But it doesn't take long for us to find out that what we really need to do is awaken the capacity to love. Whichever we start from, we mysteriously end up with the other.

6. Love

Rollo May defines love as delight in the presence of the other person, an affirming of her value and development as much as one's own.[19] This seems at first like a very simple statement, but when we consider the phrase 'as one's own' then it's quite a different story. Rollo May is talking about complicated things such as priorities, commitment, and sacrifice. Words are easy, actions are more difficult, particularly if we are to sustain them day after day. So this definition may seem abstract on its own. Can we ever really define love at all? Rudolf Steiner cautions us not to feel we can express love through definition but perhaps rather through spiritual imagery.

> Suppose a man has a loving heart, and out of his loving heart he performs a loving action to another who needs love. He gives something to that other person; but he does not on that account become emptier when he performs loving actions to another; he receives more, he becomes fuller, he has still more, and if he performs the loving action a second time he will again receive more. One does not become poor, nor empty by giving love or doing loving actions; on the contrary, one becomes richer, one becomes fuller. One pours forth something into the other person, something which makes one fuller oneself... Love is so complex a thing that no man should have the arrogance to define it, to fathom the nature of love. Love is a symbol, a simple symbol: a glass of water, which when it is poured out becomes even fuller, gives us one quality of the workings of love.[20]

Love described in this way has an alchemical flavour. It is close to the Greek definition of empathy – to feel *into*, which is a much deeper experience than sympathy, to feel *with*. The Greeks taught that if people felt true empathy with the characters in a tragedy then they would experience catharsis – a cleansing and transformation. Something of the transformative quality of catharsis is contained in love, and as with all transformations the process is long and complex. For one thing, instead of enlarging our own feelings of self, we have to feel the sorrows and joys of the other person within ourselves. In this empathy love develops out of our soul forces and overcomes egotism. One of the magical aspects of living love in this way is that it helps us on our path to maturity. We are going to make mistakes and must therefore be humble in confronting ourselves and our partners. We cannot wait until we are mature enough to truly empathize with someone before we begin to love!

We may search for a companion or companions with whom to share our journey. The image of this companion is often idealised, beckoning us on to the search in spite of the heartbreak and difficulty which may lie ahead. What is it in this ideal image of a relationship that is worth all the trouble? What is it that calls to us?

When we do find the person who corresponds to our ideal, we speak of being 'blinded by love'; but it is not so much blindness as a momentary glimpse of her ideal being, the higher being, the human spirit. The ideal of our quest is the meeting and the merging of two separate beings into one. In the words of fairy tales, 'They married and lived happily ever after'. This is a picture of a deep spiritual truth. When we marry, we join together in spirit, the two become one in a state of unity and completeness. Marriage therefore also invokes the search for our own higher self and its relationship to the divine world, to God. This search has preoccupied humanity since earliest times as is recorded in legend and song.

Unfortunately, the ideal of love has been trivialized in modern life. Billboards and commercials shout at us that we can find love by buying the right soap, the right soft drink, the alluring bathing suit, and through sex. There is little said about tenderness, understanding, forgiveness, closeness, or commitment. Teenagers who are so vulnerable to these messages then get the idea that having sex is a good way to experience closeness and warmth – that these will bring love. But they often find this doesn't work. Physical closeness brings physical closeness, which by itself has nothing to do with love at all. In fact, if we seek it over and over with different partners, we can eventually lose something of ourselves instead of gaining anything. Yet there is a widespread fear that lack of physical closeness equals emptiness. Teenagers aren't the only ones who feel this way. Many adults look for closeness through a round of sexual encounters.

We can also look for love in the early passion of a new relationship. As long as we feel the excitement of being together, and agree with each other, it is easy to love. But what happens after the passion cools and we've discovered we have differences in our outlook, in our values? Is it time to dissolve the relationship and find someone new?

The deeper capacities in the human soul that really have to do with love are seldom acknowledged. You can't talk about them on billboards or in commercials. It takes more time, it needs more space. It is easier to talk about what they are not, than what they are. What does Paul mean when he says 'Love is patient, Love is kind' in Corinthians?[21] Those were the words my husband and I chose to speak to each other during our wedding ceremony. I go back to them over and over again, because they are such difficult words to understand. I thought I knew what they meant when I said them, but as the years go by I continually return to them and ask myself: What is patience? What is kindness? Why am I lacking in these qualities?

The process of loving another human being brings about a transformation in ourselves. Our love becomes the field on which we make our way. As we learn more about loving, we learn so much more about ourselves and what our lives mean. We grow.

7. Growth

Then there is the other path – growth, changing, becoming. What is its secret meaning? The word growth has become a common cliché since the First World War. Franklin Baumer, Yale Professor, states:

> Becoming, it should be made clear, does not refer here merely to new and changing answers to perennial questions, which may be taken for granted, or even to great revolutions in ideas. It refers instead to a mode of thinking that contemplates everything, nature, man, society, history, God himself... as not merely changing, but as forever evolving into

something new and different. It disbelieves in all fixities, absolute and 'eternal' ideas.[22]

The modern human being (especially in the West) feels the need to keep changing, not to remain stagnant. This is often perceived to be a need in the physical and soul realm alone. 'Keep exercising, gather experiences.' Change doesn't necessarily lead to growth, but it presents the opportunity for it. In order for growth to occur, the human spirit has to be active, take hold, shape things and turn them inside out, transform them. Such growth can take place as a result of courageously accepting a difficult destiny, it can develop when we gain a clear perspective on our lives, realize our next step, and have the courage to take it, or from achieving respect and understanding for another human being.

The popular definition of a fulfilled life usually means having good looks, lots of money, lovely surroundings, long weekends and few responsibilities. This is the promise dangled in front of us by contemporary media images, and there are times when it is difficult to resist the allure of that promise. We have to keep reminding ourselves that the illusion is not reality. Illusion has been manufactured in advertising and film studios. On some days we might feel that every-day reality could never measure up to the illusion, yet real life is so much richer and deeper than anything Hollywood could invent (and less boring).

Is happiness the primary motivating factor in our lives? A scene from Rudolf Steiner's life gives us a possible answer. Steiner was teaching in the Working Men's College in Berlin at the time. In her memoirs one of his students describes an excursion that Steiner and some of his students took in the countryside.

On one occasion several young people walked by his side and spoke of their lives. One of them cried out impetuously, 'Why do we have so little pleasure in life, and yet everyone would like so much to be happy?' Dr. Steiner replied. 'Yes, but perhaps life is not given us in order that we may be happy.' 'Whatever else can it be for?' said the young man, quite taken aback. 'Well, suppose we had life in order to fulfil a task.' Steiner replied. These words were uttered in a very kindly tone, but with such deep emphasis that we all walked on for a while in silence, and even though I did not understand them fully, the words remained firmly fixed in my memory. Already at that time such power lay in his words that they did not fade from one's mind. [23]

In the last century, and the first half of this one, people in the West were considered strange, or at least suspect, if they spoke about spiritual or soul matters. It was fine to go to church if you wanted, but not to speak about such intimate unknowable aspects of life unless you were a religious leader or a poet. Ordinary people were supposed to pay attention to getting a good job, making money, supporting a family and making their way in life. In the Sixties people began to talk about spiritual matters openly. The outer goals weren't satisfying. Something was missing. People were having spiritual experiences and talking about them. The great interest in eastern religion awakened in people the realization that western societies were ignoring something important. The increasing use of drugs was partly an attempt to break through the hard wall of materialism to the spirit (without the hard work of inner development otherwise necessary to achieve it). The thousands of people who gave up everything they had, their education, positions, families, their things – to search for something that had no weight in this world, shook modern society. Since then life has settled down, but the interest in self-growth and spiritual matters has become a more accepted part of our lives.

We are living in a time in which many people are having spiritual experiences, often outside the confines of any specific religious structure. When they try to understand these experiences, some find traditional religion in its present form of little help. To explain these experiences, all kinds of groups, authorities, and teachings have sprung up alongside the teachings of religious traditions. This is a challenge to the old established authorities, and also means that many different spiritual disciplines and self-help groups are representing themselves as the true way. It takes careful discrimination to find one's path through the maze. Some of the traditional religious institutions have attempted to approach spiritual questions in a new way more suited to contemporary people, while other groups have reacted with fear and attacked non-mainstream approaches.

One of the most significant changes which has allowed the spirit to be acknowledged, is in our questioning of what happens after death. The recording of near-death experiences has brought some clarity and understanding to the subject, which has helped many people recognize that a spiritual world exists, that death is not a big black hole but a threshold to another state of being. This also raises questions about where we were before birth.

The search to understand such questions – what happens after death, what is the meaning of life, what is the true self, what is love – has become acceptable alongside our more immediate questions, such as what career should I prepare for, do I want a family, and how do I want to live my life. It is no longer so embarrassing to admit that we are searching for spiritual meaning. In the past, some people separated themselves from regular life and went into the wilderness to meditate for years to find such answers. Medieval knights went to battle to defend the weak, to honor a lady, to test their courage. They donned armour and used lance and sword as they fought their adversaries and strove to be worthy of King Arthur's Round Table. But those who wished to serve even higher goals hoped to be asked to serve the Grail, depicted as a cup, a goblet, a precious stone. It was said to have been thrown out of heaven in the battle between Lucifer and Michael, and later to have been the cup that caught the blood of Christ during the crucifixion.

The knights were figures who embodied the masculine quest, who did battle and overcame adversities. But the Grail Knights, in particular, are also concerned with healing and nurturing, and so unite the two journeys – masculine and feminine. This image can still offer us a path for our spiritual development in these times.

Those who saw the Grail experienced remarkable healing powers. The Grail has to do with the healing of the soul of humanity, and those who are Grail knights take upon themselves the process of self-transformation – in place of outer battles, they take on inner ones, fighting arrogance, selfishness and vanity within themselves, replacing these egoistic soul qualities with compassion, concern, interest in other people's suffering, devotion, and love. The image of the Grail Knights serves as a model of self-transformation for centuries to come. They are the archetypes of the modern selfless search for the spirit. When we go in search of such a goal today, when we take this pathway seriously, it may mean changing lifestyles. It may mean changing jobs. It sometimes means breaking up relationships as new priorities are chosen. Or the changes may be inner ones which do not reflect outwardly in a significant way. At the very least these changes cause anxiety and soul trembling as the secure foundations of life are shaken.

III
Life Cycles and Human Rhythms

To everything there is a season,
And a time to every purpose under heaven:
A time to be born, and a time to die;
A time to plant, and a time to pluck up that which is planted;
A time to kill, and a time to heal;
A time to break down, and a time to build up;
A time to weep, and a time to laugh.
A time to mourn, and a time to dance;
A time to cast away stones, and a time to gather stones together;
A time to embrace, and a time to refrain from embracing;
A time to seek, and a time to lose;
A time to keep, and a time to cast away;
A time to rend, and a time to sew;
A time to keep silence, and a time to speak;
A time to love, and a time to hate;
A time for war, and a time for peace.

Ecclesiastes [1]

1. The rhythms of human life

The leaves are turning golden, the air is crisp, the days are becoming shorter. On the hillside the ground is hard. All around us growth is slowing down. We know from past years that this autumn season will pass into winter, then into spring and summer, until once again we experience those wonderful autumn days. We take this yearly rhythm into our souls. We experience through our senses the wealth of its sights, tastes, smells, sounds, textures, and temperature changes. We hear the cracking of ice, the cry of the new-born lamb, the splendor of nature's garments. A high school friend used to sing a song as we walked down the streets of New York City. I recall only the first line, 'God painted a picture and called it the world and filled it with all of His dreams'. These words come back to me when I rejoice in the glory of sunset, the majesty of snow-peaked mountains, the gurgling of a brook bubbling through gently scented woods. We know the signs of the seasons in the place where we live and welcome them year after year. Some years a season comes a little earlier, some years later. No two years are alike. Even in parts of the earth where the signs are not so clear, where month after month is like perpetual summer, we can still perceive subtle changes if we observe carefully.

In the same way there are also seasons in our lives, called phases or passages. As well as an annual rhythm – corresponding to the seasons' round and the recurring seasonal and religious festivals of all traditions, as well as our personal anniversaries and days of remembrance – we also have many other rhythms: the seven-year rhythm, the 18.7-year rhythm, 30-year rhythm, the 33-year rhythm. Each emphasizes a different quality of the season of our soul-life. As we become aware of these rhythms, meaning and order begin to come into what otherwise seems chaotic or random. We can prepare ourselves for a new phase by understanding them. Instead of passively dreaming through life, we take a conscious hand in directing it. Then we become co-creators with the spiritual world in the shaping and forming of our biography.

A number of psychologists and thinkers have pointed to such phases of human life. Rudolf Steiner described the spiritual and planetary aspects of each phase of the life cycle. Bernhard Lievegoed, former Director of the Netherlands Pedagogical Institute (NPI), elaborated the understanding of rhythms given by Rudolf Steiner to apply to the lives of individuals and organizations. He focused on the phases of the human biography as a way of understanding our life tasks. American psychologists including Erik Erikson and Daniel Levinson also developed the principle of adult life-cycles and rhythms. Levinson studied men between 18 and 47. He said, 'Many changes can take place *within* each period. But a person moves from one to the next only when he starts working at new developmental tasks and builds a new structure for his life' [2] And no structure, according to Levinson's calculations, 'can last longer than seven or eight years.' [3]

Based on the work of Erikson and Levinson, Gail Sheehy then carried out interviews to see if people's lives confirmed the psychological theory. She presented the results of her work in her outstanding book *Passages*. For the first time information about adult life-cycles was made widely available in this popular best seller. Sheehy confirmed the existence of the seven-year periods as a basic life rhythm. She pointed out that although men and women 'are rarely in the same place struggling with the same questions at the same time', the 'fundamental steps of expansion that will open a person, over time, to the full flowering of his or her individuality are the same for both genders'. 4

The rhythms of life give us a relationship to time. They act as markers along the way and orient us to life around us. Through them we breathe in and breathe out, whether over a period of 24 hours, seven years or 'fourscore years and ten'.

> The cool wide rhythms of the night
> Linger at the break of day.
> When stillness lies with glistening dew
> On long grass blades
> My soul is like a vase of peace,
> A chalice for the rising sun.

Eleanor Trives 5

2. The seven-year rhythm

The seven-year periods or phases form the basic rhythm of human life. Significant biological changes occur in the course of each approximate seven-year period. In addition every seven years leads to the 'birth' of new elements in the unfolding individuality. Each individual incarnates out of the spiritual world, bringing qualities and needs from his own past, and will return after his experiences on earth. Each seven-year phase gradually develops into the next.

In every phase the body, soul, and spirit interweave within one dominant 'theme'. Other themes are also present, but of lesser importance. Human life is a symphony containing many different melodies and rhythmic patterns. In each rhythmic phase, elements of past phases reappear together with a new aspect. Certain themes come up again and again, but the individual responds differently depending on his particular life phase. Loneliness, for example, can be a theme throughout life, but a fourteen-year old responds differently to it, with different maturity and capacities, from a thirty-five or a sixty year old.

During our lives we experience moments of rest, moments of dynamic activity, and moments of chaos. It is quite common for a crisis to occur at the end of a seven-year phase before we pass onto the next phase. When the crisis has passed, something new can come to expression. We can observe a similar, parallel process in the plant world: in the stem of a plant we see contraction into the node and expansion into leaf, then the contraction into the calyx (bud) and expansion into flower. If we regularly contemplate this image, it can help us come to an understanding of phases in human life.

Each seven-year phase marks a new birth. The first – physical birth – is the most obvious: the child emerges from the womb, leaving behind the spiritual world where it existed as an independent entity. The following births take place in the soul and spirit, when something new is born that was not there before. This is not expressed physically but in attitudes, feelings, and capacities which arise in the individual.

In this book I will focus mainly on these seven-year-rhythms, but I will mention the lunar rhythm too, because it highlights the essential character of the particular phase we are in and helps us understand why certain questions keep coming back to meet us.

3. Other rhythms

The lunar rhythm

When a child is born the higher ego, the human being's purely spiritual aspect, stays in the spiritual world. From then on it influences and inspires the individual from the spiritual world rather than from within the human soul. What we call the ego or 'I' is only a reflection of the higher ego; some refer to it as the *lower ego*. At certain times in life we experience greater openness to our 'birth impulses', to the pre-birth intentions of the higher ego. This 'opening' occurs in the lunar rhythm of 18 years, 7 months, when the planets line up in a configuration similar to the one at the time of our birth. These times are called moon nodes. At this time – not so much the exact day as the general period around the moon node – the higher ego exerts a specially strong influence. It influences the human being in two directions: bringing will into the thinking and consciousness into the will, helping us realize our pre-birth intentions.

The **1st lunar node is at 18 yrs, 7 months.** We have an experience of the meaning of our life. It is a momentary *waking up to what we want to do in life*, why we are here. It often expresses itself in the idealism of late adolescence and the protest against what is disappointing. Many young people have such a momentary experience when they sense they are more than they seem to be. This experience which happens quite unconsciously, sometimes in a dream, fires our will to want to give something to the world. It then tends to fade in the busy-ness of life. But it still remains somewhere in the background, inspiring us to get on with our lives and do what we came to do.

2nd lunar node is at 37 years, 2 months. We gain some sense of the meaning of our life. We have passed the midpoint and are looking for something new. It may be a time when some things come to an end and enthusiasm for a past interest re-awakens (often one that lay fallow since the last moon node). But our life attitude is different now. Instead of adolescent or youthful idealism we may experience doubt, weariness and heaviness. *The stirrings of our pre-birth intentions cause us to find a new way to connect with our life-purpose.* This may lead to a change of locality, career, and way of life. Out of this change new possibilities occur. New ideas, impulses, and directions in life light up from within. The stimulus of the higher ego helps us to have renewed energy to move forward.

3rd lunar node is at 55 years, 9 months. This is one of the most active periods of our life. We have been hard at work often with a great deal of energy and drive, making our mark in the world. This period often comes to crisis with health problems. Our bodies could block our capacity to fulfil our pre-birth intentions. We have to find a way to come to terms with our changing bodies. *Out of this struggle with our health we can find new strength and power which expresses itself in our desire to direct our energy to greater goals beyond our personal ambitions.* Our higher ego again presents us with our purpose in life and inspires us to get on with it.

4th lunar node is at 74 years, 4 months. This comes during the 'years of grace' when we no longer serve personal ambitions but the life beyond. We have fulfilled or not fulfilled most of what we came on earth to do. That time is over. *Whatever we achieve now is completely out of our freedom. We are no longer working out of the past but creating our future destiny.* We become increasingly aware that what happens here on earth is connected with the spiritual world, and conversely, what happens in the spiritual world is influenced by events upon the earth. In our daily life we carry a consciousness of those who have died. Our consciousness hovers between the world of the living and the world of the dead, especially if we feel the presence of the dead very strongly. For some people this time brings an explosion of new energy and the ability to communicate the essence of their life's work.

5th moon node is at 93. This is a continuation of the 4th moon node. Because few of us reach this point in full consciousness, it is difficult to say much about it.

4. A closer look at the seven-year rhythm

Now let us return to the seven-year rhythm.

Birth to 7 years: the birth of the physical body.
From their earliest days children are like one great sense organ, taking in sense impressions of all kinds from the outside world. They turn these sense impressions into their own activity through imitation. By imitating those around them, children learn to stand upright and walk. They learn to understand and speak their 'mother tongue'. These impressions influence the physical body: if they are

quiet and soft, the child can breathe more rhythmically and relax; but when children's immature nervous systems try to process startling noises, flickering lights, and quick visual impressions, it is too much for them. They can become exhausted, tense and afraid.

Around the 3rd year children experience their own being and start referring to themselves as 'I'. Self-awareness now awakens in a rudimentary way and memory begins to develop. Although children of this age have moments of consciousness, they are in general rather 'asleep'. External sensory impressions are experienced inwardly and lay the basis for conscious ideas to be formed later. At this stage, children enter into the world mainly through their will and movements. They are always doing something. Such movement forms the inner foundation for what they will 'feel' in the next stage. Spiritual forces are at work shaping the organs and completing the physical body. The culmination of this activity is expressed in the falling out of the milk-teeth. At this time new creative powers are released for the next phase.

7-14

The physical body continues to develop, with second teeth starting to come through. Consciousness awakens further – from a state of sleep to a dream-like condition. Inner soul-life intensifies. In the earlier period, creative formative powers were shaping the physical body, but now these become available to the soul as powers of imagination and thought, as image-forming activity. Children's thinking at this age is influenced by strong feelings and personal experiences and expressed through imagination.

In the 'ninth year change' children feel a greater separation from their parents, and from everything around them which had previously been imbued with magic and wholeness. Now they begin to experience the world more objectively, and the glow of early childhood is gradually replaced by 'the light of common day', as Wordsworth says so well. An ordinariness begins to dull childhood's innate joy and spontaneity.

Around the 12th year children's thinking capacities develop from picture thinking to cause and effect thinking. They are now able to understand how and why things happen. Their strong physical resemblance to their parents may start to wane, as their individuality becomes more pronounced. The physical body begins to experience heaviness and gravity, a sense of being pulled down to earth. The larynx elongates causing the boy's voice to deepen. His sexual organs mature, and he becomes able to reproduce his own kind. The girl's body becomes rounder and softer, and through hormonal changes and menstruation prepares itself for reproduction. The changes at puberty echo changes such as the loss of teeth which occurred at the end of the first seven-year period. The forces released in puberty are now available for the next phase.

14-21

The physical body goes through great hormonal change as the adult physical body takes shape. Feeling life becomes chaotic, expressing itself in powerful highs and lows and erratic swings. The creative powers which worked on the physical body from Birth to 7, and on the soul from 7-14, are now working on the thinking. The transformation of outer impressions into inward experience leads from images to ideas. In the newness of this budding capacity, the spot-light of young peoples' thinking directs its beam upon everything around them: at first they become critical of everything, questioning and perhaps rejecting aspects of the world that disappoint them.

Adolescents struggle to use their thinking as a way of controlling their feelings and will-impulses. Thinking gradually becomes more inward, no longer needing to be stimulated by strong soul experiences. It becomes conceptual and abstract. Their glimpse of the 'higher' self around the seventeenth year gives adolescents a sense that there is purpose and meaning in life as well as disappointment. They begin to accept the contradictions of life and, with the spontaneous idealism of youth, put their energies to work for a better world. During the period of 14 to 21 the young person's character is forming. The seven character or soul types are described in a second volume of this book.

21-28

The human being begins to feel a new identity awakening as the 'I' incarnates more fully. This period is marked by strong activity of the emotional life, impulsive feelings, excitement, sensuality, sociability, and adventure. Throughout this period our 'I' tries to grasp hold of impulses and emotions in order to stabilize them. It is a time to prepare for a career and to gather experience. Our creative abilities are at the disposal of the 'I' and there is almost nothing we can't attempt. Memory reaches its peak. We begin to evaluate what is being learned as the 'I' penetrates our experiences.

28-35

The 'I' begins to enter still deeper into our soul-life, penetrating thinking. We experience life through our thinking, and through awakening to the realities of life. We feel the need to organize our lives. As we come to regard life more objectively than before, our thinking also separates us from life. As we judge everything around us, we may develop a tendency to become critical, cold, and self-righteous. This tends to lead to dissatisfaction, but also to a sense that our thinking can solve all our problems.

35-42

Consciousness is the main theme of this period. This can be a time of strength and ambition, but also of emptiness and loneliness. What we take in through our senses doesn't satisfy us any more; the body no longer excites us in the same way. Our natural spirituality fades and we feel overwhelmed by life's demands. Life can take on a routine quality, and yet we experience more and more problems. Much of what used to bring contentment no longer does. We become critical of the causes, philosophies, or religion which were important previously. **After 30, what we achieve depends completely on what we ourselves make of our capacities, how we work together with and integrate our 'I'.**

42-49

Much depends on when we experience the crisis described above. The period after the crisis (anywhere from early to late forties) is marked by a **strong period of productivity, innovation, and imagination.** New strength and new opportunities become available to us. Often careers are reshaped. We come into touch with what we really want to do in life. We can develop patience and warmth, make new friendships, and feel a new confidence in life.

The chaos is clearing and order begins to reign in the personal life. Balance is regained. The temptation during this phase is power and it takes great strength to resist it and to exercise our higher nature instead.

49-56
The problems that come during this period are met with more flexibility and humor than in the past. We have to make adjustments to life, but there can be a new vitality to do so if we are working on ourselves. There is much remembering of the past as we struggle to gain perspective. We are able to bring **wisdom and light** to bear on our challenges. Often this means taking up new possibilities, new directions, even a change of career. But whatever is done is done with **greater equanimity.**

56-63
We may now experience another burst of energy, even inspiration. Many earlier conflicts are resolved, and we are no longer so interested in power or success. Now we can enjoy the respect and confidence we have gained from life. **We are living from within, out of the depth of experience and emotional maturity.** Life has simplified. We develop enthusiasm through our own efforts. We work through our thoughts more carefully, we ponder, we consider. We go inward for insight rather than outward for stimulation. New strength is activated, new life forces are generated. New possibilities of devotion and companionship present themselves.

63 onwards is a continuation of previous phases. The processes of development which began at 35 continue and mature.

5. Smaller rhythms within the seven-year phase

There are also smaller rhythms subdividing each seven-year phase into three. The first 2^1/3 years is the 'budding' of the phase, which echoes the previous phase and announces the potential of the new one. The second 2^1/3 years is the flowering of the phase, where we see its theme in the purest form. The third period – the last 2^1/3 years – is the fruit which bears the seed. The new capacity of this phase consolidates while the seed or potential of the next phase ripens. At the end of the first third a challenge is posed, usually accompanied by a sense of loss; and at the end of the second third a compensation, a new ability arises.

Let's take the second seven-year phase (from 7-14), which I have already described, as an example. At the beginning of this phase, around 7, children have many of the same tendencies they had when they were younger. They still learn mostly by imitation, and they still see nature as ensouled, as animated, as if within each tree and flower a being is speaking to them.

Around the age of $8^1/3$, imitation becomes less strong, so that children's need for constant movement can be reined in and starts to transform into the capacity for forming inner images. The golden glow around their parents and the world starts to dim, a new sense of self dawns, and with it a sense of separation. This shows itself through all kinds of new feelings – uncertainty, fear, anger that things are unfair, feeling they are ugly, disliked, or unwanted. Instead of feeling connected with the world, the child experiences a distance and becomes critical towards the adults around him. This is generally an unhappy and restless time, but it usually passes quickly, and for most children is more than anything a foretaste and precursor of what adolescence will later bring.

At this stage children's experience of nature changes too: it no longer seems so animated and ensouled, but more objectively alive. They are often interested in planting flowers and watching them grow, and have a particularly strong love of animals. They often also love wild places – the mountains, oceans, hills and valleys. This period from $8^1/3$ to $10^2/3$ is the essence of childhood. At this time children's imaginations are vivid and alive, they love myths and legends, have a strong connection with nature, and are generally optimistic about life. They are usually well-coordinated and play actively.

Around $11^2/3$ a new aspect unfolds. The physical body which has been so harmonious begins to change. Signs of puberty appear, such as growth spurts and glandular changes. The girls tend to be about two years ahead of the boys, but there are great individual differences. Children's feelings become more connected with their growing individuality. They want to do more things on their own, and become secretive – not sharing their feelings so much with their parents but with special friends instead. A new capacity for understanding causality develops in their thinking, and they become more objective about the world. Their attitude to nature also changes. Instead of just enjoying the sheer vitality and excitement of the natural world as previously, they can now start to *know* it. This is often a time when youngsters begin to collect shells or stones, to breed animals, to learn the laws behind the natural world. This new form of thinking will be further developed in the next phase. The loss experienced around $8^1/_3$ can be partially compensated by the gain around $11^2/_3$. At fourteen this period comes to completion and the next phase begins.

In each seven-year phase we can see a similar pattern of budding, flowering, fruiting and seed-potential, though expressed in ways specific to different periods of life.

6. Broader groupings of the seven-year phases

Now we can stand back and look at the seven-year phases from another point of view. The phases fall into three broad divisions.

From birth to 21 the greatest activity is in the area of *physical maturity*. From 21-42 the greatest activity is in developing psychological or *soul maturity*, and from 42-63 the greatest activity is in beginning to develop *spiritual maturity*. This is only in potential. What we do with this depends on our own decisions.

We can step even further back and see that there are two halves to life – the years leading up to thirty-five and the years after. In the first half we are laying up treasure which we will use in the second half.

ALL THE EXPERIENCES WE HAVE IN THE FIRST HALF OF LIFE – THE ENJOYMENT OF BEAUTY, THE SENSE OF WONDER, THE UNDERSTANDING OF THE WORLD – WILL BE THE RAW MATERIAL WHICH WE WILL USE TO SHAPE OUR INNER LIFE AND INFLUENCE OUR OUTER ACTIONS.

The attitudes around us in our childhood years, the effect of our education, the influence of our relationships, the effect of physical ailments and the way they were treated, all live on into the second half of life. We can hopefully draw nourishment from them, and help in overcoming some of the traumas of later years. There is a wonderful saying, 'The person who learns to pray in childhood learns to bless in old age.'

During the first half we receive what life has to bring to us. We are students absorbing, comparing, experiencing, working with what we brought with us from the past. In the second half we give back to life. We knead the dough of the early years, rework it, reshape it, put leaven into it, and offer it up for the future.

During the first half we meet our teachers and find our ideals. We also discard teachers as they disappoint us, as they fail us. I had the strongest experience of that when I was almost eighteen. I loved the work of Carl Sandburg and idolized him. He was coming to give a poetry reading at Cooper Union Institute in lower Manhattan. I wanted to go more than anything, but I couldn't afford to give up the meager wages I earned in a part-time job at Woolworths. I was ready to run as soon as the closing bell sounded. Breathlessly I ran to the subway, took the train the few stops and then ran all the way to Cooper Union. I reached the hall just as Sandburg walked off the stage. Still not discouraged, I ran around to the back door and met him. There he stood, a tall figure in a black suit, a little bent over, his white hair parted in the middle, kindly eyes. I eagerly approached him and tried to explain that I couldn't be there for his talk and could he please tell me what he had said. (I'm embarrassed now at my audacity.) He looked at me from far off and said, 'Young lady, go chase a peanut around the corner. When you find it you'll know what I said', and walked on. I looked at the back of this man whom I had placed on the highest pedestal. All I could think of was 'He has dandruff!'

As I think about this experience today I not only think about the fall of an idol for an idealistic adolescent, but I ask myself how many times I have done the same thing to people who have approached me after I finished giving a lecture. How many times have I not perceived all that lay behind a seemingly thoughtless question? How many times have I missed the point and hurt someone's feelings, made them feel stupid? So I no longer blame Mr. Sandburg, and I hope the people I have hurt in this way will forgive me also.

In the first half of life our physical bodies are strong and active; in the second half they weaken and give signs of wear and tear. In the first half our instincts are more active and drive our feelings and actions; in the second half our consciousness is the motivating force for our feelings and actions. In the first half we long for a community of family and friends to fill our needs, and in the second half we may realize that we must do this from within and even yearn for quiet and private time.

It is easy to write down these comparisons, but they are empty words unless they become an active process. No transformation of what we have before 35 happens through wishful thinking. Each new perception and realization is born of loneliness, effort and sweat. To the outside world we just seem to be going about the daily business of living. It is an almost invisible process; our outer appearance shields the churning, boiling and turning inside-out within the soul. And only slowly, slowly, does the change reveal something new.

You might wonder if everyone shares the same rhythms or sub-rhythms at the same time in their lives. Let us look at an example from the world of nature. During my sabbatical year in Europe I was in Spain in January and February. During the warm sunny days the blossoms on the almond trees began to burst open. Golden flowers bloomed on the meadows. Spring was definitely on its way. When we reached Germany in March we experienced this again. The crocuses began to bloom, narcissi danced on the meadows, fruit blossoms turned the orchards into fields of snow. We could breathe the air of Spring once again. In May we were in Latvia and Lithuania, the Baltic countries of the cold north, where Spring finally made its appearance. Again we could rejoice in the splendor of the earth coming alive. And what rejoicing there was as people welcomed the quickening forces of growth after the long, long winter. In Spain there is a long spring and summer, a brief fall and winter, but in Latvia it is the other way around. Spring comes, soon gives way to a brief summer, and before you know it the leaves are turning and autumn is already here to be followed by a long winter. In each region there was variation in the length of the season.

There are similar variations in human lives. Within the general rhythms there are individual differences depending on the conditions and the 'gesture' of the person. Some of us experience ourselves as being always a few years ahead of a particular phase; others as a few years behind. In reading about each phase we can ask ourselves, does this shed light on my life? Have I experienced such a change? Was my attitude towards my needs and desires or towards a crisis different at different times in my life? These general laws underlying life do not detract from our unique individuality, but provide a framework, a structure within which we live our lives. Each of us relates to those laws in our own specific way and in our own time-scale. But we all get where we need to be going. How we do this and the changes we go through as we move from one phase of life to another is part of our individuality.

SECTION

PHASES OF ADULT LIFE

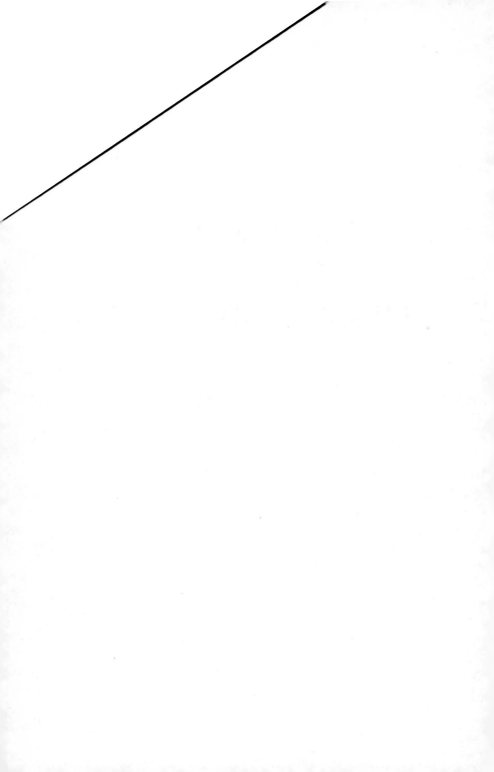

Introduction

Life, so-called, is a short episode between two great mysteries, which yet are one.

C.J. Jung [1]

We had only just arrived in Vilnius, Lithuania that afternoon. I was exhausted from a grueling eight hour wait at the Polish-Lithuanian border in the freezing cold, but we could not disappoint our hostess, Irena, who had been so excited to see us and had invited another couple to join us in the evening. The men had gone to find a guarded car-park for our van, and we three women sat in the living-room chatting. After a few minutes of this and that, Danuta and Irena said with poignancy that they felt their lives were almost over. They were only forty years old, but nothing seemed possible for them anymore. I mentioned some of the feelings I had in my late thirties and early forties, and they tearfully acknowledged that they were feeling exactly the same. Soon both were crying. These strong, creative women who had survived the terrible days of Lithuania's battle for independence, the current shortages and lack of heating, the spiraling food costs, who were excited about the new possibilities of democracy, and who had wonderful families, were crying. Why? They couldn't explain it to themselves, which was part of their problem. Each one in a different way felt life had come to a dead end. I mentioned a few words about life phases, and they grasped at them, wanting to hear more.

Is life almost over at forty? What is it that we lose? And what is being gained?

Each one of us has a unique history. We feel changes occurring through life, but are not always conscious of what they are or what they mean. It is only on reflection that we can survey the past – the paths leading to crucial turning points, the meetings with special people, the critical decisions made. In each phase of life there are laws working, like those at work in nature.

Seeds of one phase take root in the next and blossom in the succeeding one. As we try to understand these laws, perspective develops and we can start looking at life as an organic unfolding of individuality. With this comes a deeper appreciation for the richness of life in each of its stages. We come to understand growth and transformation, and hopefully can perceive what we need in order to make changes in our lives.

The changes in the first half of our life tend to happen *to* us. But after we reach the midpoint of life, around 35, we are much more involved in how we relate to the laws of development. We can ignore the changes we are going through, we can fight them, but we still go through them. When we understand what these changes are and how they benefit us, we can decide how we want to react to them. Our individuality is then much more active.

As we move from one phase to the next we are letting go of a previous way of life. Like a snake we shed our skin: something new becomes possible that was not possible before. New forces and capacities become available to us. Life phases are not so much concerned with outer events – date of marriage, when our first child was born, when we were promoted in our job – but with changes that go on in our soul life. These changes are seldom seen by others, but they powerfully influence the way we relate to the world.

Erikson divided life into three stages. First is *Intimacy,* characteristic of our twenties and thirties, when we need to develop selfless devotion. If we do not manage this, isolation usually results. The second stage, characteristic of our 40s and 50s, is *Generativity,* a process by which an individual becomes creative in a new sense. In this phase one can feel a responsibility to the new generation and become a guide or mentor. The third phase is *Integrity,* which occurs when we resolve the mid-life crisis. Erikson sees a new ego quality and another dimension of personality strength emerging after each crisis. The person never stays static. Either she will lose or gain ground.

Sheehy describes the developmental stage coming into crisis when she says, 'Crucial shifts in bedrock begin to throw a person off balance, signaling the necessity to change and move on to new footing in the next stage of development.' [2.]

We make choices we could not have made previously. We undo what we have done before. We look for new relationships. We find that something new is trying to be born. We are constantly dealing with parts of ourselves that we were not aware of. Over and over again we are given the possibility of awakening to ourselves and becoming conscious of our thoughts, deeds and feelings. When we deny ourselves these new possibilities, we box ourselves into a corner; and this will eventually throw us into turmoil.

But no matter how much we know about life, our own crises leave us hurt and confused. Knowledge *does* help, though, because it leads to understanding, and it lets us know that what is happening to us is normal and, in the long run, helpful. We can look forward to a time when we will feel better. There are also things we can do to prepare for future times of crisis and confusion; and we can come to see that even difficult situations have much to teach us, and can help us develop new capacities.

Stages of relationships

Just as each individual passes through cycles, so does a relationship. During each stage of a relationship we have particular needs and ways of solving problems. There are three basic elements to consider when we speak about relationship-stages. First, the individuality of each person. Second, the phase of life each person is in. Third, the stage the relationship has reached. In addition to these three aspects, cultural and historical expectations and the environment are also strong influences.

A chaplain I met in Ibiza, Spain, told me that he works with English women married to Spanish men. The differences in language, religion, family expectations, and roles create great stress on these couples, and the marriages are fragile. The attraction which began during romantic summer holidays weakens under the day-in day-out stresses of cultural differences.

Relationships follow similar phases to the soul development of individuals. When two people are attracted to one another, they are in the soul stage where feeling life predominates (21-28 years) no matter how old they are. After the relationship settles down to routine, feelings become less passionate, and each partner begins to step back, seeing the other person more coolly and objectively, even questioning the relationship itself. This soul stage, in which thinking predominates, belongs naturally to the 28-35 phase. If the couple survives this testing period of comparison and criticism, with its dimming of the light that illumined the other's better qualities, the next stage in the relationship is the soul stage in which consciousness or awareness predominates (akin to the 35-42 period). Here the individuals begin to look at *themselves* more objectively as well as looking at their partner in this way. During this time the challenge to the relationship is for each to see the higher self of the other (as in the first stage of the relationship) but now to gain a more realistic recognition of their partner's strengths and weaknesses. The love that blossoms during this phase is deeper and more reliable. From here on the quality of the relationship will depend upon the continued inner development of each partner.

If, for example, a relationship begins in a couple's forties, the early phase representing the quality of the twenties and thirties will be passed through fairly quickly until it enters the stage specific to the period of life the couple is in.

Where two partners are at different stages, each will exhibit aspects of his or her own stage as well as aspects of the other's stage. Let us imagine a woman in her twenties and a man in his forties. She is caught up in the adventure of life, trying to find her own identity, separate from her family and at the same time define her place in society. She is involved in herself. She may admire the experience of the older man because he is like a mentor to her (yet not her parent). She can admire his strength and know-how. He, on the other hand, enjoys the youthful spontaneous qualities of the young woman which temporarily re-awaken these old feelings in him. This works well for a while, but as the young woman comes into her thirties, she may not appreciate having him lead the way. She may reject him in her search for independence. Equally, since he is getting older, he may be wanting to concentrate more on inner aspects of life, while she, in her prime, still wishes to make her mark in the world.

A thirty-year old writer, Frank, was delighted with his twenty year-old girlfriend. Her reading of novels conjured up for her a romanticized image that she believed Frank fulfilled: the dedicated writer withdrawing into his garret to write the great novel in spite of hunger and cold. He covered the moth holes in his dark suit with shoe polish when they attended bohemian parties in the East Village in Manhattan. He, for his part, was intrigued with her youthfulness and apparent sophistication (which was an act). He felt buoyed up and stimulated artistically by the relationship. But he became too demanding sexually for her, and she realized she was not used to dealing with an older man who was more subtle than the college boys she usually dated. She wanted to end the relationship without being wholly rejected by him, and so chose to emphasize the very innocence she had tried to cover up when they first met. She dressed for their 'final' date looking like a young school-girl: long straight hair, long-sleeved simple dress, and flat shoes. When they went to a bar she ordered milk. He, confused by her new manner, escorted her home that night feeling like a cradle-snatcher. In this case the age difference did not serve either of the couple very well, although there is some humor in the way it was played out.

When the woman is much older than the man, the relationship may be successful for a while. The woman, however, is always alert to the fact that she is ageing, and so lives with the insecurity that her partner may be attracted to a younger woman. Some such relationships do work regardless of the difficulties. The man may look to the older woman for guidance, until the time comes for him to find his own way. Then both partners have to change dramatically for the relationship to succeed.

In either situation, relationships with an age difference of over ten or twelve years tend to work for a while, until the stress of the discrepancy between different needs takes its toll. That doesn't mean the relationship is not meaningful. Much depends on the maturity of both partners.

The combination of two partners from different age groups can bring much-needed support into the relationship. The older partner, whether male or female, may well have developed capacities of understanding, patience, and forgiveness which add important elements to the relationship. When both partners are in the same phase, on the other hand, they *can* have the comradeship and mutual support of experiencing many of the same aspects at the same time. But this can equally be the cause of difficulties: when both are going through the critical stage (28-35) or the more independent stage (35-42), stress and crisis can be intensified. Neither one is able to look at the relationship from a broader or more experienced perspective. Understanding or forgiveness may not yet have been sufficiently developed. In these situations egoism tends to push each partner into his solitary camp of pain and hurt. Knowing something about life phases can help a couple work through some of these difficulties.

The approach in this book

I have approached each life phase from three points of view – the individual, the couple in relationship, and people I have interviewed. In my travels I interviewed men and women whom I found interesting and dynamic. They seemed to sparkle with life, yet when we spoke I found that each had life situations and challenges that provoked crisis and turbulence. I was interested in how people worked with these situations and what they learned from them. How did they shape their lives, unite all the threads and carry out their individual destinies? It is very popular today for authors to write books debunking great heroes, showing their feet of clay, but I take an opposite view. It is clear to me that, being human, we all have our faults. We've all made mistakes and had regrets. My interest is not so much in these but in how we take hold of situations and create something positive. I have changed names and a few identifying features, but otherwise, these accounts are true.

1
Life is Ahead of Us: 21-28

In our twenties we often live in the intensity of impulse rather than through feelings which have been tempered by thought. Steiner calls this period the time of the *Sentient Soul.* It is a time when young people are building up experiences and meeting the world with vigor and enthusiasm, a time of enjoying sensations and pursuing adventures, of dreaming into the future and being full of hope and confidence. In our twenties we usually go in one of two directions: either we do what we think we 'should', what we are expected to do by our families or culture; or we rebel against what is expected, sow our 'wild oats' before settling down. Perhaps now, more than before, young people are aware of the importance of exploring their own individuality before settling down. They travel, take on jobs for the sheer experience of it rather than for career preparation, and experiment with life.

One very well-educated young man studied medicine, but decided he wanted practical experience before settling down to his medical career. He trained as an apprentice in the construction business. As he stood there with his shirt off, his tanned muscles glowing, his leather tool-belt around his waist, it was sometimes hard for me to remember that when he took a break we could talk about Greek theatre, world geography, or medicine. This was the experience he needed *now:* medicine was for the future.

A young woman wasn't sure what she wanted to pursue as a career. So she spent a year travelling around various countries visiting friends and friends' friends. When she stayed with our family she wanted the 'typical' American experience so she got a job at a fast food restaurant and loved every minute of it (for two months) before travelling to her next address. By the time the year was over she knew what she wanted to do and applied herself to it with new energy.

Two young men had never been able to concentrate on their high school studies. However, they were inspired to get to know other people and cultures. So they took off and traveled to South America, Asia, Africa, and Australia. One of them told me, 'I couldn't learn it from books, but now I have learned so much'. And he had. His knowledge of geography, history, and culture was impressive.

A young woman had her heart set on a musical career, but became pregnant. Her partner was at the university. Together they were struggling to deal with the unexpected. Life was difficult. He had long hours of study. She couldn't practise music *and* take care of the baby. She made the painful decision to postpone her musical training. Money was a constant issue, but they had hopes and dreams, and she felt the baby was a priority. So they worked through the difficult times.

In our twenties we participate in life, respond to it, rather than consciously directing it. But there are moments when our higher self lights up, when those around us can grasp who the man or woman 'in-becoming' is. Usually it is only in our late twenties that we begin to stand on our own two feet. A 25-year-old friend said to me, 'I know all about those problems, they won't happen to me!' I smiled and thought inwardly, 'Just wait'. Three years later his perspective was quite different. He said, 'I feel as if I'm coming from a different place, the same things don't satisfy me'.

A young woman had set herself the goal of a high-powered career. She finished university, went to graduate school, and landed a very good job. She was excited about her work and enjoyed the challenges, and was repelled by the idea of settling down and having a family. She played hard and worked hard, and was having a wonderful time. There was almost nothing she couldn't tackle. But as she reached her thirtieth birthday, she began to have a strange inner sensation that this could not go on indefinitely. Maybe for a few more years. But what then? Some of her friends were having babies. She joked about her biological clock ticking away. One day I was having dinner with her and she said rather testily, 'So what's supposed to happen to me? I keep feeling something different is waiting for me, but I don't know what it is. Maybe I should change jobs. I've always wanted to go into research, and I've been offered the possibility of a grant.' Her self-confidence was shaken. She couldn't fake the usual 'I'm not afraid of anything' stance, and I could sense her vulnerability for the first time.

Gradually throughout our twenties we begin to experience the results of our actions. Feelings and results interact, and we begin to wake up from the dream.

I remember canning peaches in my mid-twenties. It was a late summer's afternoon and I started thinking about life and careers. I was a young wife and mother and at my feet my firstborn child was crawling. It was long before I knew of life-cycles, but it came to me then that these were my 'at-home' years. As I thought about the future I saw the thirties as the transitional years, perhaps I would work part-time, and the forties as my professional years. There was a very settling quality to these thoughts and I felt at peace with them. Looking back now I can only smile at the satisfaction with which I laid out my goals. Even though life has taken a different course to the way I saw it, there was still some truth to the perception. Each stage in life does have its own character, we are different at different times, and react differently to life situations.

The mood of this 21-28 period is one of egotism. We are the center of our thoughts, and we feel satisfied when we fulfil our personal goals and objectives. But when we work with our higher ego to transform this attitude of egoism, when we bring spiritual forces to it, then the egotism changes from self-concern to concern about our fellow human beings. We can then experience a new level of satisfaction from our efforts to achieve something good for others as well as for ourselves.

Marriage in our twenties

When we marry in our twenties, particularly in the early twenties, we lack life experience. We have been brought together by strong emotional attraction and together we dream of building our future. We relish our similarities, focus on what we enjoy doing together, and make plans. But then life-realities begin to meet us and challenge our certainty: things don't work out as promised, there are unknown byways, our confidence is tested. Such challenges might include not getting the job we set our hearts on, being turned down from graduate school, facing an unexpected pregnancy, having a retarded or handicapped child, lack of money, and death or illness in our family. I am sure my readers can add others from their own life experiences. How we meet these realities influences our character and our further growth.

The particular stresses of the early years are not the same for wife and husband. The honeymoon period ends and conflicts begin: jealousies, disagreements – about places to live, means of livelihood, parents-in-law etc. The wife has to adjust to a different focus. When the couple was courting she was the center of attention, and her young man would think of exciting things to do or presents to surprise her with. Once married, the young wife finds herself more often catering to her husband. She may have built up an image of him as the great protector, the strong man, but now begins to see chinks in his armour, feel some doubts. Sometimes she ignores these, other times she is confused and feels guilty about having them.

There is an expression used by Congreve in *The Way of the World* which describes her change of status: *'dwindling into a wife'*. This change affects her self-image and confidence; much of her personality may have to reshape to conform to her husband's wishes, needs and demands.

Even the most sophisticated and successful career woman may still find herself trying to fulfil her husband's expectations. Every woman in love unconsciously adapts herself to what she thinks the man wants her to be. This is not done without some ambivalence. I was surprised to find this so strongly expressed in the interviews I conducted. At some point the woman may react to her submission, either justifying it or feeling she has betrayed herself.

Some women will start off being soft and pliant, sensitive to the man's moods and responsive to his wishes, expressed or implied. But once they are secure they may begin to express their more assertive side, becoming demanding and bossy – which may confuse their husbands, who don't understand this change.

One of the saddest adjustments wives make – particularly those at home – is in the pattern of emotional expression between themselves and their husbands. As the man's job becomes more and more consuming his original warmth may subside. An older woman described the daughter of her friend as 'a very dull woman'. This daughter has a PhD. in neurology, and had been involved in exciting laboratory projects in the forefront of her field. Five years later she was mostly concerned with children's naps, teething, food shopping, and the difficulties of managing a household. The daughter herself knew something was happening to her mind, but had no time or energy to give to stimulating intellectual pursuits.

The young wife who stays at home is centering her life around the needs of her husband and child. She is there to help carry out *their* dream. There is little genuine accomplishment of her own she can recognize, although she is the center of activities. Her tasks are renewable: the clothes get washed, dirtied, washed again, so too the dishes and floor. In comparison with her husband's work, hers can seem demeaning. If his job is not entirely meaningful, at least he has a paycheck at the end of the week or the chance of promotion. She faces the same routine day in and day out.

Even when women take jobs, they often just see them as temporary or as a stop-gap, a financial necessity. Their first commitment is to the family. Other women see their main job as loving a man and being loved by him, and do not wish to complicate this task in any way. When a person cannot take her job seriously, it is hard for her to take herself seriously either. Other women, in contrast, may take their jobs very seriously but then live a split consciousness between work and home.

Women at home (and in many cases, women in jobs too) often feel very isolated – especially those who were previously active in the community or at college, who were used to being active in a group. This is particularly true of a young career woman who marries and stays at home, and is then confined to a smaller circle of movement, becoming dependent on her husband as her main source of stimulation. Her needs may then concentrate on the children who can only partially fulfil them; it is an unfair, unconscious demand. This isolation causes brooding – which intensifies the isolation and leads to alienation. Depression is a major illness of women in general, and of housewives in particular.

Anne Morrow Lindberg pondered the strain on the young housewife in *Gift from the Sea*. From her personal experience she writes,

'Here is a strange paradox. Woman instinctively wants to give, yet resents giving herself in small pieces. Basically is this a conflict? Or is it an oversimplification of a many-stranded problem? I believe that what woman resents is not so much giving herself in pieces as giving herself purposelessly. What we fear is not so much that our energy may be leaking away through small outlets as that it may be going down the drain. We do not see the results of our giving as concretely as man does in his work... It is hard even to think of it as purposeful activity, so much of it is automatic. Woman herself begins to feel like a telephone exchange or a laundromat.'[1]

The young woman who is trying to approach life consciously *can* find her time at home with a child or children a maturing experience. If she can take a broad view of the responsibilities she has, she can see that this part of her life poses her with challenges in self-development. It is easy for her to get 'pulled out of herself' into constant activity, but she can work to focus herself. Taking care of young children and all the household details is a very grounding experience. She has to come to terms with details, with time-tables, with establishing a routine, with being concerned about others, with establishing an atmosphere in the home. All of this presents an opportunity for growth. What are the qualities she can develop? Patience, attention, and interest. Hilde described a situation that had occurred with her two-and-a-half year-old daughter, Anna, who was climbing into cabinets and messing up everything which Hilde had just organized. When Hilde asked Anna to come out, she of course refused. Finally Hilde became so exasperated she shook her daughter. At that moment, though, Hilde woke up. She could sense that Anna was shocked and had withdrawn from her. She put herself into Anna's shoes and felt what Anna must have been feeling. She realized how her own franticness had resulted in her losing control, and she centered herself. She replayed the whole scene in her mind and realized what she had done to contribute to the problem. Then she moved into Anna's world and began to be interested in what Anna had been doing in the cabinet. She played with her and was able to completely change the atmosphere. The bond between them was much stronger after that.

If all the different skills a young mother exercises were applied to a 'proper' job outside the home, her abilities would be recognized. It is sad that so much of what mothers do goes unrecognized;

yet it lives on in the soul of the children into adulthood. What could be more important? Mothering is a profession. As with all professions, it has moments of drudgery. But few professions have such repercussions for society. The problem is not that mothering is not significant work, but that it is unrecognized and unsupported.

The young married woman at work encounters a variety of different situations. If she does not have children, there are several patterns that emerge.

1. She and her husband can develop a partnership. They are both working, and thus divide up the chores at home. In this situation the woman's self-confidence continues to be strengthened; the couple are trying to be conscious about their situation. A sense of mutual support characterizes the relationship. There is evidence, though, that dual-career husbands (both husband and wife working) tend to feel cheated after a while. But the women are happier, feel more confident, feel good about their jobs and marriages.[2] We do not have an extensive history of dual-career marriages to look back on, so perhaps we haven't learned how and what to expect of them yet. Because more women can stand on their own financially they want a partnership, not a support system.

2. Once married, the woman adds the consciousness of the home to her consciousness of her job. Her husband may take on specific areas such as fixing the car, changing light bulbs, or making minor repairs. But his main focus is on his job and possibly a hobby, whereas his wife has to think about meals, cleaning the house, etc. Although the woman's self-confidence is not weakened, she is exhausted and sometimes resentful. Some husbands are sensitive about this and try to be more helpful. Others are happy with such an arrangement, even if they pretend not to be.

3. The third pattern is similar to the second, except that the woman feels this is how things should be. She takes on the dual roles naturally. For many such women, a job is taken temporarily or out of necessity, but they feel that their real place is in the home.

If there are children at home the situation is very different. Here are some possible scenarios:

1. *The woman wants to be home, but she cannot afford to be.* As well as worrying about her job, she thinks all the time about her child or children: illness, school vacations, babysitting or childcare, doctor and dentist appointments, as well as shopping, cooking and cleaning. If the woman is a single mother, the stress is especially great. If she is married, she may have some help from her husband, but she probably carries the main responsibility. If the children are ill, she stays home from work or leaves early. In unusual situations where the husband's work hours are more flexible, he can share this burden. One young mother put it very well. 'Until I stopped working and was home full-time, I didn't realize I wasn't mothering my children. I was just "maintaining".' Husbands tend to be unhappy with this situation. *Brothers* quotes a study in which 'Husbands with working wives were worriers. They worried about their health, both physical and mental. They worried about where they were living and whether they should move. They worried that they had fallen into a rut, both in their personal and business lives. They often found it difficult to show affection for their wives and that worried them too.' [3]

2. *The woman loves her job and wants to continue working even though she has children.* She tries to carry out both roles: loving her job *and* her children. Again, much depends on the attitude of her husband. If both of them agree on the importance of her work, they can find a way of sharing responsibility for the children and the home. Some men agree to this, but they still feel abandoned when the woman is not home, especially if she spends long hours with out-of-town appointments and travel. In general, men feel threatened by wives who love their work more than they love being at home. Women who strongly wish to pursue their careers often choose to put marriage off until they are in their thirties; or, if married, they put off having children until their thirties.

3. *The woman has a job, either part-time or flexible-time, so that she can enjoy the fulfilment of her career and still be able to focus on her children and home.* For many women (and men) this is ideal. Some com-

panies allow woman (and men) to job-share with another person. For example, a doctor has worked out an arrangement with another woman doctor that between the two of them they cover the full-time job. Their organization agrees to this, and both seem very satisfied with this situation.

4. *The woman is at home.* It is not surprising to read in the Brothers study that

> The housewives resembled the dual-career husbands in many ways. Their self-esteem was low. They were worriers too. They worried about their health and their marriage and their children. They were often seriously depressed. The single career husbands had their own worries, but these were of a different order from those of the men married to working wives. The single-career husbands worried about inflation, the possibility of war, racial violence, the energy crisis, the stock market. But their worries seldom kept them awake nights. They felt in robust good health. They looked forward to each new day and welcomed its challenge. And they considered themselves happily married. [4]

In 1993 I participated in a discussion in St. Petersburg with educated Russian women in their twenties, thirties, and forties. They all had children. Eight out of the ten women – all of whom were working – felt husbands were like children who wanted to be cared for, but contributed very little to the functioning of the home. The women, they said, work, make the decisions, organize the family, are active and go to concerts, museums, and courses, and get little support from the men. Several of the women were divorced and said their lives were hard enough already without a husband to look after like another child. When I tried to understand this phenomenon, they themselves had no answers but only questions. One woman suggested that mothers tended to pamper their sons after the Second World War when so many men were killed. These young men were not brought up to carry responsibility for the home, and therefore they did not expect to do so in their marriages either.

But these women were also very puzzled by the independent attitude they had observed in American women. One said, 'I had an American couple as a guest in my home for a week. The wife would not let her husband pour coffee for her or hold the door. She said, "I can do that myself". The woman seemed to need to prove every moment that she was independent. I don't understand it. Wasn't she comfortable being a woman?'

In some cultures marriage is clearly little more than an economic and social arrangement for the preservation of family and society. In others it is viewed as the epitome of happiness, in which two people love each other and want to spend their lives together. But although many women marry for love, they also know that one day the marriage may end. They must finish their education and have a career that can support them if their marriage breaks down. Divorce statistics make it easy to see why women feel the need to have their own careers. A woman who is also a mother experiences this need even more strongly. It has been shown, at least in the US, that when women with children divorce their financial level drops significantly, and many end up in poverty.

A married woman has other stresses to cope with, besides those involved in her relationship with her husband. She is also under pressure from society. Advertising images suggest she should be seductive, fun-loving, passive and dependent. Yet in the working world she must be aggressive and strong in order to be successful. She also has her own feeling-patterns – formed through her own education and family upbringing – and the inner, insistent voice of her own individuality. Such conflict of values can cause strain, which intensifies as a woman reaches her late twenties. Young mothers are not well-supported by society. Yet many young women are forming 'mothers' groups, viewing their role as a conscious step in self-development, committing themselves strongly to their family-role, but not just 'falling into the role' as they might have done in the past. These are modern women who understand what they are doing and why, and take it on with the same awareness and dedication they would give to a job in a corporation.

And men? Daniel Levinson described the stages in a man's life in his book *The Seasons of a Man's Life*.[5] He lists the phases of 21-35 as Onward and Upward (combining what I have described as the

21-28 and 28-35 periods), 35-43 Consolidation, 40-50 or 45-55 the Pivotal Decade, 50/55 to retirement, Equilibrium and Retirement. In the first, Onward and Upward phase, the man generally concentrates on work, marriage and family, with work as his main focus: he tries to figure out his plan of action, setting goals of achievement, trying to get to the 'top' position he thinks he deserves by the time he's 35. He is very likely to worry a great deal about whether there will be enough money to live on, especially if the wife becomes pregnant. Levinson points out that most men's picture of marriage is strongly idealized and unrealistic. They think everything is going to be beautiful, that their wives will be fantastic – as both housekeepers and lovers – even if they are also working women. Although men usually see themselves as the chief wage-earner and protector, they expect their wives to be superwomen who can take care of them as well as fulfil all their other responsibilities (work, home, children).When wives do not live up to this expectation, men often feel let down.

Men idealise having a family – especially having a son to do male things with. But they aren't ready for the sleepless nights, children's illnesses, and all the cleaning up that's involved. Their wives, involved with the realities and responsibilities of motherhood, have less time for them. The man feels he has lost his partner, and feels abandoned. But at work he still has his place. That is where he will prove himself!

In many ways, though, this is only a stereotype. Things are gradually changing as more men express interest in nurturing and in playing a full and equal part in the shared responsibilities of marriage.

Some men come to resent marriage because it is sexually restrictive and demands emotional responsibilities they aren't ready to give. They make jokes about being caught in a trap, about marriage being a prison. The traditional stag party the night before a wedding is a symbol of this attitude – the last fling before a man is locked up in marriage! Although men on the whole benefit from marriage they suffer certain subtle effects, many of which are described in The Hazards of Being Male.[6] These lie in the areas of psychological dependence and ambivalence about women in the first place. Men are often fascinated with the single unattached woman and feel suffocated by their wives. They advance and retreat on the emotional level in marriage, without even consciously being aware of this. Even so, most men benefit more from marriage than women do. The evidence shows that men survive longer when married, have better mental health, and choose marriage over and over again, even though they verbally condemn it.

Just as the young mother at home can begin to see her role in a conscious way as a path of self-development, so too can the husband and father. Coming to terms with growing up and leaving the 'single' life behind, the man can find deep inner satisfaction in his family. If he can spend some time at home when his wife is not there, he can begin to appreciate the demanding role of being 'mom'. It is not unusual for a husband left alone with the children for the weekend to respond, 'I never knew how tired you can get just taking care of one young child. I didn't get the laundry folded. The dishes are still in the sink, and I'm ready to collapse.' He can develop interest and understanding for his wife's life at home. It is especially important for husbands in their twenties to appreciate what their young wives are faced with at home with children. If they can understand the isolating nature of young motherhood and be especially helpful and tender in consequence, the relationship will be nourished.

Few of us have any education to prepare us for married life so we tend to enter it fairly unconsciously. Since the nature and expectations of modern marriage have changed a good deal, we have to be pioneers and forge a new path.

The glow of the wedding-day fades and the serious business of marriage begins: some successes come, and some failures. The couple goes through good times and bad, and every situation demands its own adjustments. Each of them begins to see flaws in the perfect image of the other. This is a period of strong emotions. At this age people react to situations on the basis of their feelings, directing themselves outwards towards the world around them. Instead of asking, 'Who am I?' as they began to do in their late teens, they switch to 'What shall I do in life?', 'How shall we shape our dreams?' and 'Can I attain the impossible?'

The young couple sees its years in the twenties as a time to build a foundation for the future, to aim towards eventual stability – even if they don't want it just yet. Most young people expect to have settled down by the age of 30. There may be some conflict during this time about how much experimentation and how much commitment should be sought. These questions are also affected by whether the wife is working at home or outside the home as well.

If they are satisfied with their jobs, working women do not become so alienated: they are stimulated by being in the world. But these women may wonder if they are missing something by not having families. On the other hand they may be concerned that having children will hinder their careers. They may worry about giving up a degree of freedom they have grown used to, or about being bored, or, of course, about the loss of income. The working single woman often shares many of the same goals as the young man except that at the end of this period she is likely to search for the man of her dreams. Many young single women in the working world behave as men did in the last decades and try to prove themselves, becoming aggressive and goal oriented. By 28-30 they may face a crisis about whether they are going to be able to change the pattern when they want to. Fear sets in that they will have to remain career women. Unconsciously, they may worry if being too successful and competitive will frighten away interested suitors.

Since the 1970s an anti-children attitude has also influenced many women, who decided to put their efforts into careers and self-advancement instead of suffering the strains and stresses of parenthood:

Years later, many women looked at their lives and came to the conclusion that something was missing. It seemed their triumph earned them the right to spend interminable days in the office, fret about the next promotion, and get heart attacks. Like men. Perhaps, hidden among all the stereotype and restraints, there was something inherently valuable in the experience of being a woman – in that disputed *difference* – that was worth preserving. Over the din of Xerox machines and the strobelike blinking of telephone hold-buttons, women were asking themselves: 'Is this all?' The very question home-bound women before them had asked of their manicured lawns and fruited Jell-O molds, working women were now asking of their hard-won careers. [7]

We all look at what we don't have and wonder what we are missing. Should I marry? Should I stay single? Should we have children? Should we wait to have children? Should we decide not to have children? These questions can throw us into turmoil.

Marriages in the late teens or twenties do not usually begin as conscious relationships. Strong emotional and physical attraction pulls the couple together. They are enthralled with their similarities, and there is a great deal of reflection or self-love embodied in this. Idealized images of marriage are very potent, surprisingly even in the children of broken or destructive families. Young people never quite believe that what they see around them could ever happen to them. Within a few years, though, many of them may be repeating the marriage dynamics of their parents. Other young people, in contrast, are so aware of their parents' weaknesses that they go to extremes to make sure they won't repeat their mistakes.

I had a conversation with a group of young mothers under 19 years of age. They had all been friends in high school. One by one, each had fallen in love; and had believed her life would be different from that of her parents. In the beginning things had been wonderful. But part of the excitement of attraction had been in escaping from problems at home. After a few months each became pregnant: the babies, who at first were welcomed with anticipation and joy, became a burden, tying the young women down at home. They still wanted to have good times, as teenagers do. Then their husbands left them. They were alone, poverty stricken, bitter. Now they felt trapped. They could no longer go out and get training (none had finished high school), could not afford babysitting, were lonely living in apartments, couldn't leave the baby (or babies) alone and could only feel despair. Their despair kept them from seeing that there were alternatives. There are programs to help young mothers finish their schooling, which provide child-care alongside education on parenting and managing a household. Such young women need someone to step in and guide them through the process of getting help, changing their lives, breaking the cycle they are in, and finding hope.

In my travels in eastern Europe I saw a different kind of situation. Because of housing shortage, the young woman (married or unmarried) often lived with her parents and got help with the children and housework. This extended family kept the woman from feeling the full burden, and gave her a sense of belonging. On the other hand, it tended to prolong her identity as a daughter rather than as an independent adult.

It is difficult to give guidance to young people in love about the difficulties that may come with early marriage. How do we know it will last? (Does one ever know?) Is it really love? What will it be like when the glow wears off? We could say that young partners are in love with love, or that they are 'ready' for love to happen. They care about being attractive to one another, seeing the highest in the other person. Emotions and ideals bring young people together, but gradually the ideals encounter, and are tempered by, reality.

The inner work of maturing is often cut short by early marriage. This may seem contradictory since the young people are having to deal with issues of responsibility: compromising with each other, putting the needs of a child before their own, facing serious responsibilities – while unmarried friends are doing what they like, when they like. Dealing with such situations does bring a sense of responsibility, but it doesn't necessarily bring inner growth. We are more likely to slip into expected roles without thinking. Our own personalities have not yet developed independently, so we bring an immature 'self' to the relationship rather than one which has learned to stand on its own, solve problems and know what it wants by passing through a necessary phase of self-centredness.

When we marry early (late teens, early twenties) a particular crisis often occurs in the late twenties. The gap between day-to-day reality and the ideal becomes unbearable. Each of us wants our personal needs fulfilled. Because of the 'romantic' tradition of our culture and because we are in love, we assume the other person can read or intuit our needs. Slowly and with much pain we find it doesn't happen that way. We become disappointed, annoyed, no longer feel the other person is so special, feel anger, and even hatred. This is one of the critical experiences in marriage and the most misunderstood. Each partner is confused and lonely, filled with ugly emotions and doubt.

Marriages in the twenties are usually based on projection. When this fades, each can seem a stranger. By resolving the projection each person becomes more integrated, but this is a long and painful process. The fact that Western society is so rooted in illusions makes couples even more confused during this period. We feel duty-bound to hold onto the earlier image of marriage and romanticism or else we think we have failed. The subtleties of love, the forms it takes as it refines and matures, have little place in the advertisements which barrage young people. Consumerism is directed at perpetuating the emotional roller-coaster of the twenties.

As time goes by there is an unsettling feeling that things must change, but that society does not really support this. The man can start to recognize the immaturity of his desire for conquest, the woman can see that her insistence on seeing the world through romantic eyes is likewise unsustainable. Both must yield to a deeper sense of loving, must be able to relinquish the old immature views without feeling they have failed to live in an 'exciting' way. This is a critical time. It is as if we are being asked to remarry now that we know the responsibilities we have accepted. If we can survive the first seven years of marriage there is a chance we can develop the capacity for intimacy which can only come after each of us has developed a solid sense of personal identity.

I don't want to give the impression that marriages begun in people's early twenties are destined for disaster. Not at all. But the challenges are greater because of the couple's inexperience. Often the shared experience of meeting these challenges, though, strengthens the young couple as they pass through difficult times. These marriages come under great strain as each person matures, and it takes a strong sense of commitment and desire to make them successful. But they do often work!

Natasha is 69 years old. She spent her childhood in the Urals, Perm and Sverdlovsk, Russia. She had one sister who is two years younger.

'All my dreams and goals were influenced by the fact that I was 20 in 1944, the war years. There was terrible hunger, more in this area than in occupied areas because the soldiers had to have food and only what was left over might be available to us civilians. My first dream was about having enough food, so as not to be hungry. I was a student on scholarship in the Conservatory, living alone, having a bed in a dormitory.'

When Natasha was fifteen her mother was arrested for political reasons and sent to a camp in the Far East. After her mother's arrest, five years went by without a word from her, no news at all. Once she got over the first shock, she started thinking what she had to do. She and her younger sister went to live with an uncle in Sverdlovsk, a kind man who cared for them. However, there was not enough room in the house, and life was very hard. She also started working. Natasha didn't stay at secondary school, but went to the music high school because it had a dormitory.

The Kiev Conservatory of Music had been evacuated to Sverdlovsk. When Natasha was 20 years old, she was studying there; near the students' dormitory was a hospital with wounded soldiers. She and other music students went to the hospital to give a concert. The room was filled with soldiers who had all kinds of injuries.

'My eye caught sight of a young soldier in the corridor. I was struck by his very light blond hair and blue eyes. The way the sun was shining reflected the lightness of his hair. I couldn't really make out his features, but I was fascinated by his hair.'

The next day the soldiers came to visit the singers in the dormitory. They came on crutches and wrapped in bandages. They began to make regular visits and brought food for the girls. Dressed in their heavy army coats they would reach down into their pockets, and take out grains to put on the table. This was very welcome. Natasha learned that the blond soldier with the fascinating hair was Sergei. She and Sergei became acquainted – their relationship became serious and they made plans to get married. She had no regular shoes (only felt slippers and galoshes) but she wanted shoes and a decent dress to attend the theater. She also wanted to look nice for Sergei. She began to give blood, and in return she received coupons. A certain number of coupons could be exchanged for a whole loaf of bread, which she sold in the market, using the money to buy a dress and shoes. But this was taking its toll on Natasha's health. She was becoming pale and thin. Because of her own weakened condition the doctors had told her it wasn't a good idea for her to give blood, but each time she told herself 'Just one more time'. It was probably her friends who told Sergei what she was doing and why; he demanded to see her arm which was covered with marks from the blood donations, and said, 'Stop this! No more!' This was a sign to her that he loved her.

Before meeting Sergei she felt uncomfortable about the way she looked although she felt secure in her chosen professional work. She thought it unlikely she would ever marry. She remembered liking a boy when she was in seventh grade. She had been worried about the angle he saw her from, from his desk – she didn't like her nose or her big lips. So she always sat covering these with her hand. Then in eighth grade when she was fifteen years old, he had handed her a German textbook with a paper folded inside. It said, 'I love you'. Her heart raced. She felt, 'Spring is coming. Everything is in blossom!'

In 1944 when the Ukraine was liberated, the Conservatory returned to Kiev, and Natasha went with it to continue her studies and graduate. She has vivid memories of Kiev in ruins. Sergei came soon after.

'Sergei and I were two very young people who didn't have anything. When he was drafted he hadn't even finished high school.'

In spite of the difficulties and hardship she remembers this time of studying music with warmth and nostalgia. She was always very active, had many friends and good relations. Her greatest longing was to become a singer. After Natasha finished at the Conservatory, she and Sergei moved to Riga. She was working and helped Sergei finish his education. Sometimes she felt that she was older than he was, as if she were guiding him. They had a child, and it seemed to her that she was head of the family. Financial problems were her concerns.

Ten years after her mother had been arrested, she was released. Now 46 years old, she sent a letter to her brother in Sverdlovsk, and he sent it on to Kiev. By the time Natasha received it, of course, she was married and had her baby. She corresponded with her mother, who asked if she could come and live with Natasha. After Natasha talked it over with Sergei, she sent a telegram to her mother saying 'Come!' When her mother arrived, Natasha found she had become an old woman with white hair.

Sergei graduated from the agricultural academy and was ready to go to Moscow for post-graduate work. Two paths had developed in their lives – his need to go to Moscow for further training, and her life in the musical world. She wanted to go to concerts, he was not interested. There were conflicts. This was a hard time for both of them, but they had the child whom they both loved.

Claudia is 64. She grew up in Berlin, the second youngest in a family of two brothers and one sister. She said she was a typical third child.

'I had less than three years of relatively normal high school, after the war broke out. I did not go to school between September 1944 and April 1946. No one did, as there were no schools open in Germany at that time. My only goal was to finish high school and pass the Abitur (examination to enter university) which I did in 1948. I wanted to go on with my studies, but I had not been a very good high school student, and my relatives said, "Oh, Claudia should get married and have a family". I had at first wanted to study journalism and literature – I loved literature, history, music, and all areas of culture; but then I changed to medicine. My father was a doctor and I had helped him with his patients many times.

'After the war, the American army which was occupying our sector of Berlin opened a German Youth Education Center to teach young Germans how to function in a democratic society. I became an active member of the German Youth Activities program. There we put on plays, participated in activities, relaxed, but most of all we had discussions which were wonderful. I had never experienced anything like them. One day I was walking across a street to change classrooms. A man came and called out, "Is Miss Claudia Buschmann here? I have a message. You are to report to the American Army Education Branch at 1 p.m. tomorrow." When I went the next day, they told me I had been awarded a scholarship to spend one year at a women's college in the southern part of the United States. We were the first group of young Germans to come to America after the war.

'When we sailed into New York harbor on a US army transport, we saw the Statue of Liberty and were amazed. We heard the Americans call her "Our Lady". It was a wonderful year, but most challenging, for no one realized how lonely and poor I was. I had a small allowance which just covered my books. I had two dresses which I washed out everyday and ironed and wore again and again. The other girls were involved with their studies, their lives, their clothes, their parties, and their dates, but no one seemed to notice that I had nothing and was alone much of the time. But I was so happy to be having this experience, and I did make a few close friends (with whom I still keep in touch). I loved the college and I loved America. I had put aside my medical studies for the year, and I enjoyed learning American literature, history, and social work; and I learned how to learn!

'Returning to Germany after this academic year, I continued my medical and journalism studies in Berlin, and after two years transferred to the University of Marburg. There I developed a relationship with Andreas, a fraternity brother* of my father, and started my doctor's thesis. I was then 23 years old. It turned out not to be a good relationship because he was constantly talking of other girlfriends, and I wanted to break it off. When I told him this, he started to cry. And so – because he was crying, and for no other reason – we went to bed. This was the first time. It hardly felt real. It did not make any impression on me. And it was over.'

After a month Claudia had several signs of being pregnant and the doctor confirmed this.

'I did not mind. I did not for a minute think, "This is awful. You have to get rid of this child". But I felt very sick. I still say today that I got to know every tree in Tübingen! I also had very little money to buy food, while my 'dear Andreas' ate in the best restaurant every day. I went to a church cafeteria for a 50-pfennig dinner every day. I had to continue some of my twelve-hour night duties in the hospital, and it was very difficult.

I did not tell Andreas I was pregnant until about three weeks later, just before I left to Berlin to see my parents at Christmas. I walked to his place. I told him: "I think I have to tell you. I'm having a baby." He replied, "This is not necessary". That was enough for me. I said, "I don't want to see anything of you anyway. You needn't be afraid," and then I took the 22-hour train journey to Berlin.

---

*Fraternities and Sororities are American college-based clubs or organizations.

'I arrived in the morning while my father was still in bed. I sat beside him, and then I told him. I was so sure he would take it as I did. But he said, "Well, it's not necessary". I could not believe my ears. Then my mother came. She was the third one who said the same thing. They were people of the 20s – perhaps they came to such decisions much more easily at that time. Then I said, "Well, I will have this baby. I have to take care of myself anyway. I don't mind taking care of the baby as well." The money my parents sent me barely paid the university fees (in those days university was not free), and I had earned every penny I needed by myself.

'My father said, "Well I'm going to send a telegram immediately to Andreas. He's my fraternity brother – he has to come at once and you'll get engaged and married." So Andreas came after two days. In 24 hours we had announcements printed so everyone got them at Christmas. The response was: "Oh, how lovely, how wonderful a fraternity engagement!" Well, everything was wonderful for everybody *else*. And when I went back to Marburg, it was the same as before. He was eating in the hotel while I was eating in the church cafeteria.

'We were married in March (you never saw photos of such an unhappy bride). Afterwards he went back to Marburg, and I went to Frankfurt because he would be coming there as soon as he finished his internship. It was very unusual at that time for a pregnant woman to be a student and to continue medical studies, and I was huge. But although it was difficult because I lived in a terrible apartment near the medical school, I got along with everyone and enjoyed my studies. But I was worn out. Andreas came to Frankfurt eight weeks before the baby came. Unfortunately I had a very bad time. Bianca was a big baby, and everything ruptured that possibly could. I had to stay four weeks in hospital. So it was not a very nice experience, but I loved this baby. I had a lot of milk and she was the easiest and healthiest baby.

'Andreas never helped me with anything. If he said, "Oh, let's go to the movies tonight," I would go and get the tickets, and if they cost 3 marks instead of 2.50 he would say, "You go back and try to sell them". I stood there in the cold night trying to sell them. If I wanted to get a hair cut or to buy stockings, I would have to ask him. So this was not very nice, but Bianca was doing beautifully, and I nursed her before and between classes. While the other medical students were having voluntary extra classes in the afternoon, I was home with Bianca. So I had to learn by books. Luckily I always liked to read, so I never had any problem with that. When Bianca was nine months old and I stopped nursing her, we had a lady who came in the morning and stayed with her till noon.'

By this time Claudia had found out how many emotional problems Andreas had. Also, his family did not accept her and said she had gotten pregnant so she could get hold of their money (of which she had known nothing). The relationship between them continued to be very difficult.

'I knew nothing could happen to improve this relationship. But fortunately my father had insisted on my finishing not only medical school, but also my internship. I completed my doctor's thesis and obtained a position in the university clinic, specializing in obstetrics and gynaecology. After fifteen months I was declared "approbated physician" and Andreas told me, "Well, that's that – now you'll stay home".

'At that point I told Andreas the relationship could not continue. I wanted to carry on with my special training, which he did not approve of. I was afraid of becoming pregnant again, so I decided to sleep in Bianca's room, closing and locking the door. Andreas had grown to like the baby, and this was a problem when I told him we could not continue the relationship. He tried everything to get her away from me. My parents, who thought the relationship could still survive, wrote me letters trying to change my mind. It is unbelievable that they didn't understand.

'Then we went through the struggle of getting a conventional divorce, a problem in Germany at that time. Andreas refused to take any of the blame; he said if he ever decided to remarry this could be a problem. I didn't realize the consequences of his refusal to take any of the blame. He did not have to pay me a penny after the divorce and the small amount he was ordered to pay for Bianca barely covered a room, a bed, a stove, a refrigerator, and bathroom. The court hearing was very brief, it took 3 minutes. The divorce was awarded and I had to take the whole blame, I was guilty of not fulfilling my marital "duties".

'Yet I loved to work, and at that time, in Germany, I was very happy to have a position at all. I got my training in the university clinic where I had to work continuously from one morning through to the following night without a break, and somehow still look after Bianca. For almost three years I only had food at night: one piece of wholewheat bread with butter, and a fried egg, and water. I became slimmer and slimmer. But Bianca was doing well, and I was making great progress in the clinic. During this time I had a marvelous relationship with a wonderful man, ten years older than me. Finally I really felt like a woman. But he was married. He and his wife had been married for a long time and had no children, and they had each lived separate lives for years. I didn't intend to marry again, but then Fritz came into my life.'

Inci, 50 years old, grew up in Turkey. She has three older sisters and four older brothers.

'It was very clear even in high school that I had to have a profession. Where did that come from? Perhaps from both my mother and my father. I don't remember my mother ever saying this, but somehow I had the feeling that she was not happy. Her life would have been different if she'd had a profession, if she hadn't had so many children. You know, at high school age, girls fancy having a man. But I said to myself, "No, don't fancy any man. He would stop you from achieving what you want to achieve." I was that scared that I would get involved with a boy.

'I think I knew I was going to be a physicist or scientist. It was quite clear because it was the easiest subject for me. I was looking forward to going to university because I was thinking I wouldn't have to work hard. History, literature, all those things were very difficult for me, but I had the feeling at that time that physics was what I wanted, that it would give me some kind of an understanding of nature, the environment.

'I used to write poems. At the age of 18 I was always writing poems. I was quite an introvert. My sisters were quite different: always playing in the street, running around, being quite active. I was a passive child who did a lot of reading. My eldest sister was already going to medical school. I used to envy Elif, my second sister, who was a scientist too. And my third sister was in political science.

'I was going to be a scientist. Nothing was going to stop me, in spite of the fact that my father wanted me to be a medical doctor like my eldest sister. It was probably my subconscious rebellion against my father's wish. In the last year of university I got a scholarship to go to Sweden.

'The only thing I had in mind was my profession, physics, nothing else. It never changed. But going to Sweden had made me much more of a political person. I started to think, "Why is Turkey so poor? There must be something wrong. Something can be changed." So a year or so later I went back to Turkey. I finished my M.Sc. degree, and then I started to be interested in politics. I attended meetings. I was 23 then. I had kept men out of my life, very consciously. I had so much fear somehow that if I were involved with a man, he would stop me. It was not as if I didn't have friends around me. I had lots of male friends and we used to go out. Perhaps I was afraid to be like my mother.

'Before I went to Sweden I had already finished my university degree, and started as an assistant. I was on leave of absence to do the practical part of my M.Sc degree. I felt I had to go back to Turkey because I had duties there. After I came back from Sweden I met an American man (I was 24 at the time). Neil was a social scientist teaching at the university. When I received a scholarship to do my PhD in England, we went to England together. I went to Cambridge. He worked in London, but we met every weekend. I was not committed to that relationship but we enjoyed being together. He respected my work. He really encouraged me to do all these things I was doing. I was in England four years, from the age of 24 to 28. I did my PhD in applied physics and then we returned to Turkey.'

Eva, 54, grew up in many different countries, since her father was in the diplomatic corps. She spent some of her childhood and high school years in Germany. She has one older brother. Eva had been sent to a Waldorf school as a child, and already at the age of eleven years loved eurythmy (an art of movement taught at the school), and dreamed of the day she would have her own eurythmy school. She felt she had been born to do this.

'I knew my dream would come true. I didn't want to do anything else. I began a five-year training when I was eighteen. When I met Peter, my friends warned me to stay away from him. He wasn't reliable, he was wild. I knew it would be the most difficult commitment I would take on in life. Yet I also recognized I had to do it. We married when I was 22 years old. It was very difficult, and we separated for two years during our twenties, but then we came back together. My training continued until I was 23. It was so intense – it was like being in a monastery: classes all day and then stage-work at night.

'Throughout my twenties I struggled with the tension between wanting to exercise my profession and have my family. From the time of my first pregnancy I felt very strongly connected to my children. Everything from then on was focused on the family. I had my first child when I was 24 and my third when I was 29.'

Nigel is a sixty-two year-old Englishman. The eldest of five children, he was the son of a doctor (a GP). His father expected him to follow in his footsteps, and looked forward to the day when Nigel would join him in his practice. But Nigel never wanted to. He knew the demands on a family doctor. Nigel was so nervous about this that he failed his exam (not on purpose). This was in 1949, and in England if you didn't go to university you had to go into National Service. He was 19 years old. He joined the RAF, and found, to his surprise, that he did enjoy the medical field after all. He pursued medical training: not as a doctor but studying pharmacy, and became a nursing orderly. After two years of pharmacy-studies, he became more interested in medical laboratory practice. He pursued this, was awarded a Fellowship and became highly qualified in bacteriology and blood transfusions. He then went to work in the National Health Service. He loved the work in the hospital in London (the same hospital in which he would have done his medical training) and felt that what he was doing was very worthwhile.

'I was very happy during this time. I moved away from home and into the dock area of London. It was a very rough area, but I enjoyed it very much. I made contact with the Mayflower Centre, which was working with troubled youths in that part of the city, and I began to do voluntary work there. I moved to the Centre and became fully immersed in their Christian missionary work, meanwhile keeping my job at the hospital.'

Daniela is 46 years old, an only child.

When she was 18 she left Germany to be an au pair in Los Angeles. For three years she lived with a family and took care of their twin girls. At 18 Daniela already had a tremendous interest in other countries and people, which has continued to this day. While in LA, she developed rheumatism in her knee, and had to have long periods of rest which interfered with her au pair work, thus creating some resentment that she wasn't fulfilling her duties. When she returned to Germany the doctors couldn't find any problem, but it took two years for the condition to disappear.

With her skills in English as well as her secretarial skills, Daniela went to a new job. Here she met her future husband Dieter. When he changed companies and moved out of town their courtship was restricted to weekends. He decided to build his own business which would include international connections and travel.

'Maybe I didn't marry for love but for other reasons, to learn languages, to travel. My eyes and ears absorbed when I traveled. At first we traveled because of business trips.'

Daniela wanted to work, but it was difficult being the boss's girlfriend and then wife. So she expressed interest in getting a job with another company, which she did. She received a good salary, but was not satisfied because there was too little work. When she tried to quit, they prevailed on her to stay. But the combination of boring work and choleric boss eventually made her start looking again. She found another job, this time as private secretary. Dieter was going on long business trips around the world, sometimes for three months at a time. Daniela was left alone in a city which she did not know, where it was difficult to make friends; but she became friends with the secretary of the senior boss. This was a woman whom others in the company didn't like, but in her own loneliness Daniela became very fond of her. The friendship with this woman, who was 20 years older, became very close and good for both of them. It was very sad when the friend died of cancer.

'I always got along well with older people. I'm still very close with the mother of an old girlfriend.'

After being married for two years, Daniela discovered she could not trust her husband. When they had traveled together, their relationship was close and exciting, but she now experienced a big gap between them as husband and wife. She found it difficult to build a relationship with him. This was her first great disappointment in adult life. After 3½ years of marriage, she began thinking, 'What could I do to get away from Germany and from Dieter?' She knew some people in Mexico so she wrote away for information. With her German/English fluency she had a very marketable skill. So she enrolled in evening school with the idea of becoming a teacher, and then travelling again. 'But at 27 I became pregnant. I was very happy about it, and felt very serious about this responsibility.' Dieter was not excited. He was focused on his business. The economy was going through a very difficult time, and this was very hard on him. The relationship became increasingly strained.

Evita, 58 years old, lives in Vilnius, Lithuania and has been very active in the fight for independence.

'When I was eleven, my father returned home from work one day and announced that he had heard on the radio that the Second World War was over. As a child I was afraid of war. I didn't understand the word. I thought war meant two groups of men who beat each other with knives. The fear of war during this time left scars in me. Perhaps my interest in politics began at that time or maybe it was influenced by my forefathers.

'For example, my grandfather had been a very courageous man. During the Czarist times until 1917, when the Lithuanian language was prohibited, he defiantly bought Lithuanian books. My father was the first recruit in the free Lithuanian army, fighting against the Polish in 1918. From 1918 Lithuania was free; and then in 1940 it was occupied by the Soviets, who pretended Lithuania wanted to be part of the Soviet Union, but the fact is the Russians annexed Lithuania. We talked politics at home. My mother secretly taught a group of children the Lithuanian language because it was forbidden. My father was the first recruit in the free Lithuanian army, fighting against the Polish in 1918. My brother was imprisoned by the KGB in 1974 when he was 49 years old, for four years. My father belonged to a secret organization whose members were willing to give their hearts and lives for the sake of a free Lithuania. So I grew up with politics.

'When I was 18 I had a boyfriend. When I was 20 we married. My only goal during that time was to let him finish his studies at university, and then I would have my turn. We did not look far into the future. Mostly we lived life from day to day. During Soviet times life was hard and confined. We did not connect with the world.

'In my 20s I knew my husband's sweetness, but he had developed a problem with drinking. In the past, drinking was just a symbolic activity for Lithuanians, and five or six men could spend an entire evening with only one drink each. But in the Soviet army my husband learned to drink glassfuls of vodka. I put all my attention on how to save him and keep him from drinking. I loved my husband very much. I wanted a normal family. I wanted nice surroundings. I wanted to finish university. I was working and gave my husband the money. I dreamed of studying myself one day. When my daughter Beruta was three, I not only worked during the day but I took my books in a bag and went to evening school. I was the top student in the group. The math teacher asked about my future plans. I told him my plan was to go to university. His eyes became large: "But you have a daughter and your family. Will you be able to do this? How? Don't you want to get a special vocational training of your own like a baker?"

Evita studied for eleven years in the evening, working during the day. Then she went to university. Evenings when she returned home were difficult. Terrible scenes took place because of her husband's drinking problem.

Pavel, born in Kharkov, Ukraine, (former Soviet Union), is 68 years old.

His parents worked for the state, his father as an accountant, his mother as a pharmacist. In the 1930s life was very hard. Agriculture had been enormously disrupted by the Soviet system. When the private farmers, the kulaks, were sent to Siberia, and the State forced collectivization of farms, production became very low. The country could not produce enough to feed everyone. In 1931 and 1932 there were very bad harvests, and people were dying of starvation. Pavel has vivid memories from when he was 8 and 9 years old, of dead people on the street. After this period life began to get better, but it was never good. In a family with such income as his, there was never any security. His parents, older brother and himself lived in two tiny rooms with no water. He remembers hauling water in buckets from a well 100 meters away. School was OK. He remembered that his teachers intentionally indoctrinated the children to believe that they had a very pleasant life. Since he could make no comparison, he believed it.

He was taught that there was one father-like person who always cared and thought about him: Stalin. He was taught that there were two kinds of people – workers, and capitalists who did not know how to work but exploited the labor of others. Religion was prohibited. If a child attended church with his parents, he would immediately be expelled from school. Religion apparently existed to confuse people, to make fools out of them, to rob them of the inner resources they needed for life. There was never any other source of information, so he was unable to dispute anything he was taught. It was a closed society. He had completed nine classes by the time the war broke out.

In 1941 the Germans entered Russia. His family evacuated to the Urals, but as they went east, so did the Germans. One of the wagons of the train his family was riding in was bombed. Pavel was only seventeen – too young to be taken into the army. But in 1942, when he was eighteen, he was drafted. He was supposed to spend three months in infantry training and then become a lieutenant. But the situation at the front was very bad and he was not able to complete the training – he was sent to the Leningrad-Volkhov front from the Fall of 1942 to Spring of 1943. So many men were killed that within six months his group had lost almost all its original members. In Spring 1943 he was wounded by a sniper's bullet in the knee. For months after the injury he didn't know whether he would survive. He was in a field hospital three kilometers from the front in an underground shelter. He developed gangrene, and the doctor told him he should agree to have his leg amputated. 'You'll feel better immediately. If you don't agree, I cannot guarantee you will live even for five more days.' Pavel couldn't imagine living without his leg, and didn't believe the doctor. All he could do was swear at him. He refused to have his leg amputated. His condition was so serious he could not be transported to another hospital. So he spent almost three months here, underground. His leg began to improve, and the doctor said, 'I see you, but I don't believe it's you. You should have died.'

The hospital was dug out from the earth. The wounded soldiers lay on beds on the earth floor. Around them girls of sixteen and seventeen were firing anti-aircraft guns. Every time they fired, the earth vibrated and the pain in Pavel's leg was intense. He became furious at the girls and shouted, 'Just stop it. I can't bear this'. One evening after dinner, a documentary movie about the war was shown in the shelter. The girls came in to watch the film. Pavel was so angry, he threw his plate at them.

When his health improved he was transported to Siberia where he remained in hospital, in a cast from chest to toes, for a year. He was released in May 1944 when he was twenty years old. The wound was still open but he could move around with crutches. His parents were still in the Urals where his mother worked in a hospital. After Kiev was liberated, this hospital was transferred back to Kiev and the family moved there. When he developed further problems with his leg he went to the hospital in which his mother worked. During his stay there, it was announced one day that there would be a concert organized by students from the music academy. Pavel attended and became acquainted with Lena, whom he often visited.

At the age of 21 he was released from hospital. Life was extremely difficult: not much food, and what there was was very expensive. He wanted to make his own independent way, separate from his family. He was seriously thinking about what to study. When the war had broken out he had still been a boy, and had only completed nine classes at school. He learned that there was training available to become a surveyor. If he pursued this career he could have his secondary education and end up with a profession. He was admitted and began the training.

Since Kiev had been destroyed in the war, the entire infrastructure had to be rebuilt. As a young surveyor he was involved in this work: constructing roads, embankments and buildings. As soon as he began working on his own, he was looking for additional work on the side to earn more money – this was not allowed, but he managed to find some. One such extra job was very interesting: Kiev had a hippodrome of international standard where horse races were held. An American who had lost a great deal of money betting on his horse, protested that the length of the track was longer than it should have been. Pavel was hired to measure the track and found that instead of 1000 meters it was indeed 1067 meters long, and earned himself as much money in these three days as he normally would in six months.

After working in Kiev for three years, he moved to Riga, Latvia where there was a great need for surveyors and where his older brother had moved. During his twenties his goal was always to find some way to make his life better. Now he had a profession: surveying for roads, rest-homes, bridges in Latvia. But he aimed to get himself a more specialized education.

He entered the Department of Hydrology when he was 24 and graduated when he was 30 as an engineer, landing himself the job of Chief Surveyor of hydrotechnical construction sites, specializing in draining land. He had married Lena when he was 23. They had struggled to find a suitable place to live, but had at last managed to rent two rooms. Then, when he was 26, his daughter was born. This was a very happy time for him.

Jerry, born in Poland, is 62 years old.

When he was eight years old the Germans invaded Poland and World War II began. When he was ten he became ill and was sent to a small town to convalesce.

'I was anti-German, yet at the same time I was very impressed by the strength of the German offensive as they made their enormous push into Russia. The propaganda was very effective and influenced me. I later became interested in German culture.'

In 1944 when Jerry was thirteen the Warsaw Uprising took place. These two months were a powerful experience.

At seventeen when he was in high school he became fascinated by India, and especially by Rabindranath Tagore, about whom he gave a talk. During this time Jerry was torn between two ideologies, Catholicism and Marxism. In his 19th year he met a man who brought him into contact with Rudolf Steiner's anthroposophy. He read everything he could get his hands on that had been translated into Polish. Over the next two years he learned German so he could read further. He saw anthroposophy as a synthesis of the most positive features of both religious and scientific culture. He kept feeling, 'I must raise myself to the starting point of anthroposophy'. He set himself the task of learning about the philosophies Steiner had referred to a good deal, and began studying Kant.

At university he studied Egyptian philology and Oriental philosophy. He was also involved in underground political activities and was arrested and put into prison for four months. This experience turned him into an anti-communist. He was expelled from university because of it, and thus had to stop his formal studies. For a while he drifted, then returned to reading and studying philosophy on his own.

Jerry was an only child. He had very good contact with his mother, and a very poor relationship with his father. His adolescence had been turbulent. In his search for something to help him come to terms with his personal problems he discovered the work of Carl Jung (just then published in English for the first time). For nine years he focused on Jung. He worked completely alone with Jung's ideas and symbols, translating his work into Polish. He also translated the works of Sigmund Freud and Eric Fromm.

Rosalind, 69 years old, came from a well-educated American family who were involved in the arts. She had two older sisters and a younger brother. Her grandfather was a painter and photographer. Her parents had settled in Chicago amongst a group of singers, musicians, and artists, and her father bought a building which became the family home as well as a music school. As a child, Rosalind was surrounded by music. Her high school goal was to become a singer. Her house was always full of students having singing lessons. Her parents were involved in founding a private school in Chicago and helping to support it in its early years.

When Rosalind was four her father died of a heart attack. His death was a traumatic experience. The family had lived very well but now everything changed: her father had no life insurance so her mother had to find work. They moved into a small apartment in the top part of the building and rented out the other rooms. From then on they always had boarders. Her mother also became a music coach, first at home and then later at music schools.

Without money to pay for tuition, Rosalind had to change to a new school, which awarded her and her brother a full scholarship. The security and confidence she had felt before her father's death was challenged in the new school setting. After three days of school she couldn't stop crying. Surrounded by many brilliant children, she felt she couldn't keep up. She felt dumb. They were wealthy, had beautiful clothes and lovely homes, and she felt inferior in all kinds of ways.

'Arithmetic saved me. I was asked to help the other children. I gained confidence. Our 6th grade teacher asked us to write poetry, do recitations. I loved that. I was proud and worked hard to do well. I became very popular even though I was shy.'

As a teenager she never had enough clothes, but she washed them, ironed them, and wore the same ones over and over. One student said to her, 'Why don't you have clothes like other people?' Although she didn't feel completely comfortable at school, there were good times at home so there was a balance. Another wonderful part of her childhood was spending every summer with her sisters and brothers at a farm which belonged to family friends.

A famous singing coach offered her free voice lessons because he thought she had a very promising voice. This has occupied her life from her 9th year on. Her weekly lessons gave her illusions of being on the way to becoming an opera singer. This was her ideal and her ambition.

After high school she worked as a clerk in the telephone room of a modelling school. One of the photographers suggested she should become a model. At that time the school was focusing on a new campaign – 'The Natural Girl – the Outdoor Girl', and Rosalind was hired as a model. She earned a pretty good salary. As a model she could arrange her own schedule and fit in her music lessons. She was 21. 'After a while I realized it was like being a prize cow at a cattle show. I couldn't stand it.' She hated the cheating and the deception that went on.

When she was in high school she had a close friend, Jeffrey. Although she had her own boyfriends, and he was the boyfriend of a friend of hers, they had many long talks. 'He really was my friend. I could relate to him from the age of sixteen on. He went to college and then joined the army. World War II was on. He was Jewish and wanted to fight Nazism. But he became sick and had trouble with his eyes. He was released from the army, received treatment and was sent to a ranch in the west for recuperation. Jeffrey got a job in advertising, and earned a good income. He was debonair, good looking, and sociable. We went to the theater a great deal. Ever since my father's death I had longed for someone to be responsible for me, to take care of me. My mother loved Jeffrey. She felt glad that one of her children at least was with someone dependable. Rosalind and Jeffrey married and several years later they had their first child, a daughter, and then their second, a son. They bought a house out in the countryside for weekends and summers.

Patrick, 68 years old, was born in the United States, of Irish parents. He had two brothers from his mother's past marriage (she was widowed), an older sister and younger brother. Another sister had died of pneumonia. Because he was in high-school during the Second World War, his main concern was to graduate, become involved in the military, and maybe later become an engineer like his father. Rather than being worried about joining the armed forces, he looked forward to it. The spirit of nationalism was at a high point, and he wanted to serve his country. He graduated at seventeen, took an accelerated program in engineering, but didn't like it, then joined the air-force.

'This period helped me mature. It was good for thinking about where I wanted to go, earning some money, and finding out who I was. I was younger than most in my unit. Others had family, and were writing home to them. I could see their desire to be home with their family. After basic training I worked in the meat and food locker, trained as a radio man and then was sent to Oklahoma for aerial gunnery training. I was assigned to a bomber that was scheduled to invade Japan. Before I was sent off the atom bomb was dropped on Japan and the war ended.'

Patrick was let out of the service, returned home and went to college. The colleges were jammed with applications from returning veterans, but luckily, because he returned to the same college he had been at earlier, he was able to enroll. But he changed his major from engineering to liberal arts and became involved with drama (in one show he played Cyrano de Bergerac). He impressed the priest – this was a catholic college – who was his mentor, and who advised Patrick to continue on to graduate school in drama since he still had some GI Bill left. Patrick had been considering drama and also advertising. After the priest spoke with him, Patrick decided to follow his advice. After spending the summer doing theater he went to graduate school.

There he met Martha who would later become his wife. After completing the course, he went to New York to begin an acting career. He began to see what an actor's life-style would be like. 'I remember someone telling me that theater is not a happy marriage but a jealous mistress. I knew the distractions would be very great. I knew my own values and morals and realized they didn't fit with life in the theater. So I said no and went to work for a film company in Princeton, New Jersey in production. I loved it, but when the company ran out of funds, I was let go. Just before this happened, my sister collapsed with an aneurism and died. She was 28 and left behind a husband and three children.'

Patrick now turned to the telephone company where his father had worked for forty years, and was employed there as a sales representative. After a year, the priest who had been his mentor offered him a job at a midwest university as his assistant, for he had established a fully recognized academic drama department there. This was a hard decision to make. Patrick enjoyed the work in advertising. He had organized several fashion shows, and gained some recognition for his creativity.

'I decided to join the priest. Martha and I were married and made our way to the midwest.'

Jack is 59 years old. He comes from a small town in Mississippi, a community where everyone knew everyone else. The elders in the town were constantly counselling the young people. It felt as if everyone was your parent. Jack attended an all-black school. Although there were challenges, he felt the strength and safety of the community He was active in athletics and drama and participated in competitions in the County. His mother had two children by her first husband – Jack and his brother. Jack knew his father, who had gone to prison when Jack was six years old.

'I went to visit him, and he told me, "Never go to jail". (He had been a suspect in a murder case.) My father felt so bad about what had happened that he didn't want to interfere with our lives. Mom remarried and had four children, but she never spoke badly about him.'

The key figure in Jack's life was his uncle Jack, who loved children.

'He said you had to keep kids busy until they had no energy left to get into trouble. He was involved in sports with kids. He solved problems. He was a genius with engines. Although he only had a third-grade education, he could do math like a whiz. He also made sure I went to church. I took his last name because I loved him so much.' (It was in choosing a pseudonym for the purposes of this book that 'Jack' said he would like that name in memory of his beloved uncle.)

In 1955, when Jack was 20 years old, his uncle Jack's first wife died.

'There were no children from this marriage so I stayed with him and helped him. He remarried and had five children. They all called me "big brother". I called Uncle Jack "Dad". We lived in a segregated society, yet we had a rich and loving community. The church and the school took care of us. On Sundays families got together after church. The mothers cooked, the kids played baseball. Then we had a potluck meal. I behaved myself. If any of us got into trouble, we'd get a whipping both at school and at home. In Junior High School I was whipped because I was caught with a group that was smoking. I had not been smoking, and I felt it was unjust that I was in trouble. So I left school. When I came home I was whipped for leaving school. I was sent back to school and was whipped again. To this day I don't smoke.

'When I finished high school, although I had been a good student, I was not ready for college. I wanted to explore the world. When I was twenty-one I was drafted. I married my childhood sweetheart before I went into the service and saw action in Korea. The regimentation of the army life didn't bother me. I was used to it. When I got out I worked for the telephone company until we went on strike. I went back into the service.

When I was twenty-one I already had a great deal of responsibility – a wife and son. With the military I had a settled way of life. I was in Japan for three years, and then in Hawaii for three years. I very much enjoyed the cultural differences I experienced. I learned how we American people have everything at our doorstep. We take everything for granted. The time in Hawaii was very enjoyable and I enjoyed getting to know the local people and observing their customs. My wife had always hoped we would get to live there so she was especially happy. During this time our family grew to three sons and a daughter. When I was 28 we left Hawaii.

Here we have the brief stories of twelve people, and we see their lives played out against very different backgrounds. The Second World War influenced the lives of five of them, each in different ways. Pavel, injured in the Soviet army; Jerry as a child in occupied Poland; Natasha, uprooted in her studies, experiencing scarcity of food and the arrest of her mother; Claudia unable to complete her high school studies in Berlin; Patrick as a young American serviceman.

During their twenties these twelve young people shared common elements. They had dreams of careers, of relationships, of families. Their interests were broad. Natasha and Rosalind studying music; Claudia and Nigel interested in medical fields; Eva in Eurythmy; Daniela – travel and languages; Evita in night school studying mathematics; Pavel in surveying and engineering; Inci studying physics; Jerry in Egyptian philology and Oriental philosophy; Patrick in drama; and Jack in the military.

Situations began to change their plans, and adjustments had to be made as each person dealt with disappointments, surprising changes such as pregnancy or failing an exam. Life still seemed exciting, though, and they had plenty of energy to accomplish all that needed to be done as they worked toward the future.

In most cases the greatest changes occurred in their relationships. Meeting their future partners, marrying, having children, finding the relationship tested, and dealing with alcoholism, unfaithfulness or changing interests, all required growth.

Nigel and Jerry did not marry during this time. They were focused on finding their careers. Nigel found his fulfilment in Christian missionary work and medical work; Jerry was involved in an inner as well as an outer search for meaning, found Rudolf Steiner's anthroposophy and Carl Jung's psychological insights. Jerry spent time in prison, learned English, and was then able to translate Jung from English to Polish.

2
Trying to Organize Our Lives: 28-35

Around the age of 28 we often begin to feel it is time to settle down and become more conscious about our lives. Living from day to day without a long-term plan does not satisfy us any more. Or we may previously have had to be too serious about life, and now decide there should be more time for fun. Whatever has been missing is what we yearn for – the most common feeling being that we need to settle down and develop roots.

At about 30, men in particular begin to experience some limitations to their physical prowess and energy. They need to work harder to accomplish what had been easy a few years earlier. They can still run and climb, but they pant and ache rather more, and they may find it harder to keep ahead of their children, if they have any. They may begin to feel pain in the lower back or stiffness in the joints, but the mind is still as agile as it used to be. Many professional sportsmen are passing their prime by 30. They have skill and experience, but not the wind nor the strength in their legs that they used to have.

Most women don't feel this as dramatically, perhaps because they are often less competitive or because they aren't sitting down as much as men with office jobs. But they, too, experience their bodies becoming softer. Their hips fill out and it's harder to maintain a girlish figure.

Besides physical changes, other changes occur at this time in our relationship to the people around us. The bold confidence of our twenties starts giving way to more sensitive awareness of ourselves. We may no longer be satisfied by just relying on our feelings: we become more inward, perhaps more subdued. It is time to become realistic and practical, to take stock of what we are doing and organize our time. Are our decisions making sense? Have we taken all the factors into consideration? Are we keeping adequate records? We begin to harness our energy to serve our plans. Our earlier idealism calms down as we get to grips with everyday life.

The force of the critical intellect is a double-edged sword: it is very helpful in organizing our lives, but can also pierce and wound other people. We step back from them more and begin to see their faults and imperfections. We can become rather cold and critical and it is easy for us to feel self-righteous about others since we may well not yet have started facing our own faults.

There is often a time-lapse involved between first judging others, then eventually getting around to looking at ourselves objectively too. But even when we start to feel the pain of facing our own weaknesses, this does not necessarily make us feel any more sympathy for others. That requires conscious work on ourselves. Developing a sense of appreciation for other people is hard work, especially because we are often reluctantly forced into it. Our own feeling of inner hurt tends to be more insistent than concern for those around us. But a mature person can be spurred on by self-doubt to feel it is time to act more sensitively and responsibly, rather than just sitting on the sidelines and criticising. A growing sense of loneliness can creep in at this time of our lives: our intellectual sharpness doesn't compensate for the strong feeling of separateness we feel.

Those who have led a single life may feel it is time to find a partner and settle down. But since we have probably become more judgmental we are not so easily swept off our feet. Our perception of others' weaknesses alternates with insight into their strengths. Is it any wonder then, that we sometimes feel like a yo-yo? We have developed a single life-style which may be very satisfying and comfortable. What will the other person bring to the relationship? We may feel very wary of a complicated situation: children from a past marriage, a career that involves much travel, perhaps an illness. We may consider such things very carefully, rather than following our spontaneous feelings and throwing ourselves into situations as we were more likely to do in our twenties.

Yet this is a very positive and active time of life. There is lots of work ahead. The calm that has replaced the emotional turmoil of the twenties is welcome since there is so much to do. It isn't surprising that radicals of the 1960s saw thirty as being 'over the hill', the point at which people stopped being trustworthy. People over 30 are not as quick to risk their jobs or their families for ideals; they seem more subdued, less reckless.

The specific choices we make during our thirties depend very much on our particular circumstances and the need to balance what has been going on in our twenties. There can be a conflict here between our previous dreams and ideals, and present realities. How can we realize both? Trying to come up with a plan is difficult as there are often no simple solutions. A woman may want to settle down and have a family, but also stay involved with interesting work. How does she do this? Are her goals compatible with her husband's?

Daniel Levinson groups together the first two phases in male adult life – what he calls the 'Onward and Upward' phase, from 21-35. This is very appropriate as the two phases have so much in common. At this time in their lives people are generally reacting to what comes towards them from outside. Levinson vividly describes the man's attitude in the first half of his thirties:

> Fatherhood is not the all-important role in a man's life. His starring role as he sees it during the Onward and Upward years is that of the promising young man on his way up. He has important tasks to accomplish. He is driven by the need for achievement.
>
> 'If I'm not making six figures by the time I'm forty, I've had it,' he thinks on the way to work. 'If I'm not executive vice-president by the time I'm thirty-five, I've had it,' he worries in the pre-dawn hours. 'If I don't own a house by the time I'm thirty... if I don't have a high four-figure balance in my checking account... if I don't have an office of my own... if I'm not elected to the club... if I'm not...' He is driven by goals that he sets himself, one after another.[1]

The inner growth that occurs during this time shows the higher self or ego is taking hold. But toward the end of this period there is often a low point. Feelings of loneliness and isolation may intensify. The realization that life's problems are not as easily solved as we thought contributes to a feeling of helplessness. Keeping busy can camouflage the growing feelings within, but not drive them away. However much we hope for some magical answer to come and solve everything, this doesn't happen. Many people experience a feeling of loss, even a sense that something is dying. Rudolf Steiner characterises the period from 30-33 as analogous to the last three years of Christ's 'valley of the shadow of death'. This implies that something in the nature of a soul resurrection may lie ahead. It is very important to have friends during this time, but to learn not to depend on them is also important. Many friendships actually weaken during this period, or break apart. We find we have different goals or interests from some of our long-time friends. We are sorry about this, yet feel we have to use our time and energy carefully. Our goals are the most important aspect of our lives now. Thus we experience gains and losses in our relationships.

Most people have a relationship with a mentor at some time in their lives. These are experienced people who recognize and encourage a young protegee's special talents. They take him under their wing, point out opportunities, introduce him to important people in their field. The protegee looks towards the mentor as a source of guidance and inspiration, as someone who has qualities he admires and wants to develop. Levinson describes the mentor for an 'ambitious young man' as a man 8 to 15 years older than him. Though wise and fatherly, he is still young enough for the two men do many things together. At some point, though, the younger man may well get fed up the with mentor's narrowness, his rules, his 'right' way of doing things, perhaps his hypocrisy. He resents his mentor and breaks away. This is an important part of his emotional development: he has to stand on his own even if it means being lonely for a time. Breaking away from a mentor is like breaking away from the father for a second time. Carl Jung vividly describes the effect on him of his break with Sigmund Freud, which occurred when he challenged the latter's theory of libido. The experience was so traumatic that Jung felt paralyzed by it:

> When I was working on my book about the libido and approaching the end of the chapter 'The Sacrifice', I knew in advance that its publication would cost me my friendship with Freud... For two months I was unable to touch my pen, so tormented was I by the conflict. Should I keep my

thoughts to myself, or should I risk the loss of so important a friendship? At last I resolved to go ahead with the writing – and it did indeed cost me Freud's friendship.[2]

The pain is felt by both mentor and protegé, but it is a necessary step for the younger man's emotional health. Until he consciously realizes what is happening he can suffer terrible feelings of inadequacy and guilt, but once the break is made he feels he has passed the test, he doesn't need the mentor because he has the confidence to face the world himself. I'm not sure I agree with Levinson about the dramatic end of the mentor relationship. Perhaps in the corporate world it has a more drastic flavor, but I know of many such relationships that ended harmoniously and were able to change in character from one of guidance to colleagueship.

Women, too, have mentors. Before so many women entered the professional world their older women relatives played this role, guiding them in traditions of homemaking and child-rearing. Here too, a time always came when the younger woman began to stand on her own feet, but usually without such a radical break – she was, instead, just accepted as an equal into the group, and her relationship with her mentor continued in a new way. In the professional world the mentor relationship is more complicated, for in fields which women are only now starting to break into, most mentors are men. They spot a talented young woman and try to help her along, meet the right people and so on. This may be complicated by the male-female relationship: the mentorship can become a subject of gossip, can become a romantic relationship or require sexual favors – but of course it doesn't have to be that way. Things are still very much in flux in this whole area, so it is too early to get any sense of the modern mentorship-patterns emerging. We will have to wait until more women move into high positions of responsibility in the professions before we can draw conclusions.

I had two mentors in my professional career, both men. The first was a college professor who guided me through career decisions, helped me apply for and be granted a scholarship for additional training (I learned years later he had personally arranged for this money through a friend), made it possible for me to meet distinguished people in my field who were friends of his, and kept me aware of openings in different locations. When I decided to stay at home to care for my children instead of pursuing my career, he remained a friend but continued to let me know what was happening in the profession. He was influential in many of the decisions I made in my twenties. I maintained a close relationship with him for over thirty years until his death, but the mentor aspect of the relationship had faded and a friendship of equals took its place.

Another mentor had been one of my teachers in my postgraduate training, but did not take on the mentor role for another twenty years. Only when he was in a particular position of responsibility and I was ready, did he begin to include me, introduce me to people, and encourage me to move into new areas.

As I have become older and more experienced I have acted as a mentor to a number of young men and women. I have had both experiences – the first, in which the mentor relationship was no longer needed and gradually changed into a friendship; and the second, the sudden break up of the relationship when a younger person wanted to break free. This second experience is a very confusing and painful experience of betrayal and loss.

The great inner challenge during this phase from 28-35 is to transform critical judgment into thoughtful consideration, allowing emotions to ripen into feelings; to take more time to make decisions, and to bring the light of the mind and warmth of the heart together in a more conscious way. Critical judgment that has not yet become thoughtful consideration is what makes many of the breaks with a mentor so painful. Critical judgment also causes many difficulties in the work place. Seeing that something is wrong is easy, offering a real solution is much harder. It is not unusual to find that people in their twenties are very critical of their employers or older colleagues who 'have sold out their ideals'. When they are given an opportunity to become responsible, they are at first very careful not to repeat their employer's mistakes. But with more experience, in their thirties, they often come to understand why those decisions were made and even find themselves making some of the same decisions. In my late twenties and early thirties I was such a rebellious person – full of high ideals. I viewed all compromise as 'selling out' and had no respect for it. I still feel something of a rebel, but I am sure many younger people see me as an old conservative who is trying to block progress.

During this period of life, then, we begin to experience our own ego shining through our feelings, our actions, and our thoughts. We gradually sense ourselves to be independent personalities, but do not always see that others are as well. This is the challenge of the 28-35 year phase: to recognize that just as the spiritual shines through me, it also shines through you. When we awaken to this knowledge and understand it fully, then we transform the experience of individuality into one that goes beyond ourselves, and can enter into a right relationship with our fellow human beings. When we are successful in this effort, then something of a higher nature flows from our souls to the souls of our fellows, and flows back again to us. We experience a reflection of the love we show to others. This affirmation of our own efforts at understanding, at empathy, and compassion allows a new level of communication to occur. But oh, is it difficult!

Challenges to relationships

There are also many challenges to relationships during this seven-year period. If the couple married in their twenties, a previously strong feeling of 'togetherness' can be disrupted by a new sense of separation. Each partner is focused on a task – profession, taking care of children, or profession *and* taking care of children. Each may be involved in separate activities for much of the time, focusing on different things. When partners begin to stand back and observe each other, not all they find will be to their liking, especially since much of the glamour and romance is gone: the knight's armour is rusty, the fair lady is a little worn! Each partner stands more naked in front of the other. And as we turn this two-edged sword of criticism back upon ourselves as well, we can have an overwhelming experience of our own faults, and be forced to ask ourselves, 'What can I achieve?, Have I found my work in the world? How can he possibly love me any more?'

The plans we made in our twenties don't fit anymore. Our priorities have changed. Becoming dissatisfied, each individual feels restricted and narrow; and turning this criticism outward, blames the other. The sense of impending crisis causes us to ask ourselves whether our partner is the right person for us.

On the other hand, life often becomes more rational, more orderly. We've established a routine. A business-like approach begins to operate in the marriage. Sex has also perhaps become routine. The couple addresses issues more logically and less emotionally. Something deeper has to arise to prevent the relationship from becoming commonplace. We make decisions about where to settle down, whether to buy a house or rent an apartment. We set down our roots. Unfortunately, these are often far from other members of our family, so that we don't have any close contact with our parents, cousins, brothers or sisters. We haven't anyone we can depend on for a close conversation, for help, for holiday celebrations. We need to try to fill this gap with friends. But it may not be the same – they may not know us in the same way. And the children don't have a sense of an extended family.

A new extended family can be built though, with friends who have similar values – especially with 'family activities' and a shared philosophy of child rearing. A new set of adopted 'uncles, aunts and grandparents' may become part of our lives, especially during the years when our children are young and we need a support group around us. Unlike our biological family, we choose these people and we stay close as long as the relationship works. Throughout the years my family has had a number of 'adopted extended families'. It was wonderful to join together for meals, go on excursions together, share child-care, plan holiday celebrations, and have long discussions. We developed a mutual support and warmth that wasn't otherwise present in our lives. Sometimes this group becomes very tightly knit; in other situations it is looser, with various configurations of close friends coming together for different occasions. But the sharp judgmental quality of the early thirties can also have an effect on these relationships, making it difficult for them to be sustained.

So although we often feel satisfied at this period that our plans are at last working out, our inner contentment with our relationships, especially with our partners, starts weakening. Additional strain is added if our social life feels too restricted. We long for something different, for some new excitement. The couple needs to get some time away to enjoy each other's company without household chores involved, to explore a new place, to wake up in a different bedroom, to go out for breakfast. We have the need to renew the sense of intimacy of marriage, to recapture the mood of our earlier love which now is so often submerged in the busyness (or business) of life.

For the woman at home, the strain at this time has a special character. The man may now be feeling very competent, and may start telling his wife to go out and do something new or different. He wants her to broaden herself rather than being mostly a mother. She often feels threatened by this: 'I'm not good enough. How will I ever interest him?' She is already feeling dissatisfied with herself, and now he too finds she has become limited and dull. She begins to wonder what her life would be like if it wasn't only centred around the home. Her husband knows he would be bored silly if he had to adopt her way of life. At the same time he likes the results of it for himself: because her life is so confined, she depends on him for exciting news from work – but he is not particularly interested in talking about it with her. Gail Sheehy points out in *Passages* that he may also be afraid that if she really became preoccupied with something outside the home, she would not care for him and feed him. This contradiction between what he wants and what he fears makes him feel guilty.

The wife often senses this and pulls away, stops being supportive as she feels more and more worried and threatened. Husband and wife often misunderstand each other just when they need each other most. She senses that he is changing and may try to become less dependent so that he won't feel trapped. She pulls away to help him, but perhaps it backfires – he feels she doesn't care and is disappointed, lost. Or the woman may frantically pursue one or another interest, but find difficulty in staying with anything for any length of time. Or, on the other hand, she may start to feel stronger and more confident, and less dependent on her husband – which may also threaten the relationship. In such situations it isn't surprising that both partners feel things have gone irretrievably wrong.

I well remember my feelings of insecurity at stepping out into the world. I had just turned 28 and decided I would begin my Master's degree. I didn't really know why, but I felt I had to do something 'important' and also be preparing for the future. I went to the university to enroll, stood in a long line, became so frenzied with the system, that I turned around and went home. I felt I had failed to face the complexities of modern life because I had been intimidated by something most 18 year-olds could handle perfectly well. Not long after, I spoke to a friend who had re-entered community college in her late thirties, and I found that many women shared the fear I had experienced that day, even to the point of being unable to ask someone where the toilets were!

This fear of re-entry at a time when self-worth is so low is a serious problem. It led me to ponder the changes I had experienced in my own life and also to re-evaluate the dynamics of marriage, particularly the woman's role. I recalled myself as a college student, active, alive, vital, interested in so many things. The world was stimulating and I felt excited to be a part of it. Then for two years my husband and I were companions in the working world, sharing experiences, feeling we were doing meaningful work together, exploring career possibilities, alive, equal to the task. Then I became pregnant and stopped working. Everything slowed down. I was alone much of the time, took long walks, became inward, brooding, occasionally visited a friend or family member, made baby clothes, did some artwork, and waited – that continual waiting for my husband to come home – and missed the previous excitement we had brought each other. After the baby came we moved out to a rural area and certain things changed, but the basic dynamic remained the same. Now the baby whom I loved occupied most of my attention. Seldom did I have intelligent conversations as I had earlier. It was hard to make friends based on anything besides children and family. Joining the League of Women Voters was a great help, but generally I felt isolated: I began to be plagued by fears and lack of confidence.

This period in our lives is the dawn of discomfort, the sense of loss, the fear of change. Comparing oneself before and after the period of 'housewifing' can be a severe shock. The fact that mothers do very important and purposeful work only highlights the fact that they need greater support to go through this time creatively. Otherwise they project their feelings of uncertainty and isolation onto the husband, become hostile to him. As well as feeling inadequate beside her husband, a wife often also sees all his faults and weaknesses, and may feel cheated and resentful.

When I look back at that time, though, as well as remembering the pain and loneliness I experience nostalgia. I did things then I haven't had peace or time for since: tended a garden, baked bread, preserved fruits and vegetables, made children's clothes, played with the children, and did a lot of day-dreaming as I went about my tasks. This inward, brooding time was developing something new in me. I was growing up. We had little money, but we were rich in warmth and family closeness.

In her book *The Brothers System for Liberated Love and Marriage,* Dr. Joyce Brothers addresses this problem: 3

> Marriage can be liberated to meet the needs of women today, to preserve the love and cherishing and excitement while discarding the restrictive and damaging aspects of the relationship.

She points out that the power of love is so strong at the beginning of marriage that the woman accepts a one-sided view of herself even though it hurts her. If a change toward equality can be effected both partners have so much more to gain:

> The answer is not to abolish marriage but to liberate it – a loving union in which each partner is as concerned about promoting the happiness and growth and fulfilment of the other as he or she is about promoting his or her own happiness, growth and fulfilment.

In Chapter 5 Brothers goes on to suggest ways in which a woman can change her view of herself, usually by cultivating a strong interest, doing part or full time work, regaining self-respect, opening herself up to a larger circle of people, and in most cases becoming much more interesting to herself and her husband as a result. Can this be done while trying also to be a conscientious full-time mother? Yes, with careful planning it can be managed. It is not easy, but it must happen if the woman feels the need for it. She cannot wait five years to become a person again. But she has to be realistic about the amount of time she has available.

Whether or not a mother should work full-time is a very individual decision. It may be right in certain circumstances: if finances require it, or the mother's individual needs; or if the couple can work out joint parenting schedules. But I cannot stress strongly enough the value of full-time mothering. I do feel that if it is at all possible the mother should be at home with the child until he goes to kindergarten. Since so much of the child's sense of security is formed during these years, it is worth the struggle – financially and careerwise – to dedicate them to the home. But if this is not possible, an extended family or older friend may be able to help out. Older people need to be needed and are often happy to be asked (if the arrangement doesn't slide into a full-time one without being agreed to). Life is more complicated today than in the past, and if we cannot be a full-time parent it doesn't help to be consumed by guilt. We have to do the best we can in the circumstances.

There are other ways for a woman to strengthen herself during this time. Making sure that we have private time of our own everyday is very helpful. Whether we use it for reading, thinking, studying, meditating, or artwork, it should be a time of inward activity. A special time in a busy day, not dictated by what is needed in the household, can be healing and balancing – even if it is only thirty minutes. Because parenting so often thrusts us into constant activity, a few moments of solitude can help us develop our sensitivity, keep our minds active and create an inner anchor. We may surprise ourselves at how much knowledge we can gain and even use later for professional use, just by taking a little time every day. Sometimes it can seem that everything in a woman's life diffuses her concentration, dissipates her energies – which does not help her sense of inferiority. Wives returning to college often feel afraid they will not be able to concentrate.

The desert a woman can pass through at this stage is fertile ground for problems. A third person may enter the relationship, an 'other woman' who flatters the husband's masculinity and offers him adoration. A man who has not resolved the earlier 'emotional' period by developing mature judgment, seeks approval from others. He does not want to observe himself with any objectivity or use his rational soul capacities to their utmost. A woman in this predicament will look for 'romance', whereas a man looks for a woman who will make him feel 'more of a man' – rather than the lesser man he subconsciously feels himself to be. A man in this situation may use a woman for his own egotistic satisfaction. The woman who is involved is fulfilling her own sensual needs or 'sacrificing herself' for him may also be avoiding facing herself. So many women who get involved in affairs with married men are ready to believe that the man has an unhappy marriage, that his wife doesn't understand him. Although this may be partially true, it is often self-delusion. The man may use this version of the facts to keep a woman's interest or attract it in the first place, or he may himself be as confused as the woman who falls for this story. Unknowingly they use each other. Very often the man ends the passionate affair and continues his marriage to this 'wife who doesn't understand him'! Women (married or not) who involve themselves in a series of affairs are failing to move beyond an early stage of maturity and need to ask themselves, What am I doing? Am I just out for sensual satisfaction or am I avoiding looking at aspects of myself? Why are these relationships not working out?

A less drastic and damaging version of the 'man as hero' for a woman who is not his wife, is when he shows excessive interest and desire to help, but without launching into an 'affair'. He makes enormous efforts on her behalf, seeing himself as a saviour of some kind, giving time, attention, and consideration in a way he has not given his wife since he courted her, while his wife wonders why he doesn't give this sort of energy to her. His feeling of self-satisfaction for his noble deeds convinces him that he is irreplaceable. Many women long for this attention from other men since *their* husbands are not providing it. Both wallow in self-pity.

This crisis period presents a challenge, but it doesn't have to weaken a relationship. If the couple can understand what is happening, if they can appreciate each other's growing individuality, a new warmth of companionship and trust can emerge.

During this period there are many opportunities for cooperation, either for the couple alone or for a family. The couple can work together planning a holiday, redesigning an apartment or house, working for social or political causes, involving themselves in the children's activities. They can sometimes, ironically, be communicating closely about such things while the marriage itself is falling apart.

If a couple cannot manage to move through this developmental step successfully, there will be a major marriage-crisis in their forties. This intellectual period of the thirties, properly worked through, can stimulate growth: the ability to see pros and cons more clearly, and a greater matter-of-factness; can provide the basis for accepting our partner as he is. The capacity for understanding grows. We learn to feel the importance of striving towards truth and facing our aloneness. The seeds of selfless love develop – but all of us do this in our own time and in our own way. Some refuse to take the necessary steps to develop new capacities, preferring instead to live in the past. People in their late thirties who still live like twenty year-olds seem sentimental and foolish as they keep searching for deep and passionate encounters.

If two people have shared years of marriage but have failed to communicate adequately, they may both build up feelings of reproach and distrust. Trust built over years of working together can bring deep joy, but it is very difficult to deepen communication without it. Marriage reflects the partners' inner development, and can only mature if they can work through the reservoir of unhappy feelings each harbors. Otherwise they get stuck. Part of growing up involves developing our own personality more strongly – which may mean temporarily letting go of doing everything together. For a while differentiation intensifies, the relationship doesn't feel the same: this is only a phase, but a necessary one. If both partners are trying to understand and support each other and have patience, the marriage will take on a new depth. When both people respect and understand each other's inner freedom, a wonderful partnership can emerge which makes it 'possible for each to see the other whole and against a wide sky'.

I was visiting a friend I hadn't seen in a while and we were catching up on where we were in our marriages. She was telling me how often she found herself apologising or explaining for her husband. She didn't know why, she could just see the little things he did which irritated someone or caused annoyance. Finally one evening a friend told her, 'Lay off, Lyn, you're his wife, not his analyst'. She said that rather than being annoyed, she was relieved. Then she was shocked at her own arrogance. What had given her the right to judge him? I don't think she is alone. One of the problems that does occur in marriages, particularly long-term ones, is the feeling you know the other person so well that you need to protect people from his faults.

A point comes in a relationship – and in this case it can be in a close friendship as well as in a marriage – when we let go. We no longer ask, Why am I with this person? We no longer add up the irritations, marking them in some invisible account book. The moment arrives when all that disappears and we acknowledge he is our partner or friend, and accept him totally. At that point we can understand, give, and commit ourselves, allowing new forces of warmth and support to develop.

Balance is the key-note of this period. If a woman has been working in the 'outside world', she often yearns to settle down and have children, to be at home if possible. If she has been at home she wants to move outward and test herself in the world. Both situations have transitional problems, both call for a new relationship with the partner. Although the problems will differ depending on which side of the front door the woman finds herself, their nature is basically identical. The way we seek balance may be clumsy, awkward, and strange, and almost certainly painful, but as Audre Lourde [4] states so graphically, 'Pain will always either change or stop'.

Gail Sheehy describes this period as one of reappraisal. A married person will question his commitment while a single person begins to look for marriage or at least a committed relationship. The inner life tries to develop as much strength as the outer demands. *A recognition that comes during this time, and that can fill us with despair, is that our intellect cannot answer all our questions about life.*

A couple who marry when they are past thirty have a somewhat different experience from those who marry in their twenties. Their ideas are more formed, their habits more set, each has a particular circle of friends and career interests. These people tend to respect each other's individuality more easily; but much humor and tolerance are needed, as each one comes with a whole set of expectations of the way things are supposed to be – including the way laundry is folded, how the table is set etc. Neither has formed the other. They are two separate entities to a much greater degree, so there is more need and possibility for respect and freedom. Second marriages also have this character; they also often bring much more complicated situations with them: children, emotional scars, expectations from the past, as well as more realistic expectations of the future; also more self-knowledge and willingness to accept responsibility when problems arise. Second marriages may give us the opportunity to learn from our past mistakes and work toward a deeper kind of relationship.

There is some evidence that people born after 1966 live at home longer or keep studying until around the age of 30. This situation may postpone the entrance into adulthood by ten years, which would mean that the attitudes described above shift into the forties instead of the thirties.

Natasha

During the time Natasha and Sergei were going through their difficulties, she had met a man with whom she worked at the Academy. They had many interests in common and both were musicians. This relationship developed in such a strong way that Natasha told Sergei she wanted a divorce. They had many late night talks, and although he very much wanted their little daughter Irina to live with him, they decided she should live with her mother. Sergei came often to see Irina, and Natasha never objected. Five years later he remarried and Natasha and Sergei renewed their relationship, but now as friends. Natasha also had a good relationship with his new wife. 'Time is the best doctor' said Natasha.

'My first marriage came out of attraction. My ideas changed with the second marriage. I loved Sergei, but the relationship with Anton was very different. Both were good people. I had more self-confidence, and I was more mature. I understood now that bright outer beauty is not the main thing.'

Natasha and Anton's life revolved around music. The whole day Natasha was at the Academy and then friends came over in the evenings to play music together. During the first three years they were very close and were always together. 'This was a very happy period. We did creative work together. We were a good couple and a good ensemble. It was an even process of growth. Everything was getting better and better in my creative life as a singer. Anton, with his experience and knowledge helped me very much. He was a wonderful musician and I had his full support. Both of my feet were on the ground. I had so much confidence.'

Claudia was working at the clinic and taking care of Bianca.

'Fritz was a senior doctor at the clinic. We were just acquainted as he was teaching me and supervising me. I had been having a relationship with another doctor during that time. One evening Fritz and I had been both on duty. I had done a difficult operation and asked him to come see whether all went well. Afterwards we were talking and he said, "It's a shame". I said, "What's a shame?" "It's too bad that you are going on with Franz." After this conversation, the other relationship ended and this one started.'

Fritz and Claudia saw each other every day at the hospital. Their love was deep and intense. He had done some important work on diagnosing breast cancer and had been asked to deliver a paper at a medical congress. Claudia translated it into English for him and when she finished she told him how much she would like to go with him to Italy to the congress. And then he said, 'You can't because I'm going with my wife'.

She was in shock and asked him, 'When did you marry?' He replied that he had married three months before. She couldn't believe it. They had already been together at this time. When she asked how this could be, Fritz replied, 'It was because I did not think Dr. Claudia Jensen would ever marry me. And if I have to leave the clinic next month there must be someone stable in my life or else I will be lost.' This was one of the most awful moments of Claudia's life. She felt completely lost and cheated. She ran out and took a taxi home because 'I was afraid something would happen to me. I was out of my mind.'

'His marriage was a most peculiar one. He had had a close, almost "married" relationship with a woman for nine years. They had traveled together all over Europe on their vacations, but they had never lived together. One particular day he had been on duty, and suddenly asked the head of the hospital if he could leave for an hour. He went out, met this woman, and they were married. Then he came back to the clinic. Can you believe this? Even if I would have decided to end the relationship with him, it would have been difficult. We continued to work together every day. And I was in love with him.'

Fritz' situation was complicated: he had been made a prisoner of war in the Battle of Stalingrad, so when he returned to his profession in Germany in 1950 he was too old to begin climbing the career-ladder. At his age he should have been a professor. He could stay at the clinic for ten years and then, because of regulations, would have to leave and go into private practice. He had been deeply scarred emotionally by his Stalingrad and POW years and he knew that once he had his own practice he would need a great deal of support. He wasn't sure Claudia would marry him and thus made this impulsive decision to marry the other woman. What else was in his mind was never clear. When he learned that Claudia wanted to be with him, he began divorce proceedings.

'Getting a doctor's post in Germany at that time was very difficult. You had to replace someone else who either had retired or died. Fritz and I traveled all over the country looking. He applied for fifteen openings, but he was always second out of about a hundred applicants. He had to leave the clinic and didn't have a new job, so just sat at home. I would come home from work and then take care of him. He went into a deep depression and would not eat anything unless I cooked it.' Claudia realized this was not a healthy situation, but she didn't know how to leave or what to do. Fritz told her, 'If you leave me I will go to the gutter'.

'I knew this was true. There was no question about it. I didn't want this to happen because I knew he was a man who had endured so much already. Mutual friends told me, "Please, please, do not marry him. We know him much longer than you."' But she did not know how to get out of it. Finally they found an office and small clinic they could take over. Fritz and Claudia were married.

'At first there was the big difference in age. I was 29 and he was 16 years older. I rather wanted an older man because I thought he would be more complete. I found out this wasn't so. It was just a misjudgment on my part because of my young age. Yet it changed in that I always felt responsible for him, even the months before we married, and this is why I didn't walk out. I always felt an obligation to look after him permanently and to make up for all the things he had suffered.'

During this time Claudia and Fritz built up a small clinic. In addition to Bianca, two other little girls were born. The family was well integrated into the life at the clinic. There were many hard times, but no matter what difficulties there were with Fritz, Claudia managed to keep everything going: her work was her great love, and she felt exceedingly happy with her three daughters. Fritz proved to be a wonderful father.

Inci

When Neal and Inci returned to Turkey from England, they married. She was 29 years old. This was an exciting time in Turkey. The Social Democrats were in power, lots of liberal ideas were being implemented. Professional women's groups were forming in Ankara.

'We women tried especially to keep democratic rights alive, to make life liveable, to be useful. For example, according to Turkish laws if a company had a hundred women working on the premises, it had to have a child-care system, but hardly anywhere had this.

'So it was one of our most important works to go and find which places did not have it and legally force them to provide a child-care system. First we organized open creches (day-care centers and kindergartens), then reading and writing courses followed.'

Although the women's groups were made up mostly of professional women at first, they concentrated their activities on nonprofessional working women. The group headed by Inci set up a women's center to which women went after their normal working hours.

'In fact, we paid the rent of the place, a small place, and cleaned and looked after it so that the women would feel very comfortable to come there and talk about their problems.'

She was then working at the university. At first her colleagues would make fun of 'Inci's little project'. But on the other hand, 'lots of my colleagues started to support me, especially women colleagues because they saw that we were doing very good work. For example, at the university there was no child-care system even though about 30 per cent of the academic staff of the university were women (400 women at that time). Now they are enjoying the child-care system. They even have a primary school now on the campus. This year a secondary school is being added. And this was *our* work.'

'During this time I was thirty years old. I was working together with Ali at the university. I fell in love, *madly*. I was working in the university, building up laboratories, having research students, and was madly in love – oh, it was the first time I felt like a woman. It was exciting. I had never allowed myself to feel like it. He was so helpless and lovely. I thought it would be so nice to cook for him, to look after him.

'I talked to my husband Neil. I told him I had fallen in love. I wanted to leave him. He said, "You are regressing. You are going back." I never listened. But it only made sense after twenty years. It was a crushing thing for Neil too. It was a difficult time because he was also getting ready to go back to America. That was another thing. I didn't want to go. I didn't want to leave Turkey. I don't know, it felt it would be the biggest crime to leave Turkey then. I had important work to do there. How could I leave?

'Neil had been right. I was regressing. I was going back to being more of a supportive woman rather than being a professional woman myself. At that time I didn't realize it, because it was *our* work. Ali and I were setting up a new faculty. Our ideal was to make a kind of Cal. Tech. in Turkey, we would attract the best people, get the funds. Twenty-four hours a day we were working there.'

Ali had become the Dean of the faculty. Inci received her position as Associate Professor which involved writing another thesis.

'I was a member of the faculty but still you know, I was not the same woman anymore. In Ankara at the faculty meeting I had my own voice, but slowly I was holding myself in more. I was getting mad, frustrated. I would not agree with many things Ali said at the faculty meetings, but I would feel reluctant to raise my voice because it would appear we were in conflict.'

At home Inci would tell Ali what she disagreed with. He would listen then, but he was not comfortable with her raising her own voice in public.

'He didn't like it that I would really have a different opinion from his. It frustrated me. Of course, it was partially my own self-oppression, I was putting myself into a secondary role. Twice a week we would invite guests who would come and give seminars in the faculty. I was the one who did the shopping, the cooking. We didn't have the guest house at that time so some of the people had to stay in our house, and Ali was no help. He was totally different from my first husband. I didn't even iron a shirt for Neil. But Ali didn't demand. He never said, "Do this for me, do that". It was me doing it, falling back into my mother's role. Why? I think there was this hope to be loved, the illusion of being loved. But the woman he had fallen in love with was a very strong woman. He didn't discourage me from being strong, but he didn't encourage me. So in a way I was still asking for his permission while I was accepting my role to be the secondary position. For example, I remember, when I was with Neil, it would never have occurred to me to worry about going to a conference and being away for two or three weeks. Never. But Ali made me feel so guilty if I would have to go to a conference abroad. He would do it in a very loving way. "Oh, how can you leave me alone?" I would feel so guilty. I would prepare meals for him for while I would be gone. I'm really horrified when I look at how slowly I slipped back into this role without realizing it.'

There was no thought of children in the marriage. This seemed very clear to Inci. Ali had two from his first marriage. Because he didn't show any great interest, Inci didn't consider having a child for herself.

'If he had wanted, perhaps I would have. No, no. I wouldn't. It was not for me. It is like earrings. I like looking at earrings, but not for myself.

'When we were in northern Turkey we were so busy. As time went on if the housework was too much I could get help. So I was not feeling it was that much of a problem. What was most important during this period was that we were working together. We were building up this faculty. I was a workaholic. He's a workaholic as well. We were a team. We were very proud of what we were doing'.

Eva

'I had my second child when I was 27 and third when I was 29. When I was thirty I went back to my career. Because I was involved in performance, the schedule was very demanding. I had most of my rehearsals in the evening. During this period I was devoted to my family, and I was trying to connect with my own professional work. The marriage continued to be shaky. We had a situation where a young woman I had known quite well moved into our house to take care of the children so I could be more involved with my work. But this turned into an affair. I was struggling with what to do. Of course, I had been warned about this problem. I wasn't ready to give up. I loved my family.'

Nigel was very happy in his career in the National Health Service. The director of the Mayflower Centre was a man who had captained the British cricket team and then been ordained. He became a mentor to Nigel, who became more and more interested in ministry work. Nigel had three strands to his life – his work in the hospital, his work with troubled teenagers, and his work in the lay ministry. They were parallel. He liked them very much. His mentor suggested that he bring together the last two and get ordained. A conference was being held in England about pre-ordination training, titled 'You and the Ministry', with no strings attached. He was interested and spoke to the person arranging it, emphasizing that he was merely curious: 'I've come to see what makes other people go into the ministry – not to become a member'. The answer was, 'Fine, come to whatever you like'.

'By the end of the conference I knew it was my next step. This was June. By October, when I was 33 years old, I began the two-year training at London College of Divinity. During this time I met Anne at a church function. From the moment I met her I knew she was the one I had been waiting for all these years.'

Daniela felt her marriage with Dieter was not working. They were still living together, but she had an inner feeling of disappointment. His reaction to the pregnancy and the baby was terrible. He blamed her and she had a very difficult time during pregnancy. After the birth of Kirsten, though, Dieter became very fond of the baby.

'Physical appearance was very important for Dieter. I kept trying to think of how to please him, but nothing worked. Nothing I did satisfied him.'

Dieter was away from home a great deal. When Daniela found a telephone number in his jacket, this confirmed her suspicions that he was having secret relationships.

'Dieter was not interested in building a home, having nice furniture, in planning our life together. I planned for a pretty long time to leave. Maybe that's why I like furniture and making my house comfortable today, more important than having nice clothing.'

She began looking for an apartment, which was very difficult at that time, and eventually found one. When Daniela told Dieter she was leaving, he didn't believe she would do it. His response was that two apartments were too expensive to maintain. At first he had hopes the relationship could be saved, but it didn't work out, and then he left.

After the separation some of their friends faded out of the picture while others stayed close and supportive, and still are to this day. Friends are very important to Daniela. She didn't have much of a family, and her parents did not offer to help. So at the age of 30 Daniela found herself alone with Kirsten. After some years she began to look for a part-time job. This came at the right moment, when Kirsten was ready for kindergarten. Mr Rheinhardt told her of an opening as secretary at the newly formed Waldorf school which he had helped to start, and she was very happy with this new job. Her life now had a strong focus – the Waldorf school and Kirsten. In many ways she threw herself into her work as a way of getting away from her own problems.

'Those were good times. I had a strong feeling of being needed. I had a close relationship with Mr and Mrs Rheinhardt, and I so enjoyed watching them with their three children. He always seemed to know what to do. This was very inspiring for me since I had the feeling I had failed at my marriage and I just wanted to do one thing well, being a mother. I felt guilty that I had not been able to maintain the marriage. I kept thinking maybe I should have suffered and kept the marriage going. It was my initiative to end it.'

She often thought about her mother's decision to stay with her alcoholic husband and to suffer terrible abuse. 'But during these years I had a good feeling. I felt free. Dieter kept coming over. We found a good way to handle all the legalities ourselves, and we didn't need a lawyer. Whenever Kirsten said she wanted to see her father, that was so.'

Then she met Ernst through a friend, by chance on the day he was divorced from his first wife. Daniela found his qualities of kindness, sensitivity, and trust refreshing. He had two children who were with him at weekends.

'He and I became close partners. He often came over and stayed. After one year I moved to his place in the country. I was 32 and I had nice dreams of living together with him to build a family.' But this dream burst again. He became jealous of Kirsten and Dieter. He wouldn't allow Dieter into the house. Daniela refused to go along with this because she thought it was bad for Kirsten.

Difficulties began between them. 'He was very hurt that I wouldn't do what he wanted. He began to say things that weren't true, and he said terrible things to me. When I went to a concert and came back after midnight, he locked the door and wouldn't open it. He had decided I should have a curfew. It was like living in the last century. Life began to take on a bizarre feeling – as if I were living in two worlds. Sometimes life was just wonderful. We had a marvelous intimacy. He gave me the feeling of being a woman. When we were alone together there was often very much feeling, softness, and tenderness.'

But he also had a very brutal side. Once he burned a mouse alive, and after that she stopped wanting to be together with him. When she was alone the dog was allowed in, but when he was there he would kick it if it tried to come in. He was also very stern with his children. If Daniela cooked their favorite foods, he became very angry and wouldn't allow it.

Things got worse. 'I couldn't stand it and moved again at 34. So once again I couldn't stand it. I never stand it. What's wrong with me? Why am I always looking for wrong people? I'm old fashioned. I don't go after men. I put my energy into handling daily life. I felt Kirsten's life had to be normal – that was my priority. Supporting her was the most important thing. I would do my best. I went to parent meetings. I was an active mother. There was no time for lethargy. I had to keep my self-discipline, be strong at work, do the shopping, etc. I couldn't get too depressed about the situation, although sometimes I had depressive thoughts. In those times Kirsten was my life-line. I started to learn to be self-confident at 34.'

Evita
Evita's life at home continued to be very difficult with her husband's drinking problems. She tried to do everything to save him, sent him to a hospital, bought medicine for him. But this didn't help.

'I had a job as a registrar in the university and at the same time I was also attending the university as a student. The students I worked with were the same age I was, and I had very good communication with them. One day I brought some old clothing to wash at the university hostel, to be used as cleaning cloths. I gave them to the different students in charge of the floors. On May 1 in the morning there was a loud knocking at my door. I opened the door and saw ten men from the KGB. They did not ask if they could enter. They came in and asked, "To whom did you give these old clothes?" I answered, "I brought them in and left them in the corridor for whoever wanted them".' She found out later that one of the students had knotted one of the cloths, dipped it in paint, and written 'Independence to Lithuania' on the wall. 'My bringing the cloths was considered politically rebellious.'

During the remaining five years Evita worked at the university, the KGB came back to her from time to time and asked about the students. They threatened to find students who would testify against her character. She told them 'You won't find enemies among the students. Look for enemies in the government where they steal, even dress up as butchers so they can steal meat from slaughterhouses.'

Around the age of 30 (1964) she experienced a powerful example of moral independence. In those days the KGB had killed a professor of Lithuanian language at the university. He was a Baltic language specialist and had been invited to go to America to a special congress. He was forbidden to go, and after protesting about this, he disappeared. For three months no one knew where he was. Then he was found in the river, dead. They had tried to make him refuse to go to the congress in America, but he wanted people to know he was being prevented from going. Again the KGB came to Evita and asked, 'What are the students saying about this?' She answered, 'Everyone, not just students, even people in the bread-queues and trolley-buses all say it's the work of the KGB.'

What kept Evita going during these difficult times? She looks back to people who helped her. She became leader of the trade union at her office. In her group there were 70 people, 60 of whom she was very close to. She opposed the Party leaders and organization. They had problems with her – she refused to do whatever they wanted. In her position of leadership she was able to have some Party people removed, even though she was taking a risk opposing their power. She had developed self-confidence and courage to face difficult circumstances.

In his early thirties **Pavel** was experiencing a happy time with his young family and his profession. 'I felt: My life is ahead of me. Everything depends on me. I can live life the way I choose.'

Then came the shock. His wife, Lena, asked him for a divorce. This was the beginning of a very difficult time for him. He had had a family, and was now alone. His parents were alive, but he had not lived with them since he was a boy. He couldn't do anything to change the situation.

He wanted to take a post-graduate course and receive more education. He was admitted to the university in Moscow. But it was a difficult time. He was 32, going through a divorce, and working very hard on his course. For three to four years he studied full-time, traveling back and forth to Riga, keeping in contact with his child.

Jerry was deeply involved in his translations of Carl Jung. He was working on the premise that neurosis during the first half of life goes underground and becomes invisible in the second half. He wanted to be sure he had penetrated his adolescent neurosis and transformed it. Based on James Hillman's work, Jerry believed he could reconcile his youth complexes and his adult ones. 'If you are conscious enough, the conflict takes a quite different course than if you just dream through it unconsciously and self-consciously. It is a moral task to become conscious of your conflicts.'

When he was thirty-three he refocused his interest in Anthroposophy. 'I'm a very critical person, but I remain faithful to Rudolf Steiner.' From thirty to 42, he was very close to a man who was his teacher in anthroposophy. He could visit him almost every day. This man was a very interesting and highly developed person. He worked as a 'smeller' in the perfume industry because he had such a sensitive sense of smell. He was also active in the homeopathic movement. Jerry admired the inner strength of this man, who had been arrested in 1952, in Stalin's era, and spent three years in prison. He was tortured and almost destroyed physically, and finally freed in 1955. 'They just couldn't break him,' Jerry said with admiration.

Rosalind
Everything was going beautifully in Rosalind's life. Then Jeffrey became ill.

'Even before that, I had to learn to rely on myself. It's never been possible for me to just sit back and be cared for. Something made me want to work, so I worked at my children's school as an assistant music teacher. Jeffrey was so good. He knew this work was important to me. From 22 to 33 we had a good life. We had two children and a close family life. Meanwhile I continued my musical studies. Then Jeffrey got the mumps. He never really felt well after

143

that. I noticed he was clumsy and knocked things over. I don't know whether he noticed it. He had always been a closed person and I never knew him well enough. I think we'll have to do it over again in our next lives. He began to have problems with his eyes again. The doctor gave him cortisone, and this affected his balance. Jeffrey became concerned about his health. His parents paid for him to see an expensive doctor and he was having tests in the hospital. One day his parents and I visited him in the hospital; and when we were returning home in a taxi, his mother started to weep. I tried to console her by saying he would get well again. She said, "You don't understand". At that point her husband sternly said, "That's enough!"

'I don't know if they were trying to protect me. Jeffrey consulted many other doctors. He either didn't know what was wrong or he knew and didn't say. Before he went to visit his parents in Florida, I had a strange experience. One evening we were sitting in bed reading. I was reading an article in the *New Yorker* about a man who became ill. He became more and more paralyzed. I read this story sitting there next to Jeffrey. My heart sank. He said, "How's that story?" "Oh, not much good." I threw out the magazine the next day. I began to worry.

'I spoke with a friend about my feelings. He advised me to go speak to the doctor myself. I did. He told me Jeffrey had Multiple Sclerosis. He said, "Don't tell him. I told him the symptoms, but I haven't used the name of the disease. The name could frighten him." Then I carried this lonely secret around with me. His parents didn't know that I knew. My sisters and brother were out of town. I was 32. I lived with the secret for about a year, then we let each other know that we knew. No one knew what MS was in those days. Some doctors thought he had a tumor and would die within six months.

'He was in Florida with his parents. I was in Chicago with the secret. I had to take care of the children. "Live in the present" I would say now. Jeffrey always lived in the future. He would say, "When I feel better we'll go to Europe. When I feel better I'll fix the house." It was a life of postponement.

'The struggles began. For a while he used a cane, then a wheelchair. His father employed him to do advertising for his clothing business. A salary came in for a while. Then the business closed. We lived on Social Security and Disability Allowance, and loans. We had a good relationship during those years, we cared very much for each other. We couldn't express our love in the usual ways. Jeffrey was very possessive of me. On the one hand he wanted me there with him all the time. On the other he said, "Of course you must go to school. Don't worry, I'm fine."'

At 28 **Patrick** and Martha moved to the Midwest. There he worked for two years teaching and directing. His career made a shift when the university asked him to work part-time and then full-time on a commercial television station at the university. He was not happy with some of his colleagues in the drama department and was eager to accept this new position. He worked as program director of the television station for the next seven years. He and Martha began their family: four children arrived during this seven year period.

Jack was in the military, enjoying traveling, meeting people. He spent time in southern California before being sent to combat duty in Vietnam for thirteen months in 1965/66. At times he thought to himself, 'I'm so near retirement, will I get through the war?' This was a totally different war from the Korean War. There was more psychological stress. The techniques were different.

'Rather than aggression out front, in Vietnam sometimes we would go for days not seeing anyone and then the troops would suddenly be wounded. The guerrilla tactics meant we never knew what would happen next, and this was very stressful. It was also difficult to experience young seventeen and eighteen year-olds fighting and getting blown to bits. Having a son approaching this age made me think a lot about it.'

Jack reflected on the new perspective of the world he gained during his years in the military. 'I saw a lot during these times. At first the Service was not fully integrated, and Blacks were in separate units. But after the Korean war the soldiers were all together on the base. There was prejudice against all minorities, but the Blacks had a specially difficult time. Black military men didn't get the promotions and they were placed in mediocre outfits. After being in Korea I was sent to North Carolina. I can still remember that at our base dances, black soldiers could only dance with black girls. When we left the base we had to sit at the back of the bus station or in special parts of restaurants. We accepted this, but it was difficult. In 1942 the first Black had been accepted into the marine corps. All the Blacks then were in basic training – all of the officers were white. During Vietnam there was an overwhelming number of Blacks in the military. By 1964 the service was fully integrated, but there were still not a lot of black officers even though many were qualified by that time.'

At the age of 31 he was sent back to North Carolina for three years as an instructor in a military leadership school there. This stimulated his interest in teaching. Then at 34 he was sent back to Vietnam for his last tour of thirteen months.

As we follow our friends into their 28-35 period, the single most apparent theme has to do with developing confidence, facing themselves and developing courage. There is a strong sense of the purpose of work, of the importance of outer activity; in several cases a couple has a working partnership with one another. It is a time when people have to face the consequence of decisions they made in their twenties.

Natasha learns that love based on inner qualities is richer than that based on outer physical attraction. She develops strength and confidence in the life of music she and Anton share and devote themselves to.

Claudia struggles in her role as single mother and doctor until she falls in love with another doctor, many years older than herself and damaged by war experiences. Despite warnings from friends, she marries Fritz. These years are filled with the joy of family and the hard work of building up the clinic; and with what she experiences as a duty to make up to Fritz what he had lost. Satisfaction comes as she experiences success in their joint efforts to make the clinic function well. Claudia's confidence grows. She is proving to herself that she can manage all the challenges, although she is exhausted by the tremendous demands she has to meet.

Inci is carried away on a wave of excitement at the changes taking place in Turkey. She falls madly in love, divorces Neil and marries Ali. They become partners in 'our work' as they build up a new university department together. She has become strong and self-confident. She realizes she is gradually losing this self-confidence, though, and becoming subservient to Ali.

Eva is devoted to her children and her career. She tries to manage both on the foundation of a shaky marriage. She realizes she has to make it on her own as she cannot count on Peter.

Nigel has found his direction – his 'real' work in the ministry – with the guidance of a strong mentor. He meets Ann and realizes very quickly she is the one he has been waiting for. He is strongly focused now on the direction his life is taking: the ministry and family life.

Daniela struggles as a single mother, but through the guidance of a patient and kind mentor, she finds meaningful work. She meets another man and dreams that this time she will have a loving relationship and family life, but again it turns ugly. She is left with the question, 'What is wrong with me?' She decides to commit all her energies to being a good mother. Through this she develops self-confidence.

Evita struggles with an alcoholic husband, raising a child, and working. She takes on more and more responsibility in her work and in the trade union, causing her to come face to face with the KGB. She develops inner strength and courage.

Pavel's dreams of happiness with his family are shattered when Lena asks for a divorce. He feels completely alone, struggling to overcome the shock of the loss. He tries to fill his life with more education. He is very busy at his studies, travels back and forth from Moscow to Riga to see his daughter. He is having a hard time, but he is busy. He is trying to gain strength to manage his life.

Jerry is deeply immersed in psychology and working on himself. He is conscious that parts of his personality are not integrated, and he takes this on as his task. Through a strong relationship with his mentor, he refocuses on anthroposophy. His interest is in strengthening himself inwardly and becoming a healing, integrated personality.

Rosalind is trying to come to terms with Jeffrey's illness. Throughout this difficult time they share a deep love and satisfaction with their family life. Rosalind's role has changed. In the beginning of the relationship Jeffrey took care of her; now she has to rely on herself and take care of him. She is gaining strength and courage.

Patrick is married, makes decisions about his career, and becomes devoted to his growing family.

Jack is in the military. He is seeing the world and meeting many situations. In Korea and in Vietnam he sees much suffering. At home he sees the contradictions in American society due to racism.

Through the inner changes our friends experience during these years, they sort out the important from the unimportant. Many of their earlier dreams and expectations have fallen by the wayside. Working together on something of meaning, making a contribution to family and society, finding inner strength and courage – these are the priorities during this time.

3
Plumbing the Depths: 35-42

We move through our lives, eyes fixed on our goals. We've got life figured out, but something's not quite right. How can we explain a sinking, lonely, empty, and uncertain feeling that sweeps over us from time to time? New and exciting experiences push these unpleasant feelings into the background for a while, but they come back when we least expect them. We can try to pretend everything is the same as it always has been, but somehow it isn't. These feelings of unease may come very gradually so that people learn to cope with them bit by bit (or at least think they do). Or a traumatic experience throws everything out of balance and they have to face the sudden shock of mid-life change.

In our late thirties or early forties we meet the results of our actions in the first half of life. Up until now we have in some ways still been children, but at this stage we become fully responsible for what we do. The spiritual world has completed its formative influence and withdraws. The 'I', our unique individuality, has thoroughly penetrated our soul life, and we stand solidly on the earth. We may feel the pull of gravity, experience a certain heaviness. We may feel moments of intense inner loneliness, even that we are 'dying' inwardly. We cannot approach life the way we previously have. It just doesn't work any more. From now on we sense that we are on our own and must act out of our free, independent will. No one can reassure us or solve our problems. No one can shield us any more from the consequences of our deeds. Decisions become more difficult. These are the years in which we are most cut off from inspiration, in which the enthusiasms and ideals of our twenties seem far away. It is from this lowest point that we can begin to consciously rebuild our lives. If we bring inner resources to meet our difficulties, new capacities and energies are released to carry us through the second half of life. How we move through the forties, fifties, sixties, seventies and beyond will have a great deal to do with how we deal with these mid-life changes.

The Valley of the Shadow: 35-42

The 35th year is often described as the cosmic midnight of the soul, the great crisis in life. Gail Sheehy[1] characterises it in this way:

> I have reached some sort of meridian in my life. I had better take a survey, re-examine where I have been, and re-evaluate how I am going to spend my resources from now on. Why am I doing all this? What do I really believe in? Underneath this vague feeling is the fact, as yet unacknowledged, that there is a down side to life, a back of the mountain, and that I have only so much time before the dark to find my own truth... (these thoughts) usher in a decade that can be called, in the deepest sense, the Deadline Decade. Somewhere between 35 and 45 if we let ourselves, most of us will have a full-out authenticity crisis.'

Sheehy points out in her later book, New Passages,[2] that this crisis seems to be happening in the mid-forties for many people born since 1966 ('the Endangered Generation'). It is too early to feel whether this change is a permanent one, or whether it is related to the particular characteristics of this generation. What is important to note is that increased longevity may have shifted the midpoint of life from 35 to 45, and that people therefore now have an increasing need to look at their sixties, seventies and eighties in a new light. We will speak more of this later.

The wonderfully emotional period of our twenties, and the more reflective time of the early thirties has led us into the situations we have to face now. During this next period we begin to look for meaning in what we have done. It is a time of evaluation and re-evaluation. Have I made the right decisions? What do I want to do with the rest of my life? How much time do I have? I used to feel the future was ahead of me, now I'm constantly aware of the past. Can I change? Should I change? Can I sense what I'm supposed to be doing here? When I look back over my life will I be satisfied with it?

We can now ask these questions in a conscious way, whereas before we were often too influenced by our emotions to allow our ego, our individuality, to penetrate them. All through life we get occasional glimpses of our own destiny. Sometimes we try to fight these insights, at other times we welcome them as affirming our own intuitions. When we grasp hold of them, we can more clearly see the overall pattern of our life. This kind of clearer awareness is described in Steiner's terms as the birth of the consciousness soul.

During this period we experience a loss of youth as physical changes make themselves felt. Now when we go out to run in the park with our children we can't keep up with them any longer. They are faster than we are. We notice that bruises don't heal as quickly as they used to, and our aching muscles are another clear sign that something is changing. The physical body feels as though it has become heavier and earth-bound. Muscle is becoming flab, the skin around our neck is loosening. Not since adolescence have we been so obsessive about checking in the mirror. Men notice the thinning of their hair, maybe a few grey hairs as well. Women notice hair appearing on the chin. It is harder to keep our weight down, our eyes get weaker and the optician reassures us that it is quite common for the eye muscles to weaken around forty. Many of the bodily functions begin to degenerate or lose their vitality. We have more trouble with lower back pain, and we find our friends are complaining about this too. As one man said, 'Seems like there's termites in the wood'. It's an odd feeling when we look in the mirror and begin to see a resemblance to one of our parents. We are surprised because we thought 'it' wouldn't happen to us. When our parents were forty they looked so old. But here we are ourselves. Remember when we thought everyone over thirty was over the hill!

But physical changes are only symptoms of the deeper changes going on within. Psychological changes are taking place as well. By the mid-thirties many of us feel 'mature' and think that we understand life, that we have established ourselves. We've made it! But with the changes that now begin to take place, we start to feel uncertain – as though the rules are changing and we don't know how to behave.

This period can be a time of loss, doubt, loneliness and self-examination: a time, above all for questioning everything. Now when we most need it our sense of humour may be least available to us.

The 35 year-old woman may well be facing inner doubt. Where she felt confidence before, she lacks it now. Where did it go? If she is out in the working world, esteemed by colleagues and excited about her work, it may be different. Especially if she waited to start her career until after she had her children, or her studies went on for a long time, or she lived with her parents and only began her career in her thirties, the crisis may not occur until her mid forties. But it will come. If she has been at home with children all through her twenties and into her thirties, she is likely to have a crisis at sometime during this phase. She may feel that she is only killing time because her life has become dull. She doesn't know what she wants anymore. She isn't sure she likes her children or her husband – usually because she isn't sure she likes herself. At the same time she wants to push herself into the world: 'Let me in. I want to be smart and important and have value placed on my time and talents too. Is it possible to pick up where I stopped learning? Do men still find me appealing? I wish someone would take me seriously. I wish someone would help me stop being afraid.'

And the 35 year-old man? Some men get into their stride during this time, while others begin to feel less and less sure. Much depends on how they evaluate their work-situation. A man who is sure of his position at work begins this period feeling strong. His plans are going along fine and life seems terrific. This lasts for some years, usually till around forty. For a man less confident in his position at work, the growing current of uncertainty comes earlier, in the second half of the thirties: What if his plans don't work out? What if he doesn't get the promotion he's counting on. Maybe he hasn't planned things right? Time is running out. He loses faith in his ideals, feeling he has to make compromises to get promotion. He can't even count on himself sexually anymore. Inwardly he feels tender, isolated, dependent; outwardly he feels vain and greedy, jealous and competitive. He doesn't always want to be expected to be the strong one. He feels panic as strongly as she feels fear. Is it any wonder that marriages can go through chaos at this time?

Doubt about everything takes over. It feels as if our will is paralyzed. One friend said it was like driving a car while stuck in neutral: we can't get into gear whatever we do. We sputter and stall and it takes time before we feel life is starting to run smoothly again. There is a lack of ease, an absence of inner light. This stage is beautifully depicted in the painting 'Middle Age' by the 19th century American artist Thomas Cole, which hangs in the National Gallery in Washington. Cole has four paintings, 'Childhood', 'Youth', 'Middle Age', and 'Old Age'. All four paintings center on a figure in a boat on a river. In 'Childhood' a young child surveys the world in all its brightness and glory. A protective angel hovers over him. In 'Youth' the mood is one of expectation and adventure: the youth looks out into the world, pointing to castles in the air. The protecting angel has stepped back to allow the young person to find his own way. In 'Middle Age' the boat's rudder has broken off and the river reveals dangerous rapids ahead. The protective angel is nowhere to be seen. The man is crouched in the boat praying as the boat heads for disaster. In 'Old Age' the boat drifts as the old man floats calmly hither and thither. The image of 'Middle Age' therefore captures the anxiety, fear, and loneliness of this period, whether it comes in the thirties or forties.

In this phase we experience the soul's helplessness. This may express itself, especially in men, in panic and impulsive decisions. Levinson calls this period the 'Pivotal' decade (roughly forty to fifty or forty-five to fifty-five), the dangerous years of passage. We need to plumb its depths or it returns to plague us until it is faced and resolved. If we grow inwardly at this time, we feel a new lease of life. We realize a new sense of power, the lost faculties return with a new quality. We feel our memory growing stronger, our self-control greater. What a relief!

The double-edged sword of this phase consists of danger and opportunity. All of us have the chance to rework the narrow identity we defined for ourselves in the first half of life. To come through the trials of this period we must re-examine our purpose and re-evaluate how to spend our strength and talents. No matter what we have been doing, there will be parts of ourselves that have been suppressed and now need to find expression. We will need to acknowledge negative feelings along with positive ones. We no longer have to ask permission from others – what we do depends on our own judgement, and women, particularly, can find this difficult.

A woman went to a very nice clothing store, one she didn't usually go to, to get an outfit for a trip. The clothes were expensive and sophisticated, quite out of her league. But they were having a sale. As she was looking at the different outfits she felt paralyzed.

What, she wondered, do these store clerks think of me? Do they know I usually can't buy clothes like this? She felt exposed, and feeling stupid, left without even trying on anything. Later she described this experience to a friend who said, 'Remember those clerks are hired to work there. They probably can't afford to buy their clothes there either. They're just normal people. Now go back and say to yourself "I deserve to have something nice." Tell yourself how confident you are.' Armed with this support she returned to the store. She kept telling herself she was confident, that what counted was how she felt about the way the outfit looked on her, not what she thought the salesgirl might be thinking. She put on an air of self-confidence as if she were playing a part in a drama and walked out jauntily with two outfits.

Another characteristic of this period is that we may have recurring dreams of our partners dying. We may be left with a feeling of sadness or guilt. What does this mean? Do I want him or her to die? No, but we are accepting suppressed and even unwanted aspects of ourselves, and preparing at a deep, gut level for the reintegration of an identity that is ours and ours alone. The patchwork quilt of personality we have built up to please family and culture dies away as we work towards becoming integrated people. But this process takes time.

We have to learn to stand on our own feet, experience ourselves as separate and valuable human beings. These are challenges that belong to the midpoint of life. It may help to remember that we came into life alone (even if we were one of a pair of twins – for each has her own birth experience). The spiritual world surrounded us in its loving protection and gradually released us to live on the earth, make our own mistakes, and find our own meaning. When we die, that too is our own experience. We cannot take our partners or our friends with us. We must face the moment on our own. So we might as well start to get some experience of being independent.

Relationships during the consciousness soul period

Our relationships become the arena for playing out these experiences. Whatever was left unresolved from earlier times comes back to haunt us now, and stronger. We have to let go of the fantasies we project onto one another. If we held on to this projection through the early thirties, we must relinquish it and separate ourselves. A sense of survival often pushes us ahead into the dark world we fear. We have to find an honest unity in ourselves. There is no substitute for self-examination in our relationships.

One of the characteristics of this period is dealing with our negative view of others. In the previous soul period we were beginning to see the faults of our partner, but the experience now intensifies. It is as if a caricature emerges, distorting positive qualities and pushing all the negative ones into the foreground. We get to know what is called the 'double' of our partner, which tricks us into doing or saying things we will regret, or things that we would hardly believe of ourselves. Our own 'double' leads us into vicious and self-destructive acts over and over again; even though we hate the outcome of these arguments and confrontations we often feel helpless to avoid them. We see the other person's 'double' far better than our own ugly side. The significant change comes when we learn to observe our effect on others and how our own good intentions are repeatedly misunderstood. We keep 'coming across' to others in a way we don't intend, then feel rejected. Why don't others see us as we really are? Why can't they see what we mean? When we begin to examine this more consciously we will perceive our own 'double' and stop seeing only our partner's. The moment we each start to face the negative aspects of ourselves is a turning point both in our own individual development and as a couple. If we consciously work through negative situations, clearly repicturing in our minds what happened, what we meant to say, what we actually said, we can begin to see where we 'lost ourselves'. Working slowly and carefully in this way, we can start seeking forgiveness for our own deeds. Instead of blaming the other, we can see how our own actions triggered the other person's reaction. Admitting our responsibility for causing pain to the other person can release amazing capacities of trust and caring. Such healing powers can bring great blessing to our lives at this time.

Instead of giving other people credit for recognizing their own faults, we often feel we have to make sure they know what they've done wrong. I found that one of the most helpful ways of improving relationships is to allow people the opportunity to evaluate themselves before others do. What a surprise to find out they are already working on their weakness! I had an on-off friendship with one of my colleagues because I found her so sharp. One day she remarked, 'Sometimes when I open my mouth and speak, I wish I could stuff my fist in it because I know how harsh I'm being.' When I heard that, I felt waves of compassion rise up instead of anger. From that moment on we had a new bond, and we could laugh when such situations occurred because I knew she was working on it. I was able to tell her of similar struggles I was having. Part of the work of this phase is acknowledging our struggles.

When a man begins to feel middle-age creeping up on him, his strongest urge is to 'escape' it, for he has an unconscious sense that facing it will require inner change. This is even more intense in him than in the woman. Some men respond to this discomfort by throwing themselves fully into work or constant activity. They feel restless, stale, burdened and unappreciated. Although the man loves his wife he may try to escape by having an affair:

> It is a way for a man to avoid the knowledge that he has passed the watershed of his life. The desperation he feels when he realizes this, and that he has about reached his limit in his chosen field, can deepen into a depression. To combat the depression he seeks conquest – sexual conquest of a young woman. And for a while this makes him feel young and vital again...Just as getting married marks a young man's emancipation from his mother...a love affair is another symbolic breaking loose from the apron strings – this time from his wife. The little boy in the man, however, expects his wife, like his mother, to keep on loving him and caring for him and turning a blind eye on his escapades. [3]

At some point, though, he must face up to the fact that he is middle-aged. If he fails to accept ageing as a part of life, he will continue to run away until he finally 'grows up'. He may issue calls for help but his wife and children don't hear them. They are busy with their own lives. The sad thing is that by the time a man faces his situation and tries to set things right, he has often lost his marriage. This pattern is so strong it has been called the 'twenty-years fracture' – 'when marriages that had seemed solid enough suddenly collapse and end in divorce.' [4] Since many marriages today are taking place in the couples' thirties, the 'twenty-years fracture' may occur in their fifties.

A woman at this point may feel 'I loved being a mother, a housewife. But I never really felt cherished. Why doesn't someone appreciate me?' She sees the problem as an external rather than an internal one. She, too, may turn to having an affair as a way to get the attention she wants and to show herself that she is still attractive. This will not solve her problem any more than it does for the man; it only causes problems for the relationship.

The professional woman who has remained single (or has divorced) during this time and has established herself in the world might say 'It took me a long time and a lot of psychic sweat to get where I am emotionally and professionally. I'm not about to let someone erode that. Life is too short so I'll stay alone for a while. There are worse things than being alone.'

Whatever our particular situation, as we work through lone- liness and inner doubt we can come to new perspectives. We begin to realize that we are independent egos who can and must decide for ourselves how to relate to the challenges of our own life, rather than doing what family or friends would do in the same situation. This brings us a tremendous burst of freedom and excitement. Percep- tion and sense of timing are heightened. Life becomes a great adventure because it is not centered only on needs and demands of the self but on something both deeper and higher. The question we now face is whether to use this new source of power for the self alone or for the world also.

A very helpful exercise is to begin to contemplate the mystery of our own destiny. We can picture the people who have entered and influenced our life in each period: friends, family members, teachers, neighbors, partners, and colleagues. Sometimes a person stepped into our life for a brief moment and said or did something that caused us to wake up, to see something differently, to feel pain, sympathy or love. Looking back we can see that this person brought us a gift. As we work carefully and slowly through this exercise we can begin to gain a picture of the invisible web of human relation- ships weaving through our lives. We begin to sense our own destiny.

This can help us cultivate the ability to recognize opportunities for helping others, for sensing the right moment for action. Then it is often possible for us to accept a relationship with friends and/or a marriage partner even when it is uncomfortable. We become more understanding of family members, more loyal to our friends, and more loving to our partner. Our whole perspective on the relationship changes and we know we are there to stay. We have to work out certain things, but there is a karmic tie which we accept and affirm. Often new patience develops; the little details become important, the thoughtful little moments that do not come out of duty but free will. At the same time strong feelings of tenderness are aroused and a new interest awakens in moral and ethical aspects of life.

Hephzibah Menuhin Hauser describes

> the tremendous and unequal division between the discipline imposed from the outside and the purely intuitive self-willing that came from choice. I learned that real responsibility has to do with what you choose to do. You can do the most difficult things all your life and they are worthwhile, if for no other reason than that you have chosen them freely. You have come to the wrong conclusion if you think that if you get rid of what is bad for you and what you hate, then you will be okay. Yes, we have to get rid of what is bad, but at the same time we have to know what we are going to use our freedom for.[5]

A couple is in for serious trouble when either separately or together they cannot find new spiritual content in their lives. If they can experience new purpose in their relationship and become conscious of their struggle they may work their way through to new aims. There is no escape from the reality of the middle-aged years even though alcohol, drugs, sexual encounters, over-eating or long hours spent in front of TV or computers may be used to distract us and dull the pain. No one can regain the youthful years, but a new attitude can help. If this new attitude has to do with bringing spiritual understanding to bear on human relationships there is much significant work ahead. Once we glimpse our partner as a spiritual individuality, the whole dynamic can change.

There are so many positive experiences that emerge from this difficult period. Perhaps the most important is clarity and honesty. We can begin to see the difference between imposing our wishes on a person, on a situation, forcing something to come out the way we want it and learning to listen to what is *really* wanted. Life is no longer a struggle for power. Egoism begins to give way to understanding. Instead of putting ourselves in the center of our experiences we will be able to perceive others and their needs.

We can also experience this as the most lonely period of our life. We no longer rely on other people to satisfy us. What we get from others in a relationship, though, will be a gift from them which can be gladly accepted. This experience of standing alone gives us independence, but does not necessarily satisfy us. What we do now comes out of the depths of our own soul, rather than from any other source. It can be very painful to realize that we have freedom but still not happiness. Our ego has emancipated itself from the emotional life (21-28) and from the intellectual life (28-35) and is now acting out of its own freedom and determining our development. 'Freedom means choosing your burden. You can exchange one burden for another, but you must carry one. If you don't carry a burden, you don't know who you are.'

Standing in the midst of this painful consciousness soul period, it is difficult to understand that joy will eventually emerge from it. Yet we pass through a transformation at this time which can release tremendous energy. Of course, it doesn't happen overnight. We constantly have to start again, but at least there is meaning in what we are going through. Whether we realize it or not, the capacity for such change has developed within the human soul by the end of this phase.

From the strengthening 'I' at the midst of the turbulent storm of this period, we can glimpse what lies ahead, what our goals in life are, and how they relate to the bigger questions in life – questions of values and meaning. A sense can arise of being part of a greater reality which we choose to serve.

A struggle characteristic of this time is that our thinking, feelings and will separate from each other and head in different directions. We may feel we can't get all three to work together or that we are coming apart. The heart and mind may work together while the will is paralyzed; or the heart and will join forces but are undirected by thought; or the mind and will act but lack warmth of feeling. Bringing all three soul forces into harmony is a major task from this time on.

Related to these three soul-forces are three necessary transformations:

In our willing we are learning to 'walk' in a new way – in other words becoming more aware of what we do, of how to direct our actions so that they pass through our hearts and minds in the service of a higher goal.

In our feelings we nurture a quality of devotion so that our hearts become activated to serve what is highest. This devotion often extends beyond our immediate family to the community and to nature. We are more awake, more open to the world. A new interest in nature often arises at this time because we are no longer just lowering our horns and charging at life, but beginning to look around and realize what surrounds us.

In our thinking we have to work to overcome the prejudices which have slotted other people into convenient categories; we have to stop giving simple reflex answers, or adhering to common opinions and 'party lines'. We need to think about how we come to our conclusions and work to be more objective. Trying to do this can be very unsettling at first.

During this period, as I mentioned, we begin to realize that our physical body no longer has the agility and strength it had before. So there is a temptation to concentrate only on the physical body, to try to retrieve some of the old vitality, forgetting that what is really needed is to activate the soul and spirit. Of course, we need to pay attention to our health, diet, and exercise; but ignoring our inner development is like building a strong shell around an empty space. Some of us get drawn in this direction and try to put off the moment of coming to terms with what life asks of us. Others are tempted to concentrate on material things. This is fine for a while but doesn't help us face the real inner questions that plague us. Others are tempted to avoid solitude – by keeping the television on, losing themselves on the Internet, drinking too much alcohol, or running around keeping busy. But these are only temporary solutions. To make any kind of progress, we will at some point have to face the loneliness and doubt in ourselves; then, from this point of deepest helplessness we can ask for spiritual help. When we gain the humility to realize we want to work together with spiritual forces or beings greater than ourselves – however we choose to express this – then we can recognize our capacity for contributing to the world. This acceptance is not resignation, but a deeper understanding of the place of human life within the larger context of world evolution. The earthly world cannot exist without the spiritual world, and we are incomplete without the recognition of the divine in life.

Treichler in his book *Soulways* sums up this 35-42 period beautifully:

> The sentient soul may be compared to a plant in its leafy stage. A plant opens up to the world through its leaves; in the same way soul life opens up to the world through the sentient soul, and like a plant is built up in the process. The intellectual or mind soul as it grows more inward corresponds to the development of flower bud and calyx. The awareness (or consciousness) soul, which opens itself up to the spirit and out of which the spirit is acting in the world, may be compared to a bright flower that reflects the light of the sun. In the second half of life, the flowering of the awareness soul will become a fruiting process and human beings will be able to give back to the world part of what they have received in the first half of life. [6]

This description may help us see that part of our challenge in the second half of life is to transform the feeling life (sentient soul) and thinking life (intellectual soul) so that they serve the new capacities developed during this 35-42 period. Up to 35 we are students of life, absorbing, learning our lessons from what happens around us. But after the midpoint of life we must develop an inner sun from which we can shine out on life.

Natasha was feeling in the prime of her life during this period. Working together professionally, receiving much attention and admiration for her work, she was known and respected in the artistic community in Riga. Every day was exciting. She was dedicated to music. She enjoyed experiencing her daughter, Irina, growing up. It was a comfort to have her mother with her. Life felt even and balanced. Until...

Claudia was now involved with the clinic, with the children, and with trying to support Fritz who had become more and more moody. These were very good, busy years.

'I knew I really did marvelous things and I really looked very nice and I knew it and felt it. It was a time I was very sure of myself. But I had decided to stay with Fritz. I felt it as my obligation for all that he had missed and the circumstances he had gone through.

'However, Fritz was so jealous during this time. Instead of being very glad to have a young and successful wife, it was the opposite. It was so strange. There was no reason for it at that time. But in everything he suspected something. Fritz kept me from seeing my closest family and friends. He even stayed away from his only relative, his brother. Today, I still say I had a husband who wanted me to tell him when I went to the toilet. And for someone like me this was unbearable.' In spite of all this, she was sure she had made the right decision to stay with Fritz. Claudia committed herself to her profession, her husband and children.

Inci and Ali were in southern Turkey building up their new university when in 1980, four years after they had arrived there, the military regime came to power.

'I was placed under arrest for eight months before I was to appear at a trial. During that time Ali was the most supportive man. For the first forty-five days I wasn't allowed to see anybody. I was taken into police custody. Of course, it was illegal. The charge was that I was connected with the woman's organization (which they now closed down). But of course that had been four years ago. I wasn't even working with it anymore. But in Turkey, since we were a legal organization, you had to give your name, address, etc. Everything was in their files. They arrested the whole women's organization, especially me, because I had been the chairwoman of the Ankara branch. What they did was just open the books and collect everybody. There was nothing they could charge us with. But what they tried to connect us with was the illegal Turkish Communist party. So they were trying to find some conspiracy between us and the Turkish Communists, but in our woman's group there were all sorts of women from religious groups and peace movements of all kinds. At that time Ali was really supportive, very very supportive.

'Of course, at first I was horrified, in disbelief. Why were they going to put me in prison? What did I do to deserve this? All the bandits, the terrorists were outside and what am I doing here? On the other hand, of course we understood what the military regime was for. Their aim was not to stop the terrorism in Turkey but to stop people who were doing things democratically. They were more afraid of the women's organization because we were doing real work. So it was a difficult time.'

Since Inci was no longer living in Ankara, she was locked up with people she did not know. The police were trying to find out whether she was still active. Their logic was that if she wasn't active in this legal organization, then she must be working underground.

'When I heard their logic I really got frightened. The press was controlled so people didn't know what was going on. At the university everybody was so afraid...they were so afraid and horrified. There was lots of pressure on the government coming from the European countries and from Amnesty International. I was chosen as the prisoner of conscience that year. I was a member of the Council of Europe Physicists group. They were going to have a meeting in Turkey, but they cancelled it. As long as I was in prison they said, "We are not going to have a meeting there." With all the pressure on it, the military regime could not last as long as it had in Chile. In Chile it lasted ten years, but in Turkey four years.

'We were in a large room like in Dachau. There were these straight benches. Usually the crime-rate for women was very low in a small town like that. There was room for 32 women and we were 120 women, and then the summer of that year they put another 100 women – 100 teachers – into prison as well because they had boycotted a day's work. They were all put into prison. It was unbearable. The toilets could not function. How did I survive hygienically? Four children were born in prison, under those unhygienic conditions, they survived. I mean it's amazing. This was the first time I realized the strength of survival.'

Keeping busy helped Inci bear the experience. 'During the police custody which was 45 days we could not do anything. We were just helping each other to heal our wounds. Lots of women came from torture. Their legs were all swollen. We had to massage them with ointments, which the interrogators would 'kindly' provide. So that was 45 days of just survival. Then they moved us to civilian prison. Normally because of the military regime they would put us into military prison. They put the men into military prison, but they didn't have a place for the women so they put us into civilian prison together with all sorts of criminals and there it felt like a paradise in comparison. We could go to toilet any time we wanted, and food was given three times a day, although there were insects in it. They would provide bread. That was the only edible thing. However, we could talk to each other and move around. The funny thing was the guards (of course it wasn't a political prison) would come and tell us their problems, how they were beaten by their husbands, their economic problems. We would take care of them too. It wasn't easy.

'There were lots of gypsies as well, rural women who didn't know how to read and write, and they wanted to write letters. They realized I was writing letters. Especially this one gypsy woman. One day she came to me and said, "OK, write me a letter" and disappeared. When she returned I said, "What should I write?" She said, "You don't need me to tell you how to write a letter. You are the professor." So I got the whole family story and her relationship with her husband, what he was doing, and how many children she had. So I wrote a letter for her. And she was surprised. "How did you know I was going to tell him that?" Every day I was writing three or four letters for different people.' Inci also taught English to a group of teachers.

Her husband had secured a lawyer for her, but the first 'trial' didn't take place until eight months later.

'The trial was so ridiculous. They made the roll call, they read the accusation in half an hour, and 25 of us were released. I was quite sure that once there was a trial I would be released. I mean they couldn't charge me with anything. What could they do? And they knew as well. What they were trying to do was postpone the trials. For example, there was another group, a radical left group, they were kept two years without a trial. That's the only way they could keep people. I didn't become a bitter person as a result of this. But what I remember is that I became much more sensitive. It created self-pity of course. After I came out of prison, during the first year I didn't feel anything. I wasn't allowed to feel anything. In Turkey people would say, "Oh, you are free now. You are now back to normal life". But I was not allowed to work because it was still the military regime. I was sitting at home translating a book, a book by Asimov. I would sit for hours. It became my life-purpose to translate that book in three volumes. So I was quite numb. I was envious of the people who were going to work. I was left alone at home and I had lots of fears. There was still a part of me I hadn't gotten in touch with. I was afraid. When people invited me to go out I was just feeling they were not inviting me because of *me*, they were inviting me because they were polite. I was also feeling that people were afraid to meet someone who had been in prison. Oh, that year when I look back was worse than being in prison. In prison I had hopes, you know, to survive and to help other people. I was busy eight hours a day, teaching people how to read and write, teaching English, writing love letters.

'I was 37 then. I still had to appear in court every month. Every month they were releasing ten people. Meanwhile we had moved back to Ankara. I heard there was a conference in my field, I had to get away from Turkey. The process was still going on so they would not let me have a passport to leave the country. I had to pretend that I was coming back so I bought a return ticket to Italy to go to a conference. Ali was going to come to Germany later for a job he had been offered. I didn't even tell my mother we were leaving, out of fear they would interrogate her and she would have to hide this knowledge.

'We left everything as if we were still living there. But later Ali came back to Turkey and cleared the house. About a year later I visited my sister in England. She said, "How was it for you?" That question, "How was it for you in prison?" made me cry for three days. Because most people said, "You are happy now. You are out of the prison. Don't look back. Just go ahead with your life." She asked me "How was it?" I didn't realize how much pain was caused by this prison experience. Ali was very supportive during the prison time but he never understood that I was carrying this pain afterwards. "This is behind you. You are abroad. Everything is ok." I don't know as I look at it now, I don't know whether that pain was only the prison experience or I was feeling something else. Maybe this is the first time I'm being honest with myself as well.

'Both the men in my life turned out to be Cassanovas, womanizers. Neil was a Cassanova too, but somehow that didn't touch me. I was having quite an independent life. Just after I came out of prison I realized Ali was having an affair, and when I asked him about it he said, "No, you are imagining things. You have to go to a psychiatrist." You know I always blame myself for all my fears. So I thought, "This man has been so nice to me, he has done everything for me when I was in prison, no other man could be so supportive. There must be something wrong with me that I am feeling like this." So all the pain lasted four or five years. I came to Germany. I got a scholarship as well. The first two years I was feeling so lonely and I couldn't understand what was happening to me. In the middle of the night I would wake up, feeling so lonely and blaming myself for it. I mean, I had a man who loved me, I believed, but I couldn't take away the loneliness. I was 41.'

Eva

'I had been struggling with the question of my career and the children. The marriage was not going well. I had to find an anchor. In my late 30s I made a decision. I would come to Vienna and join the eurythmy group. Peter very reluctantly agreed to apply for a job there as well. Now I had a double life that really required my attention – profession and family. We lived in a very tiny apartment with the three children. The relationship continued to be very strained, but I was committed to it. I kept expecting something to happen to change the situation. But it didn't. It felt as if everything was at a standstill.

Then at the end of my thirties I had a very serious jaundice condition which put me in hospital for seven weeks. I was lifted right out of my body into visions. We had someone at the house to care for the children. I was so sick I felt life was coming to an end and I would die. I decided that if I lived through this, something new would have to happen. It would be a new phase. Coming through this death experience gave me courage to make some major steps. I had lost my place in the eurythmy school because my illness dragged on for months.

'I took one of the children and we visited friends in the US for eight weeks. They told me about different courses being given and I was invited to attend. This was the beginning of a new phase of life. From the time I was 38, I felt a total change in my life. From then on I built up my own eurythmy work, but now I no longer did it as in a dream. Everything I did was conscious. I began to give classes myself and students joined me. I found many people interested in what I had to offer.

'In my early forties I felt I was in a transition period – from the tasks which brought me to earth to something new that was coming. The friendship with my children became very strong. They were now teenagers, and I felt a very special relationship to them. They and their friends made me aware that they were a very different generation. I so much enjoyed our conversations. Peter was very busy in his career. We had some good times, but there was always a feeling that I couldn't trust him. He continued to have other relationships. People would tell me about them, and it was very embarrassing. But I had known the situation when I married him.'

Nigel
When Nigel was 35 he married Anne. She had given up mid-wifery to become involved in the ministry. Together they went to work in the heart of London. During the day it was a very busy, congested area, but in the evenings the streets emptied.

'We are Townies at heart. We had decided to give ourselves in our younger years to the rough and tough. In the next 3 1/2 years we had 3 children, a daughter and two sons. Our flat was above an office building, 56 stairs up. Anne had to carry the babies. Our parish had fallen on hard times.'

When Nigel and Anne got there, only 12 members remained in the congregation. It rose to 80 in their three years there. Anne began a Mum's group and breathed new life into the church.

Before marriage both of them had had an interest in South America. They had a conversation with someone connected with the South American Missionary Society who suggested they might become a key family in Chile. It was 1971.

'I was 40 years old. We decided if we didn't do this, we would never know if it was right or wrong. President Allende was just taking office in Chile. We went and spent 9 years there.'

Daniela was focused on her life with Kirsten, but she was bothered about the breakdown of her relationship with Ernst.

'How did this happen with Ernst? I went to therapy for a short time. I found reasons. I was an only child, and I didn't have a pleasant childhood. I was not able to forget it. My father, under the influence of alcohol, was abusive, my mother was a tiny, timid, depressed woman who didn't take responsibility and make decisions. She couldn't see my pain or keep it away in my childhood. I don't have any close feelings for her, yet I'm supposed to. I had to do the good things for her that my father didn't. At least I thought I had to do these things for her. Seeing a drunk brings back all the memories of my father's drunkenness. Now it's better. I can talk about it. Those years in my late thirties and early forties were very difficult years.'

When **Evita** was forty (1974) she had just graduated from the university. She was divorced, but she couldn't get another apartment, so after the divorce she continued to live in the same flat with her ex-husband. He brought another woman (a drunken vagabond)

to live there. Both were often drunk. There were 2 rooms for Evita, her mother, and her young daughter Beruta. There was one room in which her ex-husband and his lady friend lived. They all shared a kitchen and bath. Then later her ex-husband swapped this one room with someone else who was mentally ill. This was the way he punished Evita for the divorce. There were great difficulties for many years until they could swap these 3 rooms for two separate apartments.

Evita tried to support her family by working as an engineer until 6 p.m. every day, but it wasn't enough money. So she kept her job at the university as well and worked there filling in documents every evening from 6 p.m. until 9 p.m. But when the KGB saw that she did not want to cooperate with them, they took away her university job. A meeting was staged and she was publicly chastized as though she were a member of the Communist Party, which she wasn't. This was very strange. They said she could not possibly be honest if she had enough time to work in two places. It probably meant she was not doing her engineering job properly.

Losing her evening job was very difficult because now she had no extra income. She could not buy Beruta any decent clothes. The family was very poor. The KGB found another way to punish her as well. In 1976, when she was 42, she received an invitation to visit Germany. Beruta was 16, and they were both looking forward to this trip. But she was refused permission to go since there was a likelihood they would use it as an opportunity to seek asylum. (Since she was divorced, there was no longer an incentive for her to return to Lithuania.)

Pavel moved back to Riga, working during the days and writing his thesis in the evenings. He had a very good job in a scientific institute. After his thesis was accepted his salary doubled. He remarried at 37. Life was stable again. He had a family life and a good job. His next goal was to become a full Doctor of Science (by advancing to even more professional specialization with another thesis). Pavel had also written a book on his special field. A specialist from Moscow advised him to organize this book into a second thesis. He did this and made a report to the Council of Scientists, which recommended that this book be accepted for his doctorate.

Jerry was trying to find a way to study with other people and let his ideas be known at a time when this was illegal in Poland.

'The small mission in my life was to organize young people, read and discuss together.' Until the end of the 1970s he couldn't do anything active. But he began with his friends. He introduced Biodynamic agriculture, Eurythmy, and Waldorf education into Poland. He wrote purely theoretical articles and did interviews. He brought experts over twice. (There are now over 100 Biodynamic farms in Poland.) He encouraged two or three people to study eurythmy in the West. Another person took up the initiative of establishing Waldorf pedagogy. 'I had started in1977 to prepare the ground for it. The older generation said "Don't do these public things. It's too dangerous. Stop it!"'

Rosalind was very busy, caring for her two children, and her husband Jeffrey who had Multiple Sclerosis, and working as a music teacher. 'Only once was there a real emergency. He had fallen and he called school and said he needed me to come home. This was the only time he called for help. We read together. Jeffrey was involved in the world, he read newspapers and magazines, and listened to the news on the radio. He refused to watch TV. Part of it was we didn't want it in the house with the children. He knew if we had it he would become a lump sitting in front of the TV. He teased me and said I would probably spend most of my time in front of it watching romantic movies. Jeff loved to listen to music, and at times a friend came and played the piano. These were joyful moments. The children made his life bearable.'

Around 35 Rosalind had many long talks with a dear friend who continued to be a mentor to her. He had previously been helpful in giving her advice. 'These talks changed my life. We talked about real things, about karma. I'm a very private person, and these talks helped me.

'When Jeff was in his forties, it got hard. I had to get up during the night. If his arm fell down the side of the bed, he couldn't lift it up and needed help. I became a very light sleeper and would be up in an instant. The children didn't seem to realize how hard this time was for me. I didn't want them to feel my burden, but it was difficult for me.

'During that time my life was very scheduled. By 7.45 a.m. the children were off to school. I had to have some time for myself so I set aside fifteen minutes before I brought Jeff his breakfast. I worked on meditation and reading lectures about the spiritual world. Every day I thought about what I had read as I walked to my work. That tiny bit of my own time I kept against all odds. I had the will to take this time for myself.'

Without a spiritual life Rosalind felt she would not have been able to bear Jeff's illness.

At 36 **Patrick** and his family moved back home to Boston. After two years of advancing his career he had another opportunity to become program director for a station in Des Moines, Iowa. He loved the challenge of this job, but he and Martha felt they were very far away from their family and their roots. During this time another child was born. When an opportunity arose for Patrick to become program director of a new station that would allow them to return to Boston, they took it. They had college friends in a small town on the South Shore and decided to settle in that area. Patrick's career seemed to level off. He couldn't see any further way to progress in the field he was in, and began to look around for something else. He tried to get into sales work, but nothing turned up. His eldest daughter was now twelve years old. She had friends and felt secure where they were living. Patrick didn't feel he could keep moving around. The family had to sink their roots and stay put. 'My brother-in-law spoke with me about insurance sales, and I decided to make the change and become an agent.'

When **Jack** was 34 he was sent to Vietnam, this time in Psychological Warfare Operations. He dropped propaganda leaflets to the Vietcong. During his thirteen months he had some close relationships with some of the Vietnamese who were working with the Americans. He specifically remembered an interpreter who was part Chinese, part Vietnamese. This man wasn't liked by either side. There were times the Americans had to guard him from being hurt.

Jack was interested in the local government and especially enjoyed observing the election process which was quite similar to ours. There were some war protests during that time, but they weren't as strong as in the United States.

When he was 38 he retired from the military. He went to Sacramento to join his family, began to go to college and worked as well. The adjustment to civilian life was not difficult because even when he had been stationed in the States he had always kept his military life separate from his home life. At first the students at the community college regarded him with some hostility. After all he was a Vietnam veteran and the atmosphere in the country was fairly hostile to the 'Vietnam vets'. He had many talks with his fellow college students, and gradually they began to look upon him as a friend.

As we rejoin our friends, we find that some are in a very solid, stable phase, feeling that their life has meaning and purpose. Others are facing challenges, looking inward, and asking existential questions.

Natasha in Latvia, and Claudia in Germany, are deeply involved in their professions. Respected, admired and acknowledged, they are satisfied in their professional life. But Claudia's relationship with Fritz becomes more difficult as his moodiness turns to jealousy and possessiveness.

Inci is arrested and kept in prison for eight months without a trial. She gets through this experience by keeping herself busy and concentrating on survival. It is only when she is let out of prison but not allowed to work that she hits rock bottom. She experiences self-pity, numbing fear and loneliness. She and Ali secretly leave Turkey and take refuge in Germany where they both get jobs in their professions. Inci feels safe away from Turkey. Life is stable. She has important work to do. She is however torn between guilt that her husband has suffered because of her (having to leave his country and his work), and torment because she realizes he is having affairs. She feels as if she is dying; she cries, she wakes up at night feeling unbearable loneliness, and asks, 'Why aren't I satisfied with life?'

Eva concentrates on her career and her growing children in Vienna. During a serious health problem in her late thirties, she has a near-death experience and senses that something new needs to happen. She takes one of the children to the US to visit her friends. There a new, more inward phase of her life begins. She finds that she now lives consciously where earlier it seemed she had moved through life in a dream. She approaches her career with new clarity. She accepts the marriage although she no longer has trust in it. She directs her attention toward what she can change, rather than what she cannot.

Having married later than many of the other people I interviewed, Nigel and Anne are experiencing many of the joys the other couples did in their previous life stage. They are working as a pastoral team in a run-down London parish. They have children. Their lives are focused and full. But they have always had the dream of going to South America to work in the ministry, and so they move to Chile.

Daniela experiences these years as very difficult. Her life is not much different outwardly from how it was previously: she is still devoted to mothering Kirsten and working part time. But inwardly she feels distress. She is frustrated with her life, the way she has not been able to sustain a relationship; and disturbed by the memory of the way her mother knuckled under to her domineering, drunk husband. She tries to understand herself and what the purpose of her life is.

Evita, at 40, finally finishes her university studies in Lithuania. She has divorced her alcoholic husband but has to continue to share an apartment with him. Because her salary as an engineer isn't enough to support herself, her daughter Beruta and her mother, she keeps her job at the university in the evening. Because she won't do whatever the KGB wants, though, it punishes her by taking away her university job (and thus a significant source of income) and doesn't let her leave Lithuania when she wants to visit a friend abroad.

Pavel has moved into a stable phase of life in Latvia. He has re-married, has a family life, is studying for his doctorate, and is receiving acknowledgement for his work.

Jerry has spent years on inner work and is now reaching out to others. He begins discussion groups with young people. He risks speaking out on aspects of culture which are banned by the Polish communist government. Despite the warnings of people who are afraid of the authorities, Jerry courageously introduces these ideas. He writes articles and gives interviews.

Rosalind is working, and also caring for Jeffrey, whose condition is worsening, and for her family. She finds inner courage to get through this difficult time by cultivating her spiritual life. Deep talks with a mentor help her gain perspective on the meaning of her situation.

Patrick's career has reached a dead end, and he looks for something new. The family stops moving around and settles down.

Jack is retired from the American military and now begins college in preparation for a second career. What are his goals? What should he do with his life?

The common themes of this period have to do with purpose, priorities, questioning and finding inner resources to deal with life's challenges. There is pain, but also development. Something new is slowly beginning to emerge. Each person experiences this stage differently, but inner growth seems to be the common thread.

4
Making our Mark on Life: 42-49

In our forties we enter a very dynamic stage of life. Many changes go on which call upon us to wake up and re-evaluate our lives. This time is often characterized by continuing crisis and change, and by a sense of rebirth.

It is a time when we often take on new interests or change careers, not because we are running away, but because we have come into touch with what we really want to do in life (not for ambition or for money, but to satisfy an inner longing). We are more patient with ourselves: 'I cannot expect anyone to understand me. I am just learning to understand myself'. Once we have this attitude, we are more forgiving of ourselves, our partner, and our friends. Our relationships relax and take on a new warmth. Many new friendships are made. People are attracted to us because we radiate a new confidence in life. We are asked for our judgments on situations, and we are sought out for advice.

On the other hand, we also find out that our talents do not flow the way they used to. If we keep trying to work out of our old sources of inspiration, nothing comes, the well is dry. But if we are working to transform ourselves the old talents become re-enlivened in a new way, and new ones emerge. We find we are capable of so much more than we were in the past.

By accepting who we are and working to transform ourselves, our character shines out more strongly from within. Our personality continues to become more truly individualized. We don't have to be like everyone else. We can even enjoy some of our eccentricities as long as we don't try to impose them on other people. A sense of peace and harmony fills the soul – and radiates out to other people, who are nourished by it.

After we have passed beyond the chaos and feelings of helplessness of menopause (male or female), we may experience a powerful release of physical energy which can bring problems. Indeed, **power is the**

temptation of this phase. We can be tempted to try to control other people's lives and to influence situations through the very force of our personalities. The strength of our experiences, of the lessons we have learned, makes us want to help other people do the 'right' thing. For those who do not experience menopausal symptoms as intensely as others, the feeling of power comes earlier.

We have to learn to hold back the new energy that is released during this time, transforming it instead into new capacities which have nothing to do with our own ambitions. This is difficult. We have to learn to hold back and only respond to questions we are asked, rather than overwhelming others with our strength and experience. **Developing patience** is important.

Many moral forces develop during this phase, the strongest of which is truthfulness. Have I made too many compromises with truth? Am I comfortable with the ethical decisions I have made? Have I been fooling myself? Judging our actions, our decisions, our likes and dislikes becomes part of the process of taking stock of our lives so far. Being honest about ourselves is important and also very painful.

Many of us find that an intuitive sense of our connection with spiritual forces dawns during this time. Cynics might say that a newly-awakened interest in spiritual matters is just clutching at straws as one becomes afraid of death. But this fails to take account of our emerging, deepening awareness and perception. At this time in our lives we are able to understand in a minute what younger people struggle for weeks to grasp. Spiritual ideas find a fertile soil of life experience. It is not our intellect that proves things to us now, but what we know out of the depths of our soul.

Leo Tolstoy, the great 19th century Russian writer, wrote at 45: 'I feel that old age has begun for me. I call old age the inner spiritual condition in which all the outer phenomena of the world lose their meaning for me.' [1] His aunt died later in the same year, and Author Anne Edwards writes:

> With the deaths of Aunt Toinette and Aunt Pelagya...he finally accepted the fact that his mother was dead and that there was no one who could keep her spirit alive for him. Like Aunt Pelagya, Tolstoy did not want to die. With her loss he

entered in earnest into a solitary combat with death and set out on a desperate search for the truth about eternal life. [2]

How do we relate to the obligations of life? We may have elderly parents who have special needs, family situations that are very demanding. We may be torn between obligations and personal needs, between duties and rights. How can we bring warmth and love to situations which we feel have been foisted upon us? Can we transform them by freely accepting them? How can we understand these situations in relation to our personal destiny?

In our late forties our physical bodies are usually growing less flexible while our soul forces become more so. Rigidity or flexibility-we can move in either direction. Our thoughts can harden into pedantic statements or they can fly away into fantasy. We can become hysterical, flighty, over-enthusiastic or mystical; or dull and resigned to a very conventional, materialistic outlook. Neither will satisfy us if we are really seeking spiritual growth. We must find balance by anchoring our thoughts and vitalizing them through our own inner efforts, instead of simply perpetuating what our parents believed. It is not even enough to find our own spiritual direction; we also need to think it through for ourselves so we don't become fanatical or complacent about it. Many people try to avoid dealing with spiritual questions, but it makes a big difference at this age whether we are asleep or awake to such things, for they are the source of our transformation.

We find ourselves alone more and more, which may make this a very anxious time. Many people have to face the issue of death in an immediate way – when parents, family members, or friends die – which also confronts us with the possibility of our own death.

Our attitude to death will have been quite different in earlier years. Children have no sense of it. They live in timelessness – and are only jolted out of it by traumatic experiences. Adolescents know death exists but think they are immortal. They abuse their bodies because they don't really believe they can hurt themselves. Unless a close friend becomes very ill or dies, they are unlikely to feel death's reality. In our twenties the focus is on planning our lives, not looking towards the end of it. In our thirties we may begin to think about such things as we face the abyss of loneliness, a kind of soul-death.

For some people this is when anxiety attacks begin to occur. In our forties a new feeling develops that life is almost over. We're over the top of the 'hill' and starting to go down the other side, so questions begin to haunt us: What have I done with my life? How will I look back on my life from the moment of death? Our own death becomes more real even though we know we will probably live for several more decades. For some people, though, everyday life is the source of pain and stress. They have no problem with the idea of their own death – it seems like a relief to them. But whichever way we regard death, it assumes greater significance for us.

Relationships during this phase

If we have not properly faced the changes that belong to the forties, we can expect an even bigger crisis around fifty. But whenever it comes we will, if we confront it, develop a new attitude towards life, a new purpose for living. The people close to us become especially important. Friendship is one of the great comforts of these years when we are struggling for balance. We no longer need to impress each other. We know each other too well so we might as well be straight and direct. The need for more privacy also develops during this time, and close friends or spouses will need to recognize and respect this. On one hand we have the need and wish to do things together, to share companionship, on the other we need more space. The couple has to work to find the right balance.

A man may at this time awaken to the gentleness in himself he has previously only allowed himself to love in the woman or his children, and this can be a powerful experience. Fascinated by this side of himself, he may begin to explore it the way a young woman does in her twenties. He becomes more interested in his home, in gardening, in cooking, art, music. He wants to live more through his feelings. Although there is wisdom in this tenderness it can sometimes be surprising to others if it does not seem to suit his personality. He can go overboard in sentimentality, seeming at times like a teenager with a crush on someone. His behavior can strain a relationship: the changes going on in him shake up all his connections and ways of communicating. He may become silent for long periods of time, or he may now want to talk incessantly about his latest interest. This unfamiliar experience of his own femininity can awaken in him a new appreciation of his wife and open up new areas of conversation with her, especially if she grasps what is happening in her husband and supports him.

Our late forties and early fifties is a time for discovering the parts of our personality that did not fit in with our previous image of ourselves. The danger for a couple at this period is that the woman, who now becomes more involved with her own masculine side, will reject the feminine in the man as soft or self-indulgent. He can feel like a tender flower just opening and feel unsure and a little hesitant about this. She must try not to intimidate him – yet she has different needs and it may be difficult for her to have the necessary patience. A man who has cultivated artistic activities throughout his thirties will not experience such a marked change as others.

Male vulnerability at this age makes some older men very appealing to young women. A woman who begins a relationship with a man of this age will often find in it the potential for a deep bond; this may flower for a number of years – until she comes into her thirties and starts being more assertive. He will dote on her and she will love the love that is surrounding her. It is sincere, not selfish, and comes from the inner core of his own being. A young woman in her twenties is focused on her own needs and wants and will at times use the attention and love of an older man to her own advantage, even making a fool of him.

A wife who has been intimidated by her husband's previous strength will find it difficult to come to terms with this change in him. She may have pulled back from him through the years and become resentful of his lack of interest in sharing his experiences and feelings with her. When he now yearns for companionship and gentleness he no longer finds his partner open to it – and becomes demanding and hurt. She may think to herself, 'When *I* valued those qualities you had no use for them. Now you want this experience but I have grown bitter and hard. If you had only known then what you know now, we would have been so happy. Now it is too late.' This is not an uncommon situation. The woman may be very tempted to lose herself in 'I told you so' attitudes. But if she can look deeply into herself and face her own feelings, instead of becoming callous, this can be a wonderful time of companionship. She usually feels a new sense of security at this time; and her man's need for her strengthens that.

During this period a couple can develop a new loyalty to each other which strengthens their love, which carries them through the next decades and even reaches beyond death. Remember that the challenge in this phase is power or patience. During this time of transition there is much potential for power struggles and negative attacks. Developing patience with oneself and with the other is very important.

Not every couple does find a way to transform their relationship. Through the thirties, forties, and fifties divorce becomes more and more common. In some cases an affair wakes up everyone, and helps the couple focus their energies on getting help and putting their marriage back on its feet. If they have paid close attention to what happened and why, they may be able to heal wounds and deal with issues that have been gnawing away at their relationship for decades. This takes time and often needs counselling, but it is well worth it.

It is during this period that a couple can begin to see marriage as an art form, as the most challenging and complex of all relationships we can create. **We begin to see that marriage is of our own making, and we must take responsibility for it as a labour of love.** This is the most critical turning-point in marriage. If it is not consciously grasped, even a good marriage may reach a natural end. It is during this phase that marriages assume such different qualities. The maturity of a marriage is like the face of an old person: everything is 'out front'. The scars, the joys, the fears, the tenderness are exposed for all to see. Some people have to make many compromises and adjustments which do not feel very satisfactory – but in spite of disillusionment the marriage goes on. Peace has been made even if it's not the best of relationships. For others, earlier periods of stress marked the beginning of a series of crises, resulting in progressive deterioration until separation or divorce is the final outcome. Those who manage to meet the challenge satisfactorily win through to a higher level of understanding, a greater depth.

Natasha

Life was going very well. Then at 45 came a turning-point. A decline began. She felt she couldn't sing as well as before. This brought about a loss of her sense of security. She didn't know what to do. She started working as a teacher, but didn't know if she would be any good at it. She remembered an experience she had had as a young woman in Perm: she and a friend had their fortunes told by a gypsy who said to her, 'You are a teacher'. Natasha had no connection with teaching then, but didn't forget this. It had always been there in her mind.

During the first five years of teaching, her insecurity grew. By then her first pupils had graduated from the Conservatory, and seeing the results she started to feel she really could be a teacher. As years went on she grew into it and didn't even want to sing professionally any more. She realized that teaching other people to sing well allowed her to give something and reap the rewards of her effort. 'I started my new life. Teaching had become my mission, what I could really do well.' There were also problems in her marriage. When she began her life as a teacher, she felt more independent. The relationship between Natasha and Anton became very difficult and they were nearly divorced.

Claudia had made the decision to stay with Fritz, and threw herself into the work at the clinic. As Fritz became more and more jealous she had to let him know where she was all the time. The children even made a large clock that showed where she was at any one time. Fritz never felt satisfied though. He felt that he didn't get what he wanted from life, and often had rages.

'This was an awful aspect. So I have done things not so much to please him, but to avoid his terrible reactions. I avoided doing things I knew would be right, for instance, with the clinic, just to make peace. But I was very much afraid. During the last year of his life I had three jobs, the clinic, the family, and another job I took in 1976 for the security it gave because I was so afraid something would happen to me, and then Fritz and the children would be without means. I was the main support of the family at this time. He wouldn't work very much despite the fact that he was a skilled gynaecologist and his patients admired him. Fritz was very gifted and would have made a fine artist. Now he had more time to paint. Of course, he was quite old by now. Other people his age didn't need to work. If he had not had such terrible times physically and emotionally in the war and in the prisoner of war camp in Russia he would have had more strength longer in his life. However, he had no reserves of any kind. This was not his fault.'

In 1977, when she was 48, Claudia had a very sad year. Her sister, who had lost her husband from cancer, became very ill. Claudia was with her before she died. Only a few weeks after her sister's death, Fritz was taken ill with cancer of the stomach. 'As often as my work would permit, I was with him day and night. He had a hospital bed in the living room in our apartment, which was inside the clinic. His doctors had wanted him to go to another hospital, but the girls said 'No, if Daddy doesn't want to go to a hospital he can stay here.' They were wonderful. They would be having breakfast and dinner at the table and nearby was this dying man. So he died in the middle of his family – three daughters, a wife, and two dogs. I know very well he was aware of the fact that I would never leave him. It was the first time he accepted this. So he died very peacefully.

'Within half a year I lost three people I had loved. First was my brother-in-law, then six weeks later my sister, and then Fritz.'

During the next year Claudia had to do everything in the clinic by herself, winding up both the business and medical affairs of the clinic while working full time in a state hospital.

Inci was now working in England. She was dealing with her own loneliness and the realization that Ali was having affairs.

'I had my work, but I was losing my self-confidence more and more. Even in prison I didn't lose my self-confidence. I was like a frightened child. I thought perhaps England is making me like this. I was even frightened to go and buy bread, to go to the butcher to buy meat. I was working, so most of my friends again were my colleagues. As soon as I got to work I felt good. In my own place at work I felt love and care. As soon as I came home I felt blame and guilt: 'It is my fault'. If I objected to anything Ali did, I felt guilty that he had suffered a lot because of me. He had left Turkey because of me. I never doubted that he loved me somehow. But on the other hand my inner feelings were not saying the same. Of course, my inner feelings were much more correct. Now when I look at things I should have trusted my inner feelings, but of course, we never learn to trust our inner feelings.

'I knew Ali was involved with a woman, I could feel it. But he denied it. Then he had another affair, and another. And I was feeling so bad that this man wasn't having a holiday, that he was working all the time. I would encourage him, "Ali, go have a holiday, please". Ah! I don't blame him. I blame myself. I should have trusted my feelings. I think living alone four years I've learned to trust my feelings for the first time.

'It took me some years to say, "Ali, I'm not your mother. You cannot bring all your girlfriends and say, 'Mommy, mommy, look what I brought'. If you want to see them, go and see them outside. I don't have to see them. How would you like it if I would bring my old boyfriends?" It took me years to say "Ali, no". Then he kept his relationships secret. Until the last time. I had gone away to a meeting, and when I returned he told me that when I was away he was too. This time I told him to leave. It was really painful, but it was a sudden relief. My feelings were right. I don't have to struggle anymore to get a little bit of love and affection. The pain came later, but at first it was relief.

'When I was attending a conference I went to see my sister who also lives abroad. My sister is quite interested in dreams. That night I dreamed and in the morning I told her my dream. Ali was staying in the bed. But sometimes it was Ali or my mother, I wasn't sure. But there was a child in his arms, a new-born baby. And I was very disappointed that Ali hadn't told me that he had a child. But it was my mother. I was very disappointed. I was standing in the door looking at the scene and I was paralyzed. When I told this dream to my sister I could not stop crying. I was crying and crying and crying. And the next day I came home and Ali told me about his secret relationship. Probably my subconscious was ready to accept the truth. Therefore he told me the truth. Because why did he tell me then? It's funny that someone becomes ready to accept certain truths.

'Immediately after my separation I had the feeling of my earlier years when I was 25 in Sweden and lived alone. I went back to that time. Now I have much more love and affection and better relationship with my colleagues, with my friends, everybody, people of any age. I am more myself. In the last four years I feel I have collected the parts of me which I had left behind.

'One day I was taking a shower. I remember very well. I felt, "Who's taking this shower?" Suddenly I discovered that I existed. Such awareness came, a slow process, but it came through the shower. You know when I was living with Ali I was not even aware that I existed. I was like an automatic machine, wake up, make breakfast, wake him up, take a shower, three minutes, not more. Go to work. Come back. Do the shopping. Wash. He's such an important scientist. He should not do such ordinary work. I also protected him. I did not demand. I cannot blame him that he did not do such things.

'Of course, I still love him as a person. But I can't bear to be with him for half an hour. I can't blame him. I loved him because of what he was, and I hate him for what he was. I'd sit and cry for five hours during the weekend. During the week I functioned well again. My colleagues were very supportive. I told them I was going through a separation. But during the weekends for two years I cried, and then slowly I started to discover my humor was coming back, my energy started to come back, my vitality started to come back. I had given up all those.'

Eva

'In my mid-forties I felt I was in a new phase. The two strong aspects were my relationship with my children and knowing I was working in my profession. I was busy teaching in several places. I enjoyed it and I felt I was starting to regain my old strengths. Men usually find their career in their twenties, but here I was in my forties. I had continued to do some part-time work through my thirties, but I was always working my schedule around the needs of the family. Now I felt I could find my own way and I became conscious that I was developing my own methods.

'It was extremely painful when my eldest child left home at 20. I thought I would die. I was 44. I had my work now, but I became aware that I had reached a peak in my life. I realized I had spent years building everything up and now I was losing it because I no longer had the physical stamina. This came just when I had reached a certain place of freedom. Earlier I had thought I was building for eternity. Now it felt as if I were losing everything. The children were leaving. My body strength was leaving me. But at least I did have my career. But this problem intensified because my health deteriorated and I was also dealing with symptoms of menopause. I tired more easily. I was slowing down. I couldn't count on my body anymore. In a profession which is based on movement this confronted me with a serious situation.'

At 45 Eva decided to take training in curative eurythmy (individual therapeutic exercises). This would not be as taxing physically and would give her an opportunity to use her intuitive faculties for healing. 'I had always had a very sensitive perception of people, perhaps it was even too strong. Through curative eurythmy I could use this capacity in a positive way. Now the strange thing was that as soon as I applied to be accepted into the curative eurythmy program, many students applied to be in my evening eurythmy classes. Enrolment surged. I had to pay attention to this. I felt I had to be faithful to my students. So I took part-time intensive courses in curative eurythmy while I continued giving my courses and waited to see what would happen.'

Eva had been teaching in different institutions and had evening classes, but that is very different from having one's own school with a four-year training. 'At 47 I knew it was time for me to start my own school, but where, how, when?' At the same time, she felt she didn't have the stamina and strength to carry such a training. 'This dilemma grew in me. I knew a new phase was coming in my life although I wasn't sure exactly how it would develop.

'By the end of my 40s I was developing a growing insecurity toward my body and even my place on the earth. Before, I had felt

I could do anything. No matter how difficult I could manage. But now I had to face the reality that this wasn't true.'

Nigel and Anne had decided to go to Chile where they lived under the governments of presidents Allende and Pinochet.

'We took the three children (aged 3¹/₂ years, 2 years, and 11 months). These nine years were extremely happy years.'

Anne, eight years younger than Nigel, was in her thirties. At 42, in the middle of these wonderful years, Nigel hit a low point. Under Allende civil war was looming. 'We had three children under five years of age. Food was desperately needed. Every day we stood three to four hours on line. Different commodities were given out on different days. One Saturday morning in winter after we and the three children had waited for three hours, meat ran out twelve people ahead of us. We came home exhausted, put the children to bed, and we also collapsed into bed. We asked ourselves, "We can no longer do what we came to do. Should we leave?"

This was Saturday. The next day came the answer. A Marxist student at the university had been bringing his girlfriend to Anne for drug counselling. He dropped her off but didn't stay. On this Sunday he came to see them and said 'I'm at my wits end. My parents are right-wing. I can't betray them. I can't stay at home. I don't want to take up arms. I've seen the change in my girlfriend since she has been coming to talk with Anne. I want to know about Christianity.' Nigel and Anne looked at each other and thought 'That's why we're here'. So they stayed in Chile. This young man became an active leader of a Christian group of 40-50 university students, mainly left-wing.

What had they come to Chile to do? Missionary work. They had learned Spanish with a view to planting Christianity in part of Santiago where no Protestant Church existed. Many agnostics and atheists lived there. When Nigel first went to Chile he volunteered in the hospital laboratory. As the ministry work picked up, he had less time for the hospital because he was busy with discussion groups, showing films, and responding to people's needs. His low point had been a test and a clarification of his purpose in life.

Daniela had a rough time in her late thirties, but things started to shift and move in her forties.

'Something's different now. I need time to do things, to find out things about myself. But not just about me; other people have needs. Most of the time life just goes on. But I also have very good feelings, new feelings, about being a grown up woman. That's still there, and it's getting better. I had a difficult time last year. I started feeling sorry for myself. I became sure that something's gone, I became pretty sure I would have no more children. That was very hard, but I don't feel so sad anymore. I am learning acceptance. I am getting more quiet about things that make me angry, sad, and melancholic.

'At 46 I still have problems accepting the situation with my body. Not the wrinkles but the tiredness, not to be able to stay up late or get up early. Now I work five hours, commute 30 minutes each way. I can't do everything. My work at my present job as administrative secretary in a home for handicapped children increases. My involvement there grows. But I get tired more easily.

'I see changes in my skin, I now have varicose veins. This makes me feel sad. These are things others can't see, that only I can see. Changes come suddenly, my period is not regular. This is worse. I wish it would just stop. When it comes now I just want to stay in bed. I feel helpless that I can't control my body. I have problems with my stomach and my bones. I find myself often thinking about age changes. Will life be better when I'm fifty? I think I'll be able to handle it better then. Now I'm anxious. What else is coming? I'm listening inside, trying to be aware of it, and learning to handle it. I'm trying to stay interested in many things. I don't think getting older is bad.

'My grandmother is a small old lady who finds it very satisfying to be religious. When I talk to her, she says, "I have a feeling God has decided these things. He'll bring them and He'll take them". I don't believe that. I believe, but not in a special kind of God, because of all the things going on in the world concerning religion – the killing, hurting, wars to do with religion. It just doesn't make sense to me. So I prefer to believe in the kind of God that wouldn't do this kind of thing.

'I have respect for almost all religions, but I have problems accepting any kind of religion that tells you to do or not do things. I respect somebody who tries to be a good human being in all ways including in the man-woman relationship. I try to lead a Christian life and this gives me the feeling I am religious.'

Daniela described a friend going to weekly meeting held by a priest who openly questions the church. They find him charismatic. She's afraid to go hear him. Something about his charisma bothers her. She was raised to be Catholic, but she married Dieter, a Protestant, partly in rebellion. She rebelled against the strict position of the church and did not baptise Kirsten.

'I didn't go to Catholic or Protestant Church. I use the Church as I need. I don't want to be more active, and yet I don't want to completely break with it. I somehow don't want to become committed. I'm sensitive, but I'm not active. When I'm interested in something, somehow I don't go further into it. That's a problem. Somehow I hold back. I don't make decisions that involve commitment. I blame myself that I don't make definite decisions. Where do I belong? I'm satisfied with my present life, but maybe I'm still looking for answers. As long as I'm asking, I know I'm alive.

'I'm very resistant to anyone making dogmas in life. I like to have fun without having a reason. I enjoy all kinds of music. I enjoy getting dressed up. But I'm finding I'm doing things now because I want to, not because I'm rebelling or I'm trying to please someone. I do things that make me feel good. I find I can do a lot for other people as well. This makes me feel good. In the last few years I've come to understand myself. I know I'm getting older but in my feelings I don't think I'm going deeply enough.

'I'm feeling something new, something unfinished with my marriage. I don't blame Dieter. It takes two. Maybe because he married again, I'm more tolerant when I speak with him. I've become diplomatic – this is new. In the past I was loud and demanding. I said everything that was on my mind to him. Being very honest is very important to me. I've learned that being diplomatic doesn't mean giving up honesty. I found out I can be honest with him without hurting him.

'What's to come in the future? Now I'm concentrating on Kirsten who is in her last year of high-school, and on my friends. This is a better feeling than living together with someone and yet still being alone. I'm very proud I have been able to live without a man. Many women can't.

'I feel independent. I go anywhere alone that I want to. If I want to have a good dinner, I've trained myself to go and take a table in the middle of the room. I used to be afraid, but I'm not afraid anymore. If I'm in the mood and no one else wants to go, I go by myself. I don't have a problem. This began two to three years ago. I can talk about these things with one friend Helga who is a social worker. She's showing me it's possible to continue education on your own. She's become trained in the last few years in family therapy. We meet for breakfast every Saturday morning, and she always finds a solution to problems.

'I feel I'm saying goodbye in three areas: *1)* My body is changing; *2)* my anger at the pain of my menstrual period is decreasing, and *3)* I find slowly I'm starting to depart from things that were very important to me in the past, things I was hanging onto in a very unrealistic way, such as having a traditional family (father, mother, several children). I finally realized this is not possible. I had bought the big dining room table because I always felt one day it would be filled with children. So I'm saying goodbye to not having more children. It really is not going to be. My body tells me I couldn't even carry a child over paths or down steps any more.

'I've also said goodbye to my family. Living a few hundred kilometers away from the family has changed my relationship. Things are not the same since my grandmother died. Old aunts and uncles are dying. Not much family is left. The family never visited me here, they were involved with their own houses and gardens. After some "talks" with my deceased aunt, something changed. I decided I'm not going to try to keep contact with family but I'll just accept the situation. Concerning my parents, I worry what will happen if one of them goes. I offered my parents to move nearby so I could take care of them. They won't discuss this with me. I've said goodbye to establishing a deep meaningful relationship with my parents. I just have to accept who they are.

'Up till when I was forty, these situations and thoughts made me nervous. Now at 46 I have calmed down. Maybe 49/50 will be even better. I don't have to be sad and I can accept life as it is. It's not all bad. I think the middle of life is over, and I'm beginning to accept myself. In the past when I tried to discuss my feelings with Dieter he told me I was sick because I had everything I needed in life, but I still wasn't satisfied. He said I should go to a doctor. It's normal for me to show my feelings. This is a sign of how strong my involvement is. I don't want other people telling me what I should feel. This all goes along with becoming self-confident. It is terrible I didn't have it earlier. I couldn't cry when I was small. My parents said, "Don't cry, because of the neighbors". Now I cry.

'I have many moments now in which I feel satisfied. It must be because of those moments of saying goodbye and not being in-between any more, but of knowing where I am.

'The place I still don't feel confident in is regarding education. I feel I should retrain for a different job, but I don't feel I've had a good education. I should have started earlier. But before I start something I want to know it will turn out well. But this too may change. What I'm doing at the moment I want to do. If I become unhappy with it then I will change it. My dream is to live on the Spanish island where we have a summer house, read, work in the garden, learn Spanish. I feel I could be of service there and develop the connections I have already formed (now that I have my newly-learned 'diplomatic' way). I'm becoming grateful for simple things such as making guests feel comfortable, bringing joy to people. I feel things are getting better.'

Evita was under great pressure from the KGB, but she had also developed a moral independence from them. Her main aim was for her daughter Beruta to be able to finish university, and for them both to find a way to leave Lithuania. But then Beruta found her future husband and all plans to leave ended.

In her forties Evita felt a difference in herself. She felt very strong, very brave. She felt all the world belonged to her. She was full of energy. Beruta was married. Evita herself was divorced and she had fulfilled her responsibilities. She was like a young girl – free. She received proposals for marriage but had no wish to marry. Her forties were a happy time – She traveled much, visited relatives, went to the seaside, attended many weddings. But her family still did not have a decent flat. She, her mother, her daughter Beruta, Beruta's husband, and their young son lived in two rooms.

As preparation for the Moscow Olympics, 'undesirable elements' of the population were shipped out of Moscow and relocated to Lithuania. There they were given apartments. Evita went to the government and protested that these people were given proper apartments while honest hard-working people still didn't have them. After much confrontation and struggle the family received an apartment in one of the new districts.

Pavel was trying to find a way to have his book accepted as a doctoral thesis. But it was very difficult to work through all the bureaucracy and find an institute that would have the right specialists and would be willing to do this. This didn't happen and Pavel could not achieve his goal. He was deeply disappointed. He felt during this time (from 46-50) that circumstances were stronger than he was. Everything he had done before the age of 45 had been achieved by his own efforts. But after 45 he realized that certain achievements were not dependent only on his own abilities, but were beyond his control, and that he must accept this reality.

During these years he established a normal friendship with his first wife which he still maintains. He feels that during these years he became more mature and more realistic. He realized it was better to compromise than insist on having his own way, that sometimes something stronger develops in the relationship if you give in, than if you always push your own point of view. Although he doesn't mean it in a mercenary way, he said it was like a 'good deal'. You give something and you get much more back. Sometimes it's hard to find the good you need to give to the other person. You have to look deeply into her soul to see what she needs.

Pavel pondered these questions often. He read a series of articles on marriage relationships in the newspaper. He even wrote his own article for the series but didn't submit it. 'My second wife is eight years younger than I am. She is benefitting from what I have learned from experience.'

Jerry was becoming more and more active with his interests despite the risk. What he was doing was dangerous in the current political situation in Poland.

Jerry's forties were a very active time for him. Later, in 1988-89 when it was legal, his friends also became publicly active. Meanwhile Jerry had gone more and more public. He organized two clubs, the Gnosis discussion club and a Jung club. He founded the 'Gnosis' magazine.

Rosalind

Rosalind's life centered on caring for Jeff as he struggled with Multiple Sclerosis. He never lost his optimism that he would recover. His family was his great strength. When the children became teenagers Jeff's illness was especially difficult and he became impatient with them. Sometimes he was harsh. But he loved them and wanted to guide them. When Jeff had a fever he would be out of himself: only his son would be able to reach him and bring him back. Their bond was very strong. Jeff never took drugs after he had a bad experience with sleeping pills. He was lively much of the time, bad tempered some of the time, but his mind was always clear.

'When I look back on Jeff's illness I realize how much it did for me. It made a woman of me. I became conscious of myself. I don't look back and say my life was terrible.' One winter Jeff was staying in their country house. Their daughter had finished college and was living at home. A woman had been hired to take care of Jeff while

Rosalind commuted back and forth every weekend from the city. Jeff responded very well being out in the country, and his condition improved for a while. His doctor said his family life was what kept him going. But after Christmas his condition deteriorated. Rosalind rushed to be with him many times because he was taken to hospital and the doctor said he was dying. So she became used to emergencies and crises.

'On Monday my daughter and I went to Chicago She was going to return the next day to be with Jeff. I had a strange feeling, and I said to myself, "Next weekend I'm going to stay for a longer while".' The next day, while their daughter was on the train, on her way back to care for her father, Jeff's condition deteriorated significantly.

'My brother came over to the house and saw that Jeff was feeling very low. My brother called me and told me things seemed serious. My sister and I drove up. Half way there my sister said, "Prepare yourself, he may be dying". He was dead when I got there. I really had to work this through. I wasn't there. Our daughter wasn't there. I thought and thought so much about this. Whenever I was around he picked up. I really feel he was ready to go. He chose the moment neither one of us was there. That's been hard. I regret I couldn't be there at that moment. He was going on his 50th birthday. I was 48, almost 49.'

Patrick had been pursuing his career, but around 42 he decided the family should settle in one place and put down roots. He worked in insurance sales for two years and then joined a brokerage in Boston, which allowed him to expand beyond just selling life insurance. When one of his friends started a self-funding group providing medical benefits, Patrick decided to join him.

Since first grade Patrick had been educated in Catholic schools and universities. He had been an altar boy in the Church during high school and college. He loved the Catholic Church despite its failings. Patrick and Martha's mutual faith in the Church and the importance of their spiritual life had been a strong bond between them since the beginning of their relationship.

In 1973, when Patrick was 47, a Deaconite program was restored in the Catholic church as a result of the Vatican Council in the Sixties. It was decided that this program would take place in Boston. After it was announced, Patrick's pastor encouraged him to participate. In order to enter the program you had to be at least thirty-five, and your wife and family had to agree to support you in taking this step. Martha, Patrick, and their pastor had many talks. Both of them had always wanted to serve the Church in whatever way was possible. After many discussions and psychological tests, Patrick was chosen along with 39 others, and a new stage of his life began. He started a four year program leading to ordination as a Deacon.

'Martha is my rudder. She supported it all the way. You have to keep a balance in your life between the Church, family, and work. In the training they told us the family was first, then work, then the Church. I felt 'called' to the Deaconite. It was a vocation, something I would connect with for the rest of my life. I felt the two paths of my life – my work in the world and my life in the Church – had come together. My spiritual life became stronger and more central in my daily life.'

Jack was attending community college in Sacramento after retiring from the military. He and his wife separated although they continued to be friends, and still are to this day. In college, his fellow students were the age of his children. The students had disdain for Vietnam veterans and called them 'Killers'.

'It was a hard time, and when I was thinking of quitting school, my wife heard about it and she was irate. "You will not quit school. What do you mean?" (She was a schoolteacher). Although we were going through a divorce at the time, her words meant something to me.'

Gradually Jack felt more at home in college. He reached out to his fellow students. 'The kids in college called me "Pops". They spoke with me. They were amazed at my knowledge of history.'

After finishing college, Jack worked as a custodian at the community college he had attended for two years. He enjoyed this work and spent eleven and a half years supervising campus maintenance. Then he thought about graduate school.

Learning to transform life's experiences, meeting crises in relationship, developing patience and perspective, resolving issues, finding new and more inward parts of ourselves, are all characteristic of these years from 42 to 49.

Natasha, after a happy and confident time both in marriage and career, reaches a turning-point. Her career declines and she has to move into a new role. At first she is very insecure, but in time gains strength and confidence. The marriage becomes problematic and there is talk of divorce. But overall, she develops a feeling of independence and self-sufficiency during this time.

Claudia realizes Fritz is very ill. Although she is afraid of his tempers, she maintains her strong commitment to the family. She is concerned about how they will manage if something happens to her, and so changes jobs to assure their security. She is exhausted from the extra work she takes on. During this period she loses her brother-in-law, her sister, and her husband Fritz.

Inci is still living with Ali but has not faced the truth about their relationship. She loses self-confidence, no longer trusting her inner feelings. Finally, when she discovers he is continuing to have affairs, she tells him to leave. This gives her a feeling of relief. She slowly begins to put herself back together. She experiences a sense of herself, of joy, of freedom, but most of all that she is a worthwhile, capable human being.

Eva experiences freedom as well as pain as her children begin leaving home. She wants to devote herself completely to her career but begins to suffer health problems and enter menopause. She feels her inner strength but at the same time has to face physical vulnerability. She has to develop patience.

Nigel is in Chile with his family. After a particularly harrowing time of food shortages and long queues, he hits a low point and wonders what they are doing there. The very next day, Nigel and Anne get an unexpected answer to this question and realize that their work is important. They are able to make a difference, and they stay. Their lives are meaningful to them, so they can disregard the stress.

Daniela feels something has changed. She is learning to let go, to listen inwardly, to understand herself better. As she searches for answers to deep questions, she considers several religious alternatives, but isn't sure about any of them. She is completing the mothering which has been her focus for eighteen years. Now she is free to plan the next stage of life. Even though she is experiencing physical problems and menopause, she also feels she is making progress in emotional areas. She can be more honest, she is proud that she has managed to live without a man, and that she has built a pleasant friendship with her ex-husband Dieter.

Evita was all set to leave Lithuania with her daughter, but her daughter fell in love and married. Evita decided to stay with the family and support them in any way she could. She feels independent, strong, brave and free. This is a happy time for her. She feels she has control over her own life, even though they are all crowded into a tiny apartment. She manages to assert herself and get them a larger place to live.

Pavel has to deal with the deep disappointment of failing to get his thesis published. For the first time in his life, he realizes that certain things are beyond his control. He stops fighting life and begins to listen, and accept more. He develops a friendship with his first wife, and matures in his personal and social relationships. Those things become more important than getting recognition for his work.

Jerry is very active during this period. He continues to risk danger and persecution in forming outlawed discussion clubs. He founds a magazine. He has formulated his values clearly and is willing to take the consequences for living by them.

Rosalind deals with Jeffrey's illness and death. She learns many things about herself through these experiences.

Patrick's focus becomes his religious life. He is accepted into the deaconite program in the Catholic Church. His spiritual life becomes a 'calling'. He works to create a healthy balance between work, family, and church.

Jack is at college trying to find out who he is. When he is called a 'killer', he wants to leave, but doesn't. Although he and his wife are separated, they still have a strong friendship. He respects her view that he ought not to run away. He doesn't quit, changes his way of approaching his fellow students and experiences many joyful relationships with them.

Very little of the lifestyle of our twenties and thirties shows up here. Each individual is going through a maturing process: learning lessons, resolving relationships, clarifying values, developing patience – these are more important than material rewards and high excitement.

5

The Menopausal Years –
a New Beginning

Menopause is a gateway through which we enter a new stage in life. At puberty, when a girl has her first period, she comes under the sway of a monthly, lunar influence: her body has matured and is ready for reproduction, and her emotions are closely interwoven with her physical body. In these teenage years she has times of moodiness and times when her behavior is erratic, as well as being burdened by physical aches and cramps, and feeling out of sorts. She has to get used to a new aspect of herself, about which she feels insecure and confused. She may not feel ready to leave girlhood behind her and enter upon life as a woman. During the early years of puberty this ambivalence shows – she may be mature one moment and like a little girl the next. Western culture, unfortunately, focuses mainly on the outer changes of puberty: a girl's looks, her seductiveness, her sexual prowess. She seldom finds the security and guidance of a supportive adult community of women, but must instead struggle on her own to find an image of womanhood that goes deeper than the superficiality promoted by television and movies.

After puberty and on into her adult years, a girl continues to feel strong connections between her emotions and body. Being conscious of the menstrual cycle is part of her awareness. She knows the varying emotional states called forth at different times: in the days before her period comes, at the height of her period, or in the middle of the monthly rhythm, at ovulation. Through the physical discomfort of lower back pain, tenderness in her breasts, bloating or fatigue, she is aware of one aspect of being a woman. On the other hand she may feel the excitement of womanhood, the sensuality, the self-awareness, and the enjoyment of her femininity as she enters the world of relationships.

5 The menopausal years

Women's bodies are connected with blood in four very important aspects of their lives, each of which also has something of a ritual significance: menstruation; first intercourse; pregnancy; and menopause. Each of these introduces a woman to a new aspect of herself, and affects her identity. With her first menstruation she passes from girl to woman; with first intercourse she passes from friend to lover; with first pregnancy she passes from partner to mother; with menopause she passes into a completely new stage, where she can freely choose her identity, where she is no longer defined by fertility but free to pass beyond gender to an expression of the universal human. Each of these 'rites of passage' involves its own dreams and expressions of the feminine. The age following menopause is a time at which the woman can unite feminine and masculine qualities most completely.

A woman experiences menopause some time in the years between the forties and mid-fifties. Each woman's menopause is unique, yet there are common characteristics. Her circulatory and hormonal balance is affected, causing various symptoms that can be confusing and debilitating. These physical changes create emotional chaos for some women: a sense of unease, discomfort, emotional extremes, or insecurity. It is like a counterbalance to puberty. The confusion and insecurity of adolescence – the erratic behavior, the feeling of loss of control of one's body as new and strange symptoms appear – now resurfaces at a time when women may least expect it.

The adolescent is not sure of her identity. The old familiar life is shaken at puberty as something new emerges. She feels a sense of loss, a burgeoning sense of excitement for what is coming, and a need for understanding and support from family and friends. She is unstable and longs to find a rock of strength in those around her. The changes going on within her awaken a new sense of who she is, focusing her femininity, calling her to become part of a sisterhood with other women. She belongs now to 'woman', to the stream of women going back in time, to women all over the world, to women in the future. She experiences the interweaving strands of this continuity and shares the secrets and confidences that women have always shared.

Decades later when a woman realizes she is entering meno-pause, these feelings she experienced at puberty rise up again, and she is thrown off balance. As an adolescent she looked forward to her life, to becoming an adult, to being a woman. But at menopause she often feels near the end of her creative, productive life. She looks back and considers the uncertain future. Menopause is actually rather a new phenomenon. In past centuries the average life-span of a woman was little more than fifty years, so menopause was one of the signs of old age. Life expectancy has of course increased in the 20th century – people tend to live well into their seventies – so women at menopause still have a third of their lives in front of them. Yet until recently there has been almost nothing in the way of either written or spoken encouragement to help women realize that menopause is actually the gateway to a time of new beginning – of balance, freedom, and wisdom – rather than signalling the beginning of old age.

When I visited a friend in Germany she described the symptoms she had been experiencing. Her whole life had been thrown out of balance: she had trouble concentrating and sleeping. She sweated profusely, hot flushes alternating with chills. Her body felt as though it was burning up at night, so she stood naked in front of an open window to get some relief from the cool night air. These symptoms had been going on for about two years, but had become worse in the last six months. She asked me, 'Why don't we know more about this? Why don't women speak about this to each other? I thought I was losing my mind.' The changes she was experiencing told her she was coming to an end of one phase of her life, and moving into new territory. But she couldn't see through to the other side. She only felt her present discomfort.

Such feelings are only intensified when doctors tell a women that she is 'too young' to be going through menopause, or that the discomfort 'will eventually pass'. The menopausal experience can take many years, anything between two and ten. Menopause actually means the *end* of the years of menstruation; but it is the *premenopausal* period when the body is producing fewer hormones, that brings about the most confusing symptoms. It is estimated that about 30% of women experience no symptoms, 30% have symptoms they can live with, and 30% have intense discomfort which interferes with their lives.

More has gradually become known about these changes – and hopefully this can help a woman become more patient with the process, and help her family understand her struggle for equilibrium.

She is slowly loosening the strong ties her emotions have with her physical body. Her feeling life can therefore become more objective. After menopause she can experience a new feeling of strength and self-confidence, of new capacities to draw upon which will benefit her family, her friends, and her community. She can now use the experience which has ripened over the years to bestow wisdom and blessing upon those around her.

There are three stages of menopause – pre-menopause (or perimenopause), menopause, and postmenopause. Premenopause is the time leading up to the last period. The woman's body produces fewer hormones, her skin-tone changes, her hair may thin; she may have problems with varicose veins, may gain weight and have difficulty losing it, may find herself crying without an obvious reason or forgetting something she knew only a few minutes earlier. When she goes to put the garbage in the refrigerator or folds the towels and puts them in her underwear drawer, she begins to wonder what's happening to her! She begins to worry. 'I can't remember my sister's name. Am I developing Alzheimer's?' She feels estranged from her body.

The physiological basis of menopause

Changes in the blood's hormone levels are the main causes of menopause. The word hormone comes from the Greek, and means 'I arouse to activity'.[1] The hormones act as messengers, stimulating the organs, the tissues, and the body functions.

From the girl's first period until the time of menopause, the hormone oestrogen stimulates the pituitary gland to produce the follicle-stimulating hormone (FSH), which then increases the oestrogen-level, causing one egg-cell to ripen each month. The egg is released into one of the fallopian tubes and then makes its way to the uterus.

About midway through the monthly cycle, when the egg is nearly mature, the pituitary gland begins secreting the lutenizing hormone (LH) which stimulates the egg to leave the ovary. The ovaries also produce the hormone progesterone, as well as continuing production of oestrogen during the second half of the menstrual cycle. In addition, the ovaries produce a small amount of testosterone, the male hormone. Progesterone stimulates the lining of the uterus to thicken, and the blood vessels of the lining fill with more blood so that the lining will nourish the embryo. If the egg-cell is not fertilized, the production of oestrogen and progesterone decreases, the capillaries burst, the endometrium or inner lining of the uterus passes out as menstrual flow. A new process begins.

If a sperm finds its way into the uterus and fertilizes the egg, conception occurs. Within the uterus the fertilized egg grows into a baby.

Each woman is born with a limited number of egg-cells which produce oestrogen until the cells have been used up. Oestrogen production actually begins inside the foetus when it is only 15 to 20 weeks old, and continues throughout life.

At puberty, the increased production of oestrogen in girls influences the development of breasts, the rounded contours of hips and thighs, and the growth of pubic hair. The reproductive organs mature and start to function in their monthly cycle.

Oestrogen also acts on many of the tissues and organs, helping determine height and weight, skin-tone, muscular strength, digestion, heart-rate and circulation. It influences emotional and thought reactions.

The adrenal glands, above each kidney, also produce hormones that break down into oestrogen and testosterone throughout a woman's life. As the ovaries produce less oestrogen, the secretions of the adrenal glands are changed into oestrogen by fat cells. Through this secondary source, the woman continues to receive the benefits of oestrogen for at least 10 to 20 years after the ovaries stop producing it. But less is being produced than formerly, which brings about the changes in her body.

As a woman enters her forties, the amount of oestrogen produced by the ovaries begins to decrease, and to vary from month to month. This process occurs differently in different women, thus causing a variation in symptoms. A woman may have a normal period one month, and no period for the next two months. When she does not ovulate, the ovaries do not secrete progesterone to stop the flow of oestrogen. The increased flow of oestrogen can cause abnormal bleeding and/or stimulate the growth of fibroid tumors. A constant flow of oestrogen also produces symptoms that we usually connect with our period – breast-tenderness and fluid retention. This can result in bloating and tiredness.

When a woman has not had a period for one year she is considered to be in menopause. During menopause the ovaries are no longer working, and therefore no eggs are being produced. Progesterone is no longer secreted, and so the uterus lining does not develop. Because there is nothing to shed, there are no more periods.

The hypothalamus, often called the 'brain's brain', is close to the pituitary gland, and acts as a control center for the hormone 'messengers'. When the ovaries do not respond to the pituitary gland, the pituitary 'starts shouting' and increases its production of FSH and LH. The oestrogen and progesterone levels decrease, and it is through this imbalance that problems occur.

Symptoms of menopause

In general these *can* include skin changes, thinning hair, loss of pubic hair, varicose veins, fits of melancholy, nervousness, irritability, insomnia, depression, restlessness, difficulty in concentration, dizziness, constipation, erratic changes between tiredness and energy, ringing in the ears, decreased sexual desire, feeling of fear and anxiety, crying, forgetfulness, gaining weight, nervous-system changes and increase in blood pressure. Changes can also affect the eyes – diminishing eyesight, problems with contact lenses, burning and itching, light sensitivity, dryness, a feeling of something foreign in the eyes, red lids, swollen lids, eyes feeling tired without obvious reason and a feeling of a film over the eyes. [2]

Hot flushes

The regulation of warmth – which had been connected to reproduction and the menstrual cycle – is now free, as one doctor expressed it, 'to bang around and heat you up, as though calling out, "You must tell me what I'm supposed to do."' Hot flushes occur when the balance of warmth is disturbed. They occur especially in the head, neck, arms and breasts, and can be followed by chills. Coffee, alcohol, stress, and anger can intensify this. Some women alternate between feeling they are on fire and freezing; they are continually taking off and putting on layers of clothing. Dampness from sweating may cause heat-rashes and sores, especially under the breasts. One woman said, 'I thought I finished with heat-rash when my child grew out of infancy. Now I'm the infant.' Our foreheads drip, our blouses become soaked, and we become self-conscious, wondering how noticeable it is. The physiological explanation is that lower amounts of oestrogen make the body less able to control expansion of the blood vessels. These hot flushes can occur once in a while or repeatedly during the day. Usually they last no more than three minutes, and are not dangerous; but they are uncomfortable and disconcerting. Choosing comfortable clothing that is not constricting or can be worn in layers is helpful.

Sweats

The hot flushes that occur at night are called *Sweats*. Because the woman is lying under blankets, the heat and sweat gets trapped and she can wake up feeling clammy and cold. Cotton sheets provide better sweat-absorption and reduce the cold clammy feeling. The night sweats, like the hot flushes during the day, are not dangerous, but they do interrupt sleep. Once the discomfort of the sweats has woken a woman up, she may begin thinking about problems. She may feel a lump in her throat, another menopausal symptom; worry and general discomfort may keep her from falling back to sleep. As this becomes a pattern, she loses sleep and feels tired, irritable, and depressed.

Heart palpitations

A low level of oestrogen can trigger nerves in the heart-muscle when a woman is tense or tired. This can cause pounding, and anxiety about an imminent heart-attack. She should have her heart checked. If heart disease is ruled out she can realize what is actually happening, which reduces some of the anxiety. One woman said these palpitations were like drowning in her own blood, like waves pounding on the shore. This lasted for about four months and caused her attacks of anxiety. It was only years later that she understood what had been happening.

Bodily aches, weakness, stiffness

A loss of muscle strength occurs because of decreased oestrogen levels. Muscle spasms occur in legs, back, and neck due to emotional tension and stress. Lack of exercise can cause swelling in the legs and general stiffness.

Gaining weight

Women have to adjust to the fact that their bodies don't burn food as easily as before, so fewer calories are needed. The weight-gain tends to result in a filling out and thickening of the shoulders, back, neck, waist, and stomach. Even a thin woman will find her stomach muscles weakening and a tendency to a rounder stomach.

Skin changes

The decrease in oestrogen affects the elasticity of the tissue. The skin becomes thinner and more wrinkled.

Metabolic changes

The decrease in oestrogen also affects metabolism. The digestive system slows down, resulting in flatulence, indigestion, and constipation.

Blood changes and heart disease

Oestrogen keeps the blood vessels elastic. As it diminishes, they become narrower and more rigid, increasing blood-pressure. A decrease in oestrogen may also decrease the production of good cholesterol (HDL) and increase production of bad cholesterol (LDL). This can cause the arteries to narrow, and increase the risk of heart pain (angina) and heart attack.

Fatigue

Through menstruation we eliminate toxins in our body. When we don't menstruate we don't feel as vital. Lack of a good night's sleep also makes the menopausal woman tired. She is also often dealing with worry and concern about herself and her family, which adds to her anxiety and tiredness.

During menopause it is harder to maintain good health because the body is out of balance. The activity of the hypothalamus – responsible for balancing body temperature, rate of metabolism, sleep, growth, hunger, thirst, blood-chemistry and respiration – is disturbed by erratic changes in the hormones. It sends desperate signals to the pituitary gland to stimulate more oestrogen production. But the ovaries don't respond the way they used to. The hypothalamus gets confused and cannot regulate the body in the way it had been used to. The woman's immune system is weakened and she becomes more susceptible to allergies and illness.

It is most important during this time for the woman to get rest, time for relaxation, meditation, calm. Avoiding alcohol, coffee and cigarettes is a good preventative, because these raise the acidity level in the blood, which can increase the fragility of bone-structure (osteoporosis).

There are different ways to treat menopausal symptoms. Hormone Replacement Therapy (HRT) is often the first remedy people think of. As far as we know, HRT may be helpful in preventing osteoporosis; but it may also stimulate uterine or breast cancer. No one really knows the long term effects of HRT. The artificial influx of oestrogen does seem to halt the ageing process, keeping the skin tighter, holding off many menopausal symptoms. Homeopathic remedies are also used to treat these symptoms, without any side-effects. Every woman must do her own research and decide for herself how to approach and and treat menopausal symptoms or the results of menopause. Each woman's situation is different. We owe it to ourselves to find out about the various options and discuss them with several doctors.

A woman who has had a hysterectomy that includes the removal of the ovaries usually moves quickly into menopause. If the ovaries are left intact, on the other hand, oestrogen continues to be secreted so that she goes through a more usual menopause-pattern. But because she no longer menstruates, she does not have irregular periods as a cue to premenopause and may not be as aware that her symptoms are menopause-related. One woman thought she was having a stroke or a heart attack when she experienced palpitations and hot flushes. She excused herself from a staff-meeting to look at her face in the bathroom mirror. It was bright red, and she felt anxious for the rest of the day, wondering whether her blood pressure had gone right up. Every surge of tingling in her face and neck would send her back to the bathroom mirror. Over several months this pattern repeated itself, but she never suspected it was connected with menopause. Her physician did not find anything wrong, and never mentioned menopause. Her symptoms persisted and developed into full blown anxiety attacks.

Post-menopause

After menopause, a woman's body has adjusted to a lower oestrogen level. There are, however, some conditions which do not get better. General tissue-elasticity has decreased. Oestrogen kept the vaginal walls moist, thick and elastic, but they now become thinner, shorter, narrower, and less elastic. Dryness of the vagina, which can cause pain during intercourse, can be improved with creams.

A loss of elasticity is also experienced in the muscles, ligaments, and connective tissue. Loss of tone may lead to sagging bladder, incontinence, or uterine prolapse – the uterus drops down into and even through the vaginal opening.

Hair begins to grow in the chin area. This is stimulated by testosterone, the 'male' hormone. Decreased oestrogen provides less of a counterbalance to the testosterone. Hair also becomes thinner and less vital.

One of the most serious conditions in the post-menopause period is osteoporosis. We build all the bone we are going to by the age of thirty-five. A significant loss of bone-mass occurs in the two years or so after oestrogen levels fall. Then it continues indefinitely but at a much slower rate. Taking oestrogen replacement will postpone major loss of bone, but when oestrogen replacement ends the same bone loss occurs that you would otherwise have had at menopause. So you would need to stay on HRT until you die – which isn't the way it is usually prescribed – to solve the problem altogether. The truth is that we still don't really know enough about the relationship between oestrogen and osteoporosis.

The group of women most susceptible to osteoporosis are white women (because of the lower density of their bones), who are petite, have fair complexions, and a family history of osteoporosis. Women who drink heavily, smoke, or are inactive are also more prone to it.[3]

One of the early signs is backache, which may be followed by a fracture after a slight injury. The common areas of fracture are hip, spine, and forearm. Although older men also suffer from osteoporosis, they are usually older when it begins. Once an older woman has fallen and fractured her bones, there is a likelihood this will happen again. The immobility, pain, and deformity caused by osteoporosis leave an older woman in a very difficult position. She may develop curvature of the spine, be hunched over, and barely able to walk. Fractures of the hip or spine may be fatal for such an older woman.

Emotional and spiritual changes

Once through menopause, a woman reaches a new stage of equilibrium. She regains her energy and sense of mental well-being. Mood-swings become a thing of the past. She is able to approach her life with more calm and objectivity. The frantic forties (or fifties) are over. 'We must make an alliance with our changing bodies and negotiate with our vanity. No, we are never again going to be that girl of our idealized inner eye. The task now is to find a future self in whom we can invest our trust and enthusiasm'.[4]

The woman is now in closer touch with her body's needs. She knows she needs to find moments of calm and peace. She knows she must give up habits that are detrimental to her health. She has clear choices to make, and she knows her body responds in a particular manner to the way she treats it. She develops an objective relationship to her body which allows her to see what is needed.

In giving up physical fertility, the post-menopausal woman discovers a different fertility and creativity. She can use her energy to find new ways to work, to relate, to understand. Her sense of identity is heightened and her purpose clearer.

Women pass through menopause in so many different ways. The most vulnerable women are those who depend upon their looks for their jobs – actresses, models, performers. The 'youth culture' of America is very hard on ageing women. It is not so in all cultures:

African-American women in general are more likely than white women to pass through menopause with no psychological problems. Why, I wondered? After speaking with a group of such women, they agreed that African-American women do not measure their femininity and sensuality only by how they look. Nor is their self-worth attached to their age. They don't feel they must look young and lithe. A great deal of a black woman's sexuality is defined by her spiritual strength. Middle-class black women come out of a matrilineal tradition. They have not been as pampered as middle-class white women or put on a pedestal and catered to. Instead, they gain in prestige as they enter middle age. They grow more and more confident. The standard of what is sexually attractive is different so that these women continue to feel desired and attractive in their middle years. What's more, sensuality for the African-American woman is not related to the European-American anorexic body type. [5]

So much of how we feel in these later years depends on our expectations. If we think that once past fifty we are old, old is what we will feel. But each phase of older age has its own uniqueness. A woman in her fifties has very different qualities from a woman in her seventies – both can have much to offer.

It is all to do with keeping active and vital. Sheehy cites the ten-year study by Cecelia Hurwich, PhD candidate at U.C. Berkeley, of women in later life: *Vital Women in their Eighties and Nineties*. The women had remained creative, active and productive into old age. They all had a nonconformist frame of mind, had mastered the art of 'letting go' gracefully, continued to live in their own homes and keep up with the community or worldly projects that had been of interest to them, retained close contact with nature, and multigenerational group of friends. By post-menopause these women had already faced their fears of ageing and death. Freed from those anxieties, they could now contribute their energies, insights, and knowledge to the community.

> Coming through the passage of menopause, they reach a new plateau of contentment and self-acceptance, along with a broader view of the world that not only enriches one's individual personality but gives one a new perspective on life and mankind. Such women – there are more and more of them today – find a potent new burst of energy by their mid-fifties. [6].

209

The expression 'wise woman' has been coined to describe the woman who has passed through menopause and is free of the past. She is now able to realize her talents and pursue her interests. Although she is having to slow down and apportion her time more realistically, she has intense energy which she can maintain over long periods. She has self-confidence and a sense of the new perspectives opening to her. She is more realistic about her goals and realizes something of the innate spiritual dimension of her nature. Her strength comes out of substance and depth. People seek her out for advice for she inspires respect. Her new-found identity shines through her eyes and makes people happy to be around her.

Male menopause

The changes a man experiences during this time are not as obvious. Changes in his emotional life do not seem to have a physical cause, although a decrease in the production of testosterone does occur. Men's bodies age faster than women's, according to British endocrinologist Dr. Katharina Dalton, and middle-aged men do not get the new burst of energy that post-menopausal women do. A man's emotional life has never been so bound to his body as the woman's, and he is likely to have had greater objectivity in his feelings throughout his life. But during this time of change, his relationship to his feelings does alter. They grow stronger, and there are times when he is now at the mercy of them – an unfamiliar experience for him. Women tend to become more assertive and confident while men grow more tender and vulnerable. This can take up to ten years for a man to come to terms with. Not that there is crisis all the time, but high points and low points, usually including one very low, or crisis point. This is referred to as 'male menopause.' It can be a very unsettling experience, and has only recently been recognized by doctors and psychologists as a real condition, since it isn't obvious in the same way as a woman's menopause.

Once the menopausal crisis is resolved for man or woman, a new equilibrium is regained, and each can look forward with new power and perspective to the coming years.

6
Reassessing our Priorities:
49-56

During these years we have a good vantage point for looking back over our lives and gaining perspective. We draw closer once again to our childhood experiences and are able to see our parents in a new way. Interest in our family and 'roots' may become very strong during this time. Why was I born into a particular family, country, nationality or culture? Removed from the personal intensity of the earlier years, we may now be able to understand these connections more objectively, as part of our karma. What have I learned from these experiences? What can I contribute?

Through developing an understanding of our relationships, struggles, and accomplishments, we are able to bring **wisdom** and light to bear on them. One of the benefits we can gain from studying the past is a deep sense of **gratitude** for all that has been bestowed on us. But we should also be wary of losing ourselves in sentimentality.

By the time we enter this phase, middle-age is a fact of life. Many of the strong emotions of earlier stages seem far away and even a bit silly. In fact, it's hard to remember some of the reasons for our disagreements with friends or partners. We find ourselves forgiving those who caused us great pain. It becomes more important to *understand* past events than to rekindle the emotions that once belonged with them, and to make peace rather than hold old negative feelings against people. By now we have worked through many of our previous ambitions, desires, and intentions and can see them from a different perspective. The strong urge to compete has considerably diminished. We begin to value new and different ways of living and relating. Freedom can emerge from all these changes – the freedom to reform ourselves, to be independent in our relationships, to live according to our own values. We can re-assess our goals and outer success with a certain amount of calm detachment and inner well-being – rather than, as we may earlier have done, in frantic attempts to fill a void in our life.

Yet those weaknesses we have not faced and tried to deal with in past phases will now become even more insistent. Unwillingness to look at ourselves objectively and accept criticism will only block our further growth. The longer we fool ourselves and deny responsibility for our behavior, the harder it gets to change it. Our ability to be flexible is decreasing during this period, yet we have an increasing need to hold onto a positive image of ourselves. This condition creates a log-jam in our soul life. New possibilities cannot arise for us until something begins to move. And that 'something' has to grow out of the darkness and depths of our soul life. Our higher ego has to penetrate with its light the darkness of fear and resistance. Our own blockages, the obstacles we have created, prevent us from imagining what freedom from such burdens would be like – we get used to living in fear. It is much easier to hold on to all our anxieties than to accept that we have transgressed – that we have been thoughtless, aggressive, harmful, greedy, selfish, lazy, self-deceiving, controlling, manipulative and so on. In the Middle Ages such behavior was characterized by the 'Seven Deadly Sins' which plague every human being. We modern folk usually picture ourselves in terms of our highest self, what we are striving to become; and the realization that we are actually very far from our aims and ideals can be an extremely painful one. If we have been outwardly successful, we may have discovered that success has not, after all, brought us happiness. So what is really worthwhile in life? We may find that our success has been bought at a price which we now question. We may feel that our colleagues and our family do not appreciate the sacrifices we have made to attain this position. We have to begin to face our past behaviour – where we perhaps justified our actions for the sake of achieving success, or blamed other people for our failures. If we have not achieved the dreams of our youth, we have to face this too.

The big question during this period is whether we will have enough flexibility to learn from the past, or become too rigid and replay past errors. Each attitude has repercussions for our own development and for those around us. If we don't make progress with our inner life and come to peace with it, then the 'mid-life crisis' continues and we are not able to use our energy in a meaningful way or establish equilibrium.

One of the most common symptoms which follow this period of reassessment is a career-change as part of a total change in life-style. Those who have pursued a single career for twenty years or so, may now find it has gone rather stale on them. They may consider new possibilities, usually more oriented to deeper interests than money and success; a secret hobby, an artistic or outdoor interest, a caring profession. Occasionally this means more schooling or retraining at a time when intellectual faculties seem to be waning. We have already proved ourselves in the world yet are now being asked to do it all over again, and at a time when we may anyway be feeling insecure. Making such changes requires a certain flexibility; a degree of risk, financial loss, or loss of position may be involved For this we need a great deal of support from our families and friends.

Often it is the man who goes through this change most dramatically. He is likely in the past to have been the 'provider' of a particular life-style, so changing careers at this point may also affect the lives of everyone in the family. Perhaps he is looking for something more inwardly satisfying or perhaps he wants more security and less risk. The house may be sold, holiday vacations disappear, family savings get used for daily living. The children are usually most affected by this if they are still at home. They are often confused by the changes in their father, and may find it hard to be supportive and sympathetic at a time when they are understandably thinking about their own lives. It is a strong wife who can keep her family together at this time, adjusting to these changes with patience, and nurturing her husband at the same time.

Where the woman has been mainly home-based and feels the need to make changes while a child is still at home, her decision also involves a rearrangement of family life. Everyone has to do more chores since the wife/mother has changed her focus. All the family members are more on their own, and the feeling of being nurtured weakens. On one hand there is more work for everyone to do, but on the other there is pride that 'mom' is paying attention to her own life. It is also quite possible that a wife is preparing for a new life at the very same moment as her husband. The dynamics of this double rearrangement of life-style will also have a strong effect on the marriage. The husband and wife can become a mutually supportive team, sharing their fears and comforting each other as they enter new territory; or they can pull apart moving in opposite directions, now finding little in common with the other.

Usually single parents with children still at home don't feel the freedom to make any radical change until their parental responsibilities are fulfilled. This puts particular stress on a woman who knows she needs to change her life in some way, but feels pressured by her circumstances to maintain the status quo.

If the woman has been at home, keeping house and caring for the children, a change comes when the children leave home. This is often referred to as 'the empty nest syndrome'. This can be a serious crisis if our whole life until then has revolved around our children's needs and an image of ourselves as homemaker. As the children leave, one by one, we may feel abandoned, and unsure of what to do next.

Other women can hardly wait to have time for themselves again. After a period of adjustment to the new situation, they can begin to do something about their own lives. Some people return to school, find a job, start a business or volunteer for community work. Once fears about not being up to it or of being rejected have been overcome, most people begin to feel strength and excitement. Some women, though, go through stress because they feel they have nothing of value to show after twenty years at home. Their skills may be outdated, companies are often not interested in employing women in their fifties: weight problems, wrinkles, health problems or heavy responsibilities at home sometimes make us seem an unattractive proposition. We cannot compete with 'go-getters' in their twenties; but on the other hand we should remember that we do bring a sense of stability into the business-world, which can be very valuable.

Children leaving home can be a challenge to the couple's relationship. An 'empty space' is suddenly there between the man and woman. It can be a delightful experience to get to know each other again, to have time for each other; or it can spell the ruin of the marriage if a couple discovers that their relationship has deteriorated and was only held together by routine and concern for the children.

During this time our inner relationship to our family changes – both to our grown-up children and to our own parents: we more easily accept our children as they are, rather than feeling they 'represent' us. If parents and children have drifted apart, parents at this age may feel the need to re-establish connections, to make up for previous failings. That does not always meet with instant success, and can instead re-open old scars and cause a good deal of pain and misunderstanding. It takes personal courage and clarity to let the past 'sleep' and move forward without casting blame and poking in old wounds. Every little conciliatory gesture on either side needs to be appreciated as a step forward.

If our own parents are still alive, we find our relation to them also undergoing change. We may have more understanding of them than we did in the past. We may seek opportunities to heal old wounds, let by-gones be by-gones. We begin to take a long view of life, which motivates us to heal our relationships. This is not only an outer act: such an intention includes changing our inner attitudes. It means developing patience and understanding and valuing another person's viewpoint as much as our own. It may also often mean caring for an older parent, experiencing the pain of watching a competent, independent person whom we have loved, lose physical and psychological capacities, which in turn brings up questions of how to deal with old age and death. Should we have our elderly parent(s) come to live with us – how will the siblings work out these arrangements between them? Many old rivalries and unpleasant feelings between sisters and brothers may be revived as they work out how to care for their ageing parents. It's not unusual for the moment at which our youngest child leaves home – when the possibility of new freedom dawns – to coincide with having suddenly to deal with the needs of an elderly parent. The deep bonds we have with our parents can be renewed as we see them through their later years.

Becoming grandparents is another major step in our lives. Some of us joyfully celebrate this step while others feel reluctant about it. The connection with our grandchildren awakens our feeling life. It elicits a special kind of companionship that is unlike any other. The younger child and the older adult can communicate in a way that is not always possible between parent and child, though of course everything depends on the kind of grandparent we are thinking of. Grandparents of this present generation don't so easily fit the picture they had of their own grandparents. In today's era they are often busy professional people. Such relationships need to be cultivated over time, through many shared experiences. The great physical distances between grandparents and grandchildren in our mobile society present great obstacles to such closeness. But the relationship that grows out of special efforts is well worth it.

In some cases grandparents find themselves becoming surrogate parents to the grandchildren because their daughters or sons have had their own problems and have moved back home (or never left), or because the various generations are living together. Here, too, we may need to put aside our own needs and meet what is asked of us.

While many people come through this life-phase with equanimity and peace, others are confronted by the question of whether life is worth living at all. They may be hounded by bitterness, jealousy and a longing for past excitement. They may decide to get whatever joy out of life they can, and break long-term commitments in a 'last fling', seeking satisfaction outside themselves. This may be a blind alley – it doesn't really solve the problem of how we face life from here on. Or it might also possibly be a necessary change, one that is apparently immature and self-serving, but which gives us the very experiences we need to embark on inner changes.

The marriage relationship itself is likely to be more relaxed. We are used to each other now and can tolerate small annoyances with humour. Companionship becomes the central element. If a couple can support each other through all the changes that occur at this time, their bond becomes deeper. If one of them is undergoing stress and uncertainty, it is an opportunity for the other to be stronger and more sensitive. Yet it is also a time when years of bitterness and hurt can haunt us. We may walk around with our personal lists of unfulfilled promises and expectations. The temptation is to become ensnared in self-pity.

The physical body is making its presence felt, is less reliable now. Illnesses from earlier times may return with greater strength. We become more careful about diet and exercise. We go to the doctor more often. Our feeling of vulnerability intensifies. We may be more conscious of life and death as we go about our daily routines. We have more to be afraid of than in the past, but also more ability to deal with the fear so that it doesn't paralyze us.

Childhood traumas cause more problems during this period. Early traumatic experiences are woven into the body itself, and in our late forties and fifties the imprint of the fear we once experienced resurfaces as physical ailment. If children feel the world is good and safe, they can develop capacities while being fearless – camping, climbing, etc. Venturing into the unknown becomes an adventure. But if our sense of life and innate feeling of safety has been damaged (through abuse, the death of a sibling or parent, frightening experiences, or shocks) we lose that unconscious sense of safety. Our possibilities in life are limited because fear rules us and we are too frightened to venture beyond the safety of home and familiar places. Such premature vulnerability holds children back from many experiences. Some, though, will become daredevils and take all kinds of risks to overcome it. This is true also of older people – there are those who in their fifties drive too fast, jump out of parachutes, go rock climbing, etc. Some do it for the sheer adventure, some to overcome fear, others because they have made peace and accepted death.

Fear of death can be very intense during this time. People who have had such fear attacks describe them vividly: they imagine dying in an airplane or car accident whenever they travel. On airplanes they immediately check out the emergency exits, look for the emergency medical facilities. Their hearts race, they turn cold inside. When they stay overnight in a hotel they have trouble falling asleep because they are sure they will die in the night.

Others succumb to the fear of death because of changes in their bodies. Sudden appearance of chest pains, high blood pressure, a darkening skin mole, a lump, will send chills down the spine and evoke images of hospitals and funerals. These experiences confront us with our mortality. But what are we actually afraid of? Of pain, the process of dying, death itself, of what may or may not come next? If we are able to work through these fears consciously, we can arrive at a great sense of freedom, and start accepting whatever life brings.

On my 50th birthday I developed pneumonia. All plans to celebrate were thrown out the window as I lay shivering under the covers. During the weeks that followed there were very low points when I was sure I was dying. The worst moment came one afternoon when I was alone in the house and became terrified that I would not make it through the afternoon. I limped over to my neighbor and good friend, and in the weakest, mousiest voice whimpered, 'Can I stay with you for a few hours?' She settled me into her bedroom, armed me with a strong cup of hot peppermint tea, and checked in on me every few minutes. Her warmth and caring helped me come through that terrible afternoon. During my recovery I felt I could not concentrate on anything for very long. The sound of the television or radio was like salt on an open wound. I was supersensitive to everything in the environment. What I could do that helped heal me was to read poetry and copy out my favorites, paint simple color washes of blue, yellow, and red, and to sleep long hours. I never knew I could sleep so much. The following meditation on fear was very helpful and I worked with it regularly:

> We must eradicate from the soul all fear and terror of what comes out of the future. We must acquire serenity in all feelings and sensations about the future. We must look forward with absolute equanimity to everything that may come, and we must think only that whatever comes is given to us by world direction full of wisdom. It is part of what we must learn in this age, namely to live out of pure trust, without any security in existence, trusting in the very present help of the spiritual world. Truly, nothing else will do; if our courage is not to fail, let us discipline our will. And let us seek the awakening from within ourselves every morning and every evening.
>
> Rudolf Steiner [1]

I had other low points when I felt terribly vulnerable, but I was able to work my way through them with prayer and meditation. Day by day I became stronger, yet I still had a feeling of being unprotected and uncertain about life.

A friend suggested that I try writing the biography of my first 21 years. As I began it I could only feel negative experiences looming over me. I remembered what I had *not* had in life, the sadnesses, the experiences that had caused scars. I remember saying to my husband in a most melancholic tone as I began this exercise, 'Oh, I've had a sad childhood'. As I sat in my study and began typing out memories, I had a remarkable experience. I began to see that the sadness in my childhood was no one's fault. Much of it was within my own mind and never shared with my parents. They never knew of my fear of a murderer I had read about in the newspaper when I was five years old. They didn't know of my recurring nightmares after my brother died in an automobile accident. As I wrote about these experiences, others began to push their way through: wonderful, gentle moments, memories of my mother singing her favorite song, of a special teacher, of visiting my cousins in the countryside. I began to feel happiness and enthusiasm, but not yet understanding. As we ate dinner during those evenings I would exclaim that my childhood hadn't been awful after all. As I worked further with my autobiography a pattern began to emerge. I saw that I had been protected and guided in most unusual ways. For example, ours was not a religious family so I knew nothing of God or prayers. But in school we had learned a song about what to do when you get lost:

Remember your name and address and telephone number too.
So if one day you lose your way you'll know just what to do.

The song goes on to tell that we should go to the first policeman we meet and tell him we are lost, but that we know our name and address. It's a rather innocuous song, meant to teach six and seven year-olds the importance of knowing such information. But for me it became a prayer. When I was frightened I sang that song to myself. It filled a need as surely as the most holy words could have done. I felt the protection of a guardian angel over me. As I looked back I saw how special people entered my life just when I needed them, how they brought me gifts of love and understanding. As the days went by and I continued to fill out details of the autobiography, my heart grew lighter and more open. I was filled with appreciation and joy. I bounded into the living-room and exclaimed, 'I had a wonderful childhood'. I meant the word 'wonderful' in its real meaning. I was filled with wonder for the way spiritual forces work their way even into the darkest corners. I made copies of the autobiography, which by now had become a good-sized book, and gave them to my children for Christmas that year.

Through working on my own biography I found a sequence, a progression through three types of experiences – first the facts of what happened, then the feelings about these facts, then understanding them. Often our feelings predominate, and often they have grown one-sided through years of viewing everything from a certain unconscious perspective. When we home in on the *facts* of our experiences instead of the feelings we have come to associate with them, the feelings begin to alter: we realize we have falsely judged someone or misremembered a situation. I came to see this as a helpful way of dealing with current day-to-day problems as well.

In discussing how different men come through the 'Pivotal Years' (from 40/45 to 50/55), Brothers points to three different groups. The first group consists of those who had an unhappy childhood, particularly during the Depression and Second World War. They know how bad things can get and are not frightened by difficult times. They appreciate the stability of a family and home and are not longing to have every desire fulfilled, tending to approach things in a realistic way.

The second group of men have a strong sense of responsibility to other people. They are sought after for advice and guidance, for comfort and perspective. They are kept busy and useful. Their efforts in helping others and in improving the community and the world continue to make their lives meaningful and interesting. They come through these years in a healthy way. 'With both these groups, it is the old-fashioned virtues that seem to keep them on a steady course – altruism, hard work, courage, perseverance, compassion, responsibility, a deep sense of duty.' [2]

The third group is somewhat different. These are the men who never had much ambition, optimism, confidence, or interest in working with other people. In addition, they didn't harbour strong resentments, anxiety, hostility, or frustration. They seemed hardly touched by difficult times: '...the less a man has going for him, the happier he is'. Since they never set their goals very high, not achieving very much in life was not a disappointment. 'It is man's reaching for the stars that tends to make him unhappy and dissatisfied during these troubled years. When he realizes he is middle-aged and probably never will reach those stars, it is a hard blow at a vulnerable time.' To come through these years in a happy frame of mind, though, is not necessarily wholly positive. It is the way in which we overcome our earlier needs and desires that is important for our growth, not that we never had them at all.

It is my experience that women generally come through this period more easily. If they have had children, they are similar to the group of men who 'have a strong sense of responsibility for other people'. The years of caring for children, of being concerned about their health, their friends, schools, teenage boyfriends and girlfriends – in other words their emotional and social development – leave women less focused on their own needs. Because they continue to gain much pleasure and satisfaction from the relationships with their children, their sense of accomplishment is stronger than their sense of failure or loss. This relates to a comment the great anthropologist, Margaret Mead, once made: 'Women can enjoy an irreversible achievement by giving birth to a child. Men have nothing like that. The only way men can realize themselves is through their work'. [3]

Women who do not have children probably fit into groups similar to the ones characterized above by Brothers – those who are strongly goal-orientated, those who are embittered and disappointed, and those who have neither strong goals nor particularly strong feelings.

The challenge of these years is to try to retain flexibility rather than growing rigid and set in our ways. Will we develop new perspectives? Will we learn from experience? Will we find inner stability or get stuck in the way we have always done things? Can we find a rhythm to our lives so that we avoid rushing frantically all over the place? Can we find a healthy balance in our lives? This period is devoted to **finding beauty in the art of living**, to shaping and harmonizing the 'given' circumstances of our lives with what is growing from within our soul and spirit.

Natasha had gone through a difficult time in her mid-forties. Now she felt great strength and confidence. She continued to teach voice. She was sure she was doing what she was meant to do. There were difficulties at times within the marriage. Anton brought up the idea of divorce, but they worked it through and stayed together. When she was 55 he died suddenly. The experience was very traumatic and it took her several years to accept it.

After Fritz's death, and the closing of the clinic when she was 49 years old, **Claudia** experienced a great change in her life. 'I was completely drained from the experiences of the past few years, and I moved into an apartment by myself. The girls were at the end of high school and in university, and they lived close by. We saw each other regularly. I had earlier joined another organization as a doctor and I was with them full-time, but I didn't have the responsibility of a whole clinic. This is when I started a personal life again, especially with Rolf. We had known each other for more than a decade. He had been a surgeon in our clinic and had become a friend. During that time he was having many difficulties at home and the clinic was like a family for him. He brought a change to the whole institution with his skills and personality. He was always there when someone was needed. I had been carrying the responsibility not only for obstetrics and gynaecology, but also for surgery. As Fritz had slowly become weaker, Rolf had assisted him in surgery and took over when Fritz became too exhausted. Since Rolf had left his teaching position in medical school, he set up an office.'

As Rolf was unfamiliar with all the bookkeeping and organization, Claudia was able to be very helpful to him and set up the office. For several years they had a mutually supportive relationship.

'After I closed the clinic, our relationship changed. It was by chance that he and his wife lived close by me. His children were all grown and had their own families. He came over every evening and had dinner with me and then went home. Things were still very difficult at home with his wife, but he didn't feel he could leave her permanently because of her illness. Rolf and I did some travelling together. This was a very new and different kind of relationship for me, but my eldest daughter objected to it. Now that I was responsible only for myself, I could choose what I wanted to do. But now here was this daughter who wanted to cherish forever the memory of her step-father. She and I did not have a very nice relationship during this time.

'For many years the relationship with Rolf was very nice. I was never very sure of him and this was nice for me. I don't like men I am very sure of. Then I had trouble with my heart when I was 52. I was having other health problems as well. Although I went to several doctors and dentists they couldn't find anything. Then when I was 53 we discovered I had severe problems with my teeth. I was transferred to another dentist, Dr. Z., who immediately saw what had to be done. Because of my heart trouble I would have to be in the care of a cardiologist as well.

'That is how I met Dr. Z. This was the most surprising thing. I came in the office and he examined me. He said after ten minutes "All this has to be done. This, this, this. Do you agree or not?" I was so happy that there was someone who for once said, "This is the fact. Would you agree to have this done?" So after three days he started. Dr. Z. did four root canals in one sitting. Afterwards he went behind the chair, (and he does this probably with everyone), and took my head in both his hands and rubbed it gently. At times when he checked up on me I felt and looked extremely awful. Then he would rub my head. I just was melting.

'One afternoon, just by chance, he came to the hospital and checked on me. We talked and talked for hours and told each other things we had never told anyone before. He told me his first name was Arne. The next day he came again. Then three days later I was dismissed from the hospital. When I developed a fever at home I called him when he was on duty at the hospital. He could leave since he had a beeper and said he'd come by to check on me. I opened the door and he opened his arms. I was in them. He laughed and danced with me. He threw himself on the sofa on his back and continued laughing. It was wonderful. Nothing had ever happened to me like this. He was called back to the hospital and as he left he looked at me and said, "This is what I have been dreaming of for 20 years. Why for heaven sake does there have to be an age difference of 18 years?" Our relationship became very intense. I was always trying not to be a mother to him, but I know in some ways I have probably been a substitute mother for him because his mother had died earlier. I was experiencing a happiness I had never experienced before.'

Inci had just separated from Ali and was going through the painful process of divorce and trying to find her own way.

'Of course, in the beginning it was very painful. We had to see each other again and again. We had a house in Turkey which we had to sell. We used to meet outside in a café. It's strange that you meet the man you were closest to in your life in a café like a stranger and you separate like a stranger! Last year he came to visit at Christmas. It didn't hurt to separate from him this time. He writes me letters. It seems he hasn't been able to form a steady relationship with anyone.

'One book opened my eyes very well. It's called *Cassanovas and Their Dependent Wives*. Suddenly I realized that it's like a disease, like an addiction. Before I read this book, I used to blame myself: I hadn't been a good wife. He had to go out to look for other women. Sometimes when I was with Ali I had the feeling that he was expecting a miracle from me. Whatever I did wasn't enough. Nothing I did worked.

'A friend said "How could you fall in love with him? You just have to run away from a man like that". Why am I attracted to that kind of man? I don't know, but I have a theory about it. You know coming from a big family, my mother having so many children, she would have interest in this child, in that child, while she was looking at me. In fact that was something I liked about Ali, that when we were in a group he was always showing interest in other people. I would hate a man who was only interested in me and who was not being polite and sociable. I look at my friend Nina who chooses a man who is always totally focused on her. He doesn't look at any other woman, not even from the side of his eyes. I would find such a man very boring.

'I don't regret the time I spent with Ali. I had some beautiful moments with him, very exciting times feeling like a woman. I never felt like that with other men. We did lots of things. We had creative work together, and he's a nice person. I wish I had never married him, that I never had an affair with him, but that I had him as a friend. It would be fun. He's intelligent, he's charming.

'Now I'm very reluctant to let anyone come and live with me, or get close to someone, because I'd hate it if I'd slip back. I'm not quite sure yet of my own needs. You know, even if I have guests in this house I realize that I ignore my own needs, so much so that I lose contact with myself. If I have guests I make sure I wake up before them to dress, I cannot relax and be myself. I feel I have to take care of them. Until I learn this I cannot get close to anyone. I can't blame anyone. My guests aren't expecting me to do this. But it is the whip inside me. But slowly I'm learning to control myself. I did something I'm very proud of. When my sister and her husband visited me last week, I had an appointment with a hair-dresser. I said, "I'm disappearing for two hours. I have to go to the hair-dresser". I would never have done this before. I have to learn to respect my needs. That doesn't mean not to be a caring person, but there should be a balance somehow. It seems that I can lose that balance very quickly. I don't know if a man feels that way too.

'But this is a good time in my life. Since my separation, my work is much better. First, I have more time and I have a clearer mind, and most of my energy doesn't go into thinking "What is Ali doing, Is Ali coming home, is he not coming home, what time is he coming home?" My sleep is much better. He used to come home at one o'clock in the morning. Especially the last four years with Ali I was very very irritable. I don't know. I hated myself. I have started to like myself again.'

When I asked Inci whether there had been any spiritual influences in her life, she answered 'Through divorce, separation and all the pain I went through, I learned to respect my feelings. Spirituality means to me to trust my own feelings. Perhaps in the past my career as a scientist pushed my feelings into the background, but now I find they help me to make more rational decisions and rational experiments. Rather than just doing, I'm following my feelings more.'

Eva entered this phase knowing she was taking a new step. She was living with the question of whether or not to start her own eurythmy school, and at the same time facing the weakening of her physical and life-forces.

'I think it has now become clear that I must begin the school. I have a wonderful group of people around me who would be the faculty. The students are asking for it. I am still open to other possibilities, but it is looking clearer that I could make at least a four-year commitment. In my fifties I feel I am finally standing on my own feet. I have no obligations anymore. I can really choose to do want I want to do.

'The marital relationship has also gone through changes. I've come to realize that Peter's problem is his own situation. I used to feel I was the problem. I wasn't attractive enough. I wasn't interesting enough. But I have come to see in one way this has nothing to do with me. I knew he had this problem when we married. Reading the book *Women Who Love Too Much* helped me understand this kind of problem more. From time to time there is a problem. I learned last year that he had a thirteen-year relationship with a woman. This was very traumatic. Our children, who had not been involved in knowledge of this in the past, found out and they even took sides for a while. That has been resolved now. But even today when the telephone rings and it's a woman's voice on the phone, my knees get weak.

'I respect his work, his enthusiasm. I enjoy him. We live together and support each other, and we have great regard for each other's capacities. We share the family experiences and the relationship with our children. But now I could live somewhere else and see him only from time to time. I feel I have fulfilled my commitment to our relationship. I'm not interested in having other men in my life. I want to do my work.'

Nigel and Anne had been in Chile for nine years. When Nigel was 50 years old the family returned to England because the children were ready for secondary school and both sets of grandparents were in their 70s.

'Back in England no one knew us. Our parents had all retired to the same town in East Anglia. We were given a parish in a village in North Essex, a village with thatched cottages and an old Norman church. It was very difficult. We realized village life was not for us at all. Eighteen months later we went to the vicar and asked for a change. He suggested different things, but it was not for another eighteen months that a move came. We were in the village for 3 1/2 years.

'Among the possibilities was Cambridge. This was the right thing. We stayed there 7 1/2 years (from the time I was almost 54 to 61). We were happy there. Projects, couples groups, young peoples' groups, the homeless, AIDS counselling. This period took the children through their teenage years.'

In 1984 Evita turned 50. She felt young in her soul, she still had her figure, and she felt good. Her mother, who had been alert and lively to the end, died. Her daughter Beruta was pregnant with a second child. Earlier she had met Herbert in Germany where he worked in the government archives. They began to write to each other and formed a friendship. He was ill. He had had two strokes – one had been ten years before their acquaintance. His wife and two sons didn't allow him to eat with them because he could not eat properly since his stroke. When she learned about these circumstances, she was upset. Herbert was very emotional, frustrated by his physical limitations, and got tired easily. Evita invited him to visit her in Vilnius. He came for a visit, and while he was there her daughter Beruta had a second child. In spite of all of their own difficulties, the family treated Herbert with warmth and compassion. He responded very happily to this and said, 'This is like heaven'. Then she made a big change in her life. She decided to marry him. For several years they all lived together until she was able to secure an apartment of their own.

Evita is still very active in politics, is always fighting for progress. She remembers that when she was a girl of 12 or 13 she had two girlfriends, with whom – although they never did it – she planned to write a proclamation to stick on every tree in protest at the Soviet system.

She also recalled that around this time (1947, when she was 13) her father told her the KGB had shot a man. They didn't bury him, but put a stone around his neck and threw him in the river. In spring when the ice on the lake broke, her father told her to go for a walk along the bank of the river and keep an eye out for the man. She saw something shooting up from the lake and ran home to tell her father. He could not swim, so he gave her the keys to his boat. She rowed around the body and discovered it was a headless man. Her father organized all the neighbors. They retrieved the body and buried the man in the forest. She remembered this event for many years even though she couldn't speak about it.

In 1989 (when Evita was 55) someone tried to shoot her when she was walking from the canteen to her office. It was just before February 16 (the day commemorating Lithuania's first independence in 1918). After the shooting she asked a policeman to look for the bullet. He destroyed the wall the bullet had hit, so there was no evidence of anything. The policeman asked permission to come to her apartment to have a conversation with her. He came in while she was watching television – a program showing a meeting of Soviets in which an organization was protesting about the separation of Lithuania from the Soviet Union. She was very nervous about what had happened and was taking some medicine. The policeman asked if anything was wrong with her health. She replied, 'Everything is all right with my health, but I can't stand seeing such a meeting'. He didn't mention the shooting. She said, 'What are you interested in? Why are you here? You are not a policeman. After what you did to the wall, even Sherlock Holmes could not find anything. You are from the KGB.' Although she was in danger, she felt strong and unafraid of him. There were many such events during these years.

For twenty years **Pavel** was head of the Economics Department in the Academy of Sciences. In most cases a person had to be a member of the Communist party to become the head of a department. But in his case the Council of Scientists decided his work was so significant that the Academy would receive recognition and esteem by having him as head of a department. Pavel gave lectures and made recommendations for changes that would remove responsibility for the economy from the Communist party. Although some of his recommendations were not appreciated by the Party he was not afraid, even when the KGB came to question him. He told them they had to study to understand his special field; or otherwise they could go and ask the Vice President of the Academy their questions. Because Pavel was recognized and respected by high officials of the government and the Party, he could 'spit on the KGB'.

At one point he wrote an article criticizing some aspects of the economy in Latvia. The Communist Party in Moscow communicated its dislike of this article to the Communist Party of Latvia, and Pavel was called in and questioned. It seemed he had criticized some Latvian drainage-methods, but criticism was not allowed. The Latvian Communist Chief was also angry that Pavel had sent the article to a Moscow newspaper without getting prior approval. Pavel and his director were brought before the Council of Ministers and a large audience. The Minister read every word of Pavel's article. Whenever he came to the word 'we' he stopped and said, 'but we didn't say this' and 'we didn't say that'. Pavel was ready to stand up and shout, 'Finish this or I'm leaving'. But he is now grateful to the Director who restrained him quietly and told him, 'Close your mouth!'

Pavel never became a member of the Communist Party – he declined to join in spite of many attempts to make him do so – but he tried to avoid conflict with it. 'You needed to have two faces, depending on whom you spoke to.'

Jerry had been taking risks, organizing talks, holding group meetings. His friends had warned him against it, but he continued. He spent these years in a very active way. He was writing, translating, organizing activities, appearing on television, working with groups of young people, holding discussions. He was constantly busy. He never married, but felt very fulfilled by his work and his activities.

Rosalind

Rosalind's life changed significantly after Jeff's death. She worked full-time with teachers and parents as well as being the registrar of the school. She did whatever needed to be done. She took on major responsibilities.

'I had very good friends, and we did many things together. I had the school, my family, and my friends. I was shy, yet socially I got along very well. These were full years. I worked very hard. My family attitude was "We've had blows in life, but we never let it stop us".

'After Jeff's death I wanted to change my apartment, but it was rent-controlled and I could not afford to give it up. Our house in the country was paid off.

'A few months after Jeff's death I had a dream. The gist of it was that he was there in the house with me. He was going to go outside. I was so happy to see he was well, as he had been in the past. I saw he had a little problem. Then slowly he became more and more incapacitated. It became cold. In the end I picked him up like a baby in my arms and I carried him in. Everyone was there, as at the funeral. In the end I realized he wasn't alive anymore.'

For so many years Rosalind had built her life around Jeff and the children. One day several months after his death she was doing some errands when she suddenly realized, 'I don't have to hurry home. I can even go to a movie if I want.' She began to experience a sense of freedom she had never had before.

Patrick found his greatest strength during these years in his family and in his role as a deacon in the Catholic church.

'I felt I had to devote myself to my family, to provide for my children in whatever way I could. When we had crises, and we had our share, I turned to spiritual help to give me the strength to meet the problems. There is no substitute for placing these problems in the hands of the Lord. It gives you peace, relieves the anxiety. If you are tense, this works against you and you aren't able to think clearly about the problem. But prayer gives me peace and relieves much of the anxiety.'

Patrick said that his role as a deacon had required him to be more conscious of his behavior. 'I can't raise hell now. People are looking up to me.' He found that people seek him out to talk to him about their problems.

Jack heard about a graduate-school program that interested him. The counsellor at the college advised him to go ahead, and he won a scholarship and became a very capable student.

When he was fifty-three, Jack lost his eldest son (thirty-three years old) to illness. He was deeply affected and needed a break from work, so took leave for one year. The support the family members gave to each other helped them all through it. Jack especially appreciated this. The death of Jack's eldest son was a special blow to his youngest son, who had looked up to his elder brother like a father when Jack was away from home, on tour in the military.

While Jack was on leave, he received a call from the City Recreation Department where he had volunteered in the past. He became a Recreation Leader with children from kindergarten through sixth grade. He resigned from his job supervising the maintenance of the community college and worked for three years as a Recreation leader. He loved this work, especially the drama, the cultural awareness programs, the trips to museums and farms with the children. Meanwhile he began doing maintenance in the evenings at an independent school. By now Jack had five grandchildren.

Our friends are moving into a new stage, developing a sense of freedom, changing roles, and finding perspective in relationship to the past. Wisdom and gratitude emerge as new capacities.

Natasha resolves marriage problems and is achieving success in her second career. Her husband Anton has a heart attack and dies quite unexpectedly. She must now find a way to relate this event to her life.

Claudia, free after Fritz's death, develops several relationships and experiences tenderness and caring in a new way. She experiences her femininity after years of stress and worry. Even though she has concerns about the age difference with Arne, she decides to enjoy the happiness of the relationship for as long as it lasts. This is a significant role-change for her.

Inci continues to gain perspective on her life. She is grateful for the good times with Ali although she is happy to be free of the relationship. She is working on herself, balancing her personality, and feeling joy in life.

Eva feels she is finally standing on her own feet. She has fulfilled her obligations and feels free. She has come to peace in her relationship with Peter – she can live with him or do without him. She appreciates their common interests and connection, but she is not interested in putting up with appearances and manipulation. 'I just want to do my work.'

Nigel has returned to England so the children can attend secondary school and college/university. He is looking for the right place to work that suits his and Anne's sense of mission. They devote themselves to service and are intimately involved with the community in which they live.

Evita feels free of her family responsibilities. She forms a long-lasting friendship with a German man. Despite his health problems, she consciously takes on caring for him and they marry. She becomes very active politically: with the break-down of the Soviet Union, Lithuania has the chance to be free. She faces the KGB with courage and defiance.

Pavel is recognized for his significant work and is appointed Head of the Economics Department. He maintains his independence from the Communist Party, though many others in his situation give in and join.

Jerry continues to be active, expanding his activities to include television interviews and public appearances. He feels fulfilled in his life although he never married. His activities are now legal and he is being recognized for his courage and contributions.

Rosalind is finding her new life after Jeff's death. After a dream in which she more clearly accepts his death, she realizes she is free to do whatever she wants.

Patrick appreciates the spiritual help his family receives when they have problems. He finds his role changing as people turn to him for help and advice.

Jack is granted a scholarship to graduate school. He suffers the loss of his son which affects him very deeply. He withdraws as he tries to deal with it. During this time he receives a call to work with children as a recreation leader. He accepts the work and it helps him overcome his grief. He moves into a career devoted to young people.

Dealing with loss, changing roles, finding inner strength, and experiencing freedom are themes we see in this phase.

7

Getting Older, Getting Better?
The Active Years:
56-63 and beyond

There's no fooling the mirror any more so we have to accept that we are now 'mature' adults. Young people look up to us with respect (or compassion), but inside we may still feel as if we're eighteen. We notice that even middle-aged people give us seats on the crowded bus or address us with formal politeness. If we have worked through the challenges encountered in previous stages, many earlier conflicts will have been resolved, or are in the process of being so. We no longer have to prove ourselves. Leaving stormy emotions behind, we relish a new-found peace, calm and simplicity, and can enjoy the respect and confidence we have gained from life. We are living out of the depth of our inner experience and emotional maturity. With the seasoning of our emotional life, another burst of energy pours out in the late fifties.

One of the big changes in the fifties is developing enthusiasm through conscious effort. When we were in our teens, our twenties, and our thirties also to some extent, enthusiasm was spontaneous. As we committed ourselves to causes, followed our interests, gave time and energy to activities we believed in, we could feel the fire in our bellies. We could stay up all night folding envelopes for a political campaign, travel into dangerous places to work with needy children, go on expeditions in jungles and deserts, adopt orphaned children, race around the world on airplanes to attend conferences and nego-tiations. Our bodies cooperated. We could tolerate stress and strain. We seldom became ill, or if we did we soon recovered and consid-ered it part of the price of doing what we knew needed to be done.

But as we get older this changes. It's not that we are less concerned about the world, but we don't get carried away so easily.

Our bodies have become more of a hindrance and our responsibilities at home weigh on us more. And something inside us has changed. We don't get so spontaneously excited by our ideals. The challenge now is to develop a new kind of idealism, what Steiner calls 'achieved or mature idealism'. Now the ego, the 'I' must develop its own enthusiasm: we can no longer depend on outer stimulus for our ideals, but must achieve them through our own effort, and so in a real sense cultivate the independence we strove for in adolescence. Our inner work can allow a sense of goodness and morality to shine out from our soul, as we come to feel the pain and suffering of others as though it were our own. In this phase one of the major challenges is to be truly concerned and interested in others rather than wallowing in our own pain.

If we respond to life with egotism rather than empathy, these new moral forces do not develop. Instead our emotional life takes hold of us, stirs us up and whips us around. We may become much more temperamental, moody, and ill-natured. It is as if the emotional swings of adolescence had resurfaced in a fixed and rigid form; idealism distorts into pessimism, bitterness and self-indulgence.

How do we fathom the great mysteries of life? Am I living the biography I came here to live? Am I worthy of being an example to others? Such provocative questions may stimulate reflection in our quiet moments. At this stage of life we focus on perspective – gaining distance to look back and evaluate, taking the time to wonder, to appreciate, to find joy in simple things.

This period of 56-63 is also a time to prepare for our later years. Retirement can allow us to enjoy life at a slower pace, but it can become boring for men or women who have been very active, especially for the male. There is a proven correlation between death and retirement: analysts have discovered a peak in the male death-rate about two years after retirement. How we plan for this time is important. From 56 to 63 it is helpful to start thinking about what we will do when we retire. Developing new interests (or interests that have been on the back-burner for years), strengthening relationships with family and a few good friends, having a social life so that we don't become isolated, all goes a long way towards an active and creative experience of the retirement years. I'll return to this in the next chapter.

From the forties onwards, and increasingly through our fifties and sixties, we begin to experience a need to transform our desires. Our present technological age presents us with an array of so many interesting, beautiful, efficient **things.** It is easy to constantly want something new that we don't really need. As we get older, though, all the things we have gathered round us become rather a burden, so that we feel an urge to simplify our lives, to shed some of the objects that have followed us round for decades. Or, on the other hand, we may continue to gather and collect more and more, like a squirrel laying up a store of nuts, in which case we should perhaps ask what need all these things are satisfying in us. There does come a point for almost everyone where a surplus of outer objects doesn't satisfy anymore. Of course we enjoy having some old 'friends' around – furniture, photographs, books. But the acquiring stage seems to be past. This is worth remembering when we give gifts to grandparents. A special little gift which will make life easier for them may often be appreciated, but time spent with their children or grandchildren is likely to be even more precious.

My children used to dream up wonderful I.O.U.s for grandma – going for a walk together, cooking her a meal, going to a movie together, making popcorn together, playing cards. I often remember the words of an old friend who told me her husband was very stingy when it came to buying 'things' for his children, but generous in providing experiences for them – camping, going to concerts, exploring places on holiday. He felt that the latter was better investment for their future. As a grandparent myself now, I gain so much more pleasure out of a thoughtfully displayed book of photos of my grandchildren or a telephone call than a piece of jewelry or a blouse. By the time we are in our fifties and sixties, we know the kinds of things we like and it isn't so easy for others to choose gifts for us.

When we look at marriage in the late fifties, sixties and beyond, we find a new quality of **devotion** emerging, whose depth and richness is a metamorphosis of early love, and sheds radiance over our later years. The love of partners and friends has a depth at this period that can rarely be experienced in earlier years when we are orientated so much more towards the outer world. Appreciation and tolerance also characterise this phase. Companionship is the most powerful element of our relationships from now on, whether it be with a marriage partner or a good friend. This companionship or friendship is the anchor that makes all the difference in the way we live, especially with those old friends with whom we have shared years of experience.

During this phase we are confronted by a choice between interest in things of the spirit or superficiality. We need to try to discern what is essential and what is not. Can I see new possibilities? What must I do to bring about necessary changes? We can experience continually new and deeper perspectives. Life becomes ever more meaningful, more precious, more a gift that we can graciously receive.

Natasha

'I look back now and I see that there have been three periods in the life of wife and husband. In the first period there is great love. You don't notice the drawbacks of the other person. Everything is O.K. In the second period you get to know the person better. You still love him, but you notice the drawbacks. This is the hardest time. The third period is when you have overcome all these feelings and come to the conclusion not to be so emotional and react so emotionally about everything. You learn how to forgive, and then you can remain friends. During the 2nd stage I was very self-critical. I felt lonely, I felt insulted, I didn't want contact, I wouldn't talk to anyone about it. Earlier I had been betrayed by a woman friend and so I didn't trust sharing such feelings.'

Natasha realized that in her life the 3rd stage only came after the death of Anton. His sudden death in 1979 when she was 55 was a shock. After his death she couldn't get a good night's sleep for a very long time. In her mind she went through their life together and re-evaluated it. She was examining herself from outside. She realized where she had failed or been at fault, and felt, 'If only I could have thought then as I think now, I would have done things differently'. After his death she started writing poetry about him, and felt his presence around her.

In the Russian Orthodox Church there are three significant times after a soul departs. At the 9th day the soul lives among the living. On the 40th day the soul leaves the earth. One year after death, the soul is at peace. Natasha had a series of dreams which coincided with these times.

'On the 9th day I had a dream in which I saw him. I was walking on the stairs in the Academy. He was in the hall. I came up to him, but in the dream I thought to myself "But he's dead! But he's alive! Maybe I dreamed he died."

I asked him, "Did you come to your classes?"

"Yes," he replied. He was wearing summer clothes.

I asked him, "You didn't die?"

"What are you talking about? Of course I'm alive."

I felt wonderful: "He's alive. It's a dream that he died."

On the 40th day I had another dream. I saw Anton. He came in wearing winter clothes, but no hat. I came up to him, pretty sure he was dead. Yet I wasn't surprised to see him. "How are you?"

"Not too bad, but it's very cold there. That's why I'm in my winter clothes."

"But you died, haven't you?"

"No, this is the second time you asked me. I'm alive."

Around one year later I had the third dream. I saw him. We were sleeping, two blankets as usual, two pillows on our wide couch/bed. I touched him, felt him. "Is it you?"

He had a beard. I felt his face. I said, "I'm here. But you died. Is that true?" I felt his beard.

Then he said, "What's going on? This is the third time you've asked me. I didn't die. I'm alive." The touch was so real. He turned away and left. I saw him leaving. He disappeared. I woke up and immediately I tried to touch him, but no one was there. It had seemed so real. I can still feel his beard. It was around three or four in the morning. I felt he really was there. It was a little scary. I was sorry it was a dream.'

After that Anton appeared in her dreams often. He was always leaving for another woman. Natasha would wake up in tears, realize it was a dream, and feel relieved that it was. Several times she dreamt they were going to divorce. He wanted it, not her, and she was in grief. The suffering in her dream was greater than it would have been in life. After such dreams she would go to church and light a candle for him even though he was an atheist. After Anton's death and after her mother's, she started going to church more often, not to the services, but for inner quiet and to light a candle and think about these two people close to her who had died.

'I don't trust priests. Not all are sincere or even sincere believers. People should communicate directly with God not through priests. If you really believe in something to which you are connected (maybe God really created us all. It can't be proven), then you can communicate with Him yourself. Belief that lives on within you is enough. My relationship with God is personal.

'Everyone has a kind aspect. I believe a person has two cores in her, good and evil, but if a person has a weak character then circumstances can force her to be evil. When a person is growing up she begins to understand and begins to differentiate between good and evil. She realizes it is easier to be bad than to be good. To be kind and good, people have to sacrifice something. If a person has a strong enough character she can struggle and resist something which would lead her to evil. There are two ways in life. One is the hard way, overcoming difficulties. This leads to kindness. The other way is the easy way, having few difficulties. The person adapts herself to life, but doesn't care about others. Our attitude towards life and people begins with which way we choose.'

Claudia was struggling with her new relationship with Arne, a man 18 years younger than herself. What about the relationship with Rolf?

'This was difficult. I was never able to be with two men. I had to finish the physical part with Rolf. So he knew something was wrong. He behaved badly. He had at least ten other women during these years so it was ridiculous for him to be jealous. For years I had been the one waiting for him, and he would either show up late or not at all. So the way he behaved was ridiculous. He became very demanding of me and started speaking roughly to me. I liked to return from Frankfurt to Cologne ahead of time just to have the distance between Rolf and me, because I would not tolerate this behavior any more. We liked each other and understood each other. We could share many other things. Our good friendship came back much later, but first he was terrible. He never knew about Arne. When I had set up my apartment in Cologne, Arne came the next day to help me get settled.'

Their relationship deepened and became more intimate after she started to work in Cologne. Claudia experienced great joy in their relationship. She thought at that time, 'I will never be bitter when this ends'. She was radiant. 'I just flowered. Everyone noticed it. I was working all the time, yet people wondered why I was so bright and happy. Before this I had begun to feel old. Now I was looking young again.'

The relationship ended in a very unfortunate way. 'I knew he had a growing relationship with another woman. He had wanted me to meet her. One day I stopped over at his apartment, and he said, "By the way Thea is coming. I would like you to meet her." I said "You should have told me before. I'm going at once." I never put on any make-up or anything when I was with Arne to look younger. I was completely natural. But knowing another woman was coming I might have done so.'

Then Thea moved in with Arne in 1987.

'This was difficult because she was pathologically jealous. No woman can escape his charm but it doesn't mean too much. She did not know about me. I told myself, "Well, I'm going to take this as long as it's working". And he felt the same. So he came to see me at my place rather frequently then. By the end of the year Thea decided to move out. Arne asked me if for Christmas he couldn't come with me when I was going to Majorca. We had never done anything like this before. He felt so awful because he realized that he wanted to marry Thea, but he pictured her having many children, and that he would become fenced in. So we went to Majorca together. We had separate apartments there. We were not always together during the day, but we did see each other quite a bit. Then he left to go back while I stayed. Then something terrible happened.

'An acquaintance of mine, a woman who had been there at Majorca when we were, and who lived in Frankfurt also, called him and made a joking comment about us, but I didn't know this. Arne called me one night. I didn't know if he had been drinking. For over an hour he told me terrible things. I was weeping. "What are you talking about? People are saying things? You were the one who asked me to take you, I didn't ask you to come." He kept talking. So I started to cry and from January until the middle of the summer I wept much of the time. I had to wear sunglasses. When I was home I would cry all night. I was dried out. It was an awful time. Such a wonderful relationship had such a terrible ending. I knew it would end some time. I had pictured myself visiting him when he was married and had a family, taking care of the children. Now it was all over.

'About a year or so later I went to see him again as a dentist. I started to cry, which was awful. He always treated me completely correctly as a patient. I continue to see him from time to time professionally. He is very nice when I come. He kisses my hand or my cheek. He went back with Thea and married her. He had to promise her never to call any of his former women friends. He could have ended the relationship so differently. It's all right now. If I need some help I know I can call him. Rolf and I call each other once in a while, but our relationship was never the same as it had been. So since January, 1988, when I was 59, I am a lonely wolf.

'I don't think I have been through any serious changes within myself, except that I have become a very sad person. When I left my other job in Cologne to retire, this was the first time in my life I was really alone. I had years of experience when I was not left alone. So I like to be alone, but I don't like the fact that the only people I talk to are the bakers, the cleaners, the butcher. It's a terrible sadness, it's almost dangerous. If it had not been for my daughters and grandchild I don't know what would have become of me during that time.'

Nigel and Anne were living in Cambridge.

'When our oldest child, Nadine, left home to go to college, it was traumatic. I drove her to Birmingham University, took her to the boarding house where a group of young women would live, looked after by the landlady. She was 17½. We said goodbye. I couldn't believe it. We left her there. It hadn't registered in my mind what it would be like without her. On the drive home of several hours, I didn't say a word. This was the initial shock and the beginning of a new relationship with my daughter. Anne had come to terms with it better. She is more extrovert and practical. She had thought it through earlier – what would life be like without Nadine? I hadn't realized how different it would be.

'By 1990 we had accomplished what we had come back to England for. The children finished secondary school and we were with our parents through their last years. We still felt a nudging towards South America, we had left our hearts in Chile. We now felt released to go overseas again. Since I had been with the church 25 years, I had a sabbatical and we went back to Chile for three months; we stayed in the same house there and worked. It was fantastic. We had so many good friends there. But there was no opening. We asked ourselves whether we should give our later years to South America. We made ourselves available, but for a year no offers came.

Then out of the blue an offer came from the Intercontinental Church Society, to be a chaplain in Ibiza (a Spanish island in the Mediterranean). The chaplain was retiring. We were told to go for a week and see the situation. We'd be nearer the children than if we were in South America. We did go. Everything went fine except there were so many retired people. We asked ourselves, "Are we ready to devote ourselves to retired people?" We decided to come. The longer we've been here, the more the scope has expanded. We still serve a high proportion of retired people. In addition, there are about 20 families of British woman who married Spanish men. There are great cultural problems, and very few of these marriages are successful. Disillusionment tends to set in after a few years. If a British man marries a Spanish woman, they tend to go to England. These marriages have a better chance. But with the other situation there are two problems. The men usually don't know much English, and they are Catholic while the woman is usually not.'

Nigel and Anne began a couples group, providing a non-threatening situation in which problems could be shared, with meetings once a month. They have a potluck for the first hour, then discuss a topic such as: Christianity and other religions. Now they have begun a children's group in response to requests. They give two non-communion services a month and two Anglican services. They have been quite happy in Ibiza, but now a big decision awaits them. With the Anglican Church's decision that women can be ordained as priests, Anne is thinking of going for ordination. Nigel had thought they'd stay in Ibiza until he was 65 and then retire from the parish, but still offer work. It looks as if Anne's decision means a move back to Cambridge as a base for the next stage of their lives. They will leave Ibiza when Nigel is 63.

Nigel and I were discussing some of the big changes in his life. Getting married at 35$^{1}/_{2}$ presented a great challenge.

'I had been a bachelor, set in my ways, independent of my family. It was a shock. I had always wanted to get married, but I hadn't found the right person. I knew right away that Anne was exactly the right one, but I had to learn to share and yet have an independent life within the marriage context. I had to learn that we could do things together, but we needed to keep our own hobbies. Both of us love classical music, but we didn't play an instrument. Anne likes rock and roll. I've learned to tolerate it. Anne learned to play guitar and chirango in Chile. She loves to paint and draw. I love ornithology. We both like tennis. On our day off, we combine these. We drive to a part of the island. I go birding. She sketches, draws, or takes photos. Then we have a meal together in a restaurant. Respecting each other and finding a balance between our individuality and our life as a couple has been the most important challenge.

'My parents were very close to each other. Both of them loved tennis and classical music. They taught us that there is a basic need in the pattern of human institutions – man and woman need each other. There must be a physical as well as a mental and intellectual attraction. They have to be able to think on the same wave-length. Family is very important to me. I can't possibly think of marriage without children. The family gives children a stability; children give marriage stability.

'As we think about our later years, Anne has plenty of time ahead of her. I'm in very good health and can still serve. There is no way we can retire to where the children will definitely be living.

Their jobs may take them to different places. Nor is retirement only controlled by nice climate and an easy life. We have seen retirement as a time to be picking up on our relationships with our friends as well as serving the needs that come up. Cambridge is the place where we have many good friends. Very few are members of our church. Friendships within the church can cause jealousy within the parish, and in our training we were told to avoid that. Our friends are in the age-bracket of 50-65. We can get old together.

'I've had several moments when I felt I had met my destiny. These were connected to my relationship to Christianity. First there was an experience when I was eight years old. I was brought up in a Christian family, but wasn't committed to it. I realized that although I was part of a family, I had to make my own relationship to God. God loved me and I was special as a person. My family had gone to the beach at Filey, Yorkshire, for a holiday. We came across a beach mission, with a pulpit and pews made out of sand. University students were running the mission. I saw it as attractive and wanted to listen. My parents said they'd walk on and pick me up on the way back. I listened. "Christianity is all about people who make a point of decision to receive Christ into their life; others do not. That is the difference, there are not good people and bad people, but those who have received him and those who have not received him." Then he continued: "Tomorrow I'll put a little box here. You can write me a note, tell me who you are, if you like." I did. He came to visit me and I made a conscious decision to become a Christian.

'The second time was the call to ordination. I was not living an unfulfilled life; on the contrary, everything was wonderful. I was doing useful work. I loved my three tracks – weekends in the Christian ministry, weekdays working in the hospital, and with teenagers in trouble. But God called: "Put this aside so you can get special training for ministry." First comes the Call and then comes the Testing. God had been preparing me for something I didn't realize, somewhere else. At various times I have been very conscious of God's presence. When things have been hard, for example, that time in Chile, I have said, "Well, God called me here. I am being tested. I can't go back on this call. God got me here and is using me." In my own human strength I couldn't have attempted the work in Chile with three young children. I am a homebody, I love my home and family in the UK. Yet there was this call. But God doesn't let a person down. "WHOM GOD CALLS, HE EQUIPS" is very telling. He's enabled me to rise to the call.'

When **Evita** looks into the mirror she is pleased with herself. Even though she has put on weight since she had a hysterectomy, she accepts her age. She would not want to be a girl of 30. Two days ago she saw herself in a video and realized she had become a little older.

'Every period of life creates its own beauty. It creates a new space for the human being to live her life. In this space, the first place was reserved for my family. All the rest of the space was filled with politics.'

Evita's bravery continued to show itself. The following is one example of this:

At the beginning of the Second World War a terrible tragedy occurred. There was a prison beside a pine wood in Lithuania. The German army was approaching, and on the last night before it arrived, the Soviets brought seventy people – teachers, farmers, and students – from the prison into the pine wood. They didn't shoot them because the sound of guns would have been heard, but bludgeoned them to death with guns, and left their bodies. On 23 June 1941, the Germans arrived and people told them what had happened. The Lithuanians took away the dead bodies to bury, photographed by the Germans. Parents buried their dead adult children in graves and put monuments and flowers there.

In 1945 when the Soviets returned they leveled the graves and monuments. If anyone so much as breathed a word about this massacre being the work of the Soviets, they were taken to Siberia. The KGB said the Germans had done it. Evita was a child at the time of this atrocity, and was told to stand in the meadow while her parents went to see to the corpses. She could hear the women weeping at what they found. 'We could never tell the truth about this tragedy,' she remembers.

In the terrible days of Brezhnev she told many secret things to people, but discreetly. At her office she told some trusted people about what had happened in the pine woods. When independence was regained, a newspaper reported the truth about this tragedy. Some of her colleagues at work came to her, kissing her, crying because she had been courageous enough to tell them the truth when she could have been imprisoned for it.

Although independence was proclaimed in 1991, the KGB was still strong. She wrote a long text about this atrocity for television, but such things were still not allowed to be broadcast. The only mention of her text was an announcement on television that she had written a letter which had been passed to a museum at Kaunas. A little while later she received a letter inviting her to a strange meeting, which she felt was probably a KGB ambush. It might have come from one of the perpetrators of the crime, or at least from someone who wanted to get rid of her. Evita was the only person still alive who knew about the KGB connection. She didn't go.

How was her marriage with Herbert progressing? They became close companions. 'Young people marry for love. I remarried because I was afraid of loneliness. In spite of his illness, Herbert has a good heart. We have had a very difficult time financially. For two years he did not receive his pension from Germany and nothing from Lithuania. He had nothing, not even clothes. I bought clothes for him. I had said in the past, 'I don't want to marry again'. So what did I do? I married a poor and a sick man. But I trust him.'

Evita became very active in an organization fighting for Lithuanian independence. When she spent days and nights in Parliament, Herbert never tried to stop her going, even though her life was in danger there.

On January 13, 1991 sixteen people were killed at the TV tower. The day before, Evita had been at Parliament. In the evening she couldn't stand it any longer and had returned home, her feet badly swollen. She and her son-in-law had planned to go to the Parliament building. As she lay on her bed, the shooting started in the city center. She telephoned her organization to say she was coming, but they told her not to come to the TV tower or to the House of Parliament. She could do other things to be helpful. She could telephone the German Embassy in Moscow since many of the telephone lines were cut (and all radio and television communication had been cut off). Evita called Moscow to try to give the world objective information about what was happening. She asked the German ambassador to communicate this news to Edward Shevardnaze and to ask him to pass it on to Mikhail Gorbachov. Two days later lots of announcements and statements reached her, written by Boris Yeltsin and Landsbergis, asking Soviet soldiers in Lithuania not to shoot Lithuanians. But at that time Yeltsin was not yet allowed to speak on TV to make his plea.

So Evita and Herbert went to the Soviet army base in Vilnius to pass on these pleas to them. Since Herbert was not Lithuanian it was thought best for him to remain outside, on the corner. Evita offered Yeltsin's statements to the soldiers and they invited her to come into the base through a special gate. She went to a small window where a Soviet officer sat, greeted him and told him why she had come. He did not want to accept the documents through the window. 'Come in,' he said. Although she was afraid, she went in. She greeted him and asked him to distribute these statements and pleas among the soldiers. Leaving the army base, she couldn't even feel her legs for fear. Herbert, himself very frightened, waited for her at the corner.

Six months later, in August, 1992 the Putsch occurred. Evita had spent all night at the House of Parliament, listening to the radio. Very early in the morning she heard that Mikhail Gorbachov had been taken away. Something was going on in Moscow. She called the Prime Minister, asked him to wake up, saying that something strange was happening. Then she spent all day and the following night at the House of Parliament. People streamed there from all over Lithuania, many even sleeping on the grass. The Lithuanian Independence Army gave an oath of allegiance to fight for Lithuania to their last drop of blood. There was no fear. Priests were there. People were on their knees praying to God not to forsake Lithuania. The House of Parliament is near the bridge, so when Soviet tanks rolled from under it the sound echoed all around, increasing people's sense of dread.

The next day Evita was given more proclamations and asked to distribute them to mail boxes in the apartment houses. Herbert helped her carry these heavy stacks of proclamations. In one of the houses, a door opened, and a Soviet officer came out and asked sternly what she was doing. 'We brought you some letters,' she replied. He tried to take all of her pile, shouting he would shoot them both. As they went down the staircase, he followed them shouting.

'Herbert and I went to another house, but now we left if someone opened a door. We were very frightened while we were doing this. We returned home and had some coffee. Then I went alone to the District office.' They offered to have one of the men from the office accompany her this time, but when he heard it was dangerous, he refused. She asked him to at least help by folding the leaflets for her to put in post-boxes. She started off alone, but then he followed after all and joined her. They were now much more discreet as they went from house to house, and although they were afraid, they managed to finish the job, and then, trembling, ran to her house. Herbert made coffee and they calmed down. When she meets this man today, he says, 'Good day Partisan, when will you be given a medal?'

When we spoke about these events, Evita emphasized that she had not done everything alone, but was a small part of a large movement. All Lithuanians had had a share in it – everyone did what they could at that moment. Some, for instance, brought food from home to those at the House of Parliament. There was an enormously strong sense of brotherhood. 'If they could gather all our tears it would be an ocean.'

Evita has hope for the future. She sees that Lithuania is now part of the wider world and must always be so.

'This temporary government is not forever. It is like a ribbon from the Soviet period that will vanish. Time will correct it. The new generation will go on and see the world through other spectacles.'

But she is concerned about the stress on families. 'When a family is stable, then the land is stable. Then children can see what is normal and from that they can build the future.' We must help children understand why we live, to treasure the past, to plan for the future. They must know about ecology.

'Existence is not life. What we had was existence. People had no minds of their own. They couldn't think for themselves. Now it is very difficult for these people. Many parents are letting their children do anything they want as part of the new democratic way of life. But children must have moral discipline. They must know there are certain things they can do, and other things they cannot do. They should not feel they can do whatever they like. I am older. My time is the late afternoon. The next generation must take over.' As Evita says this, her blue eyes sparkle. She is filled with enthusiasm about life.

Pavel retired from the Institute and then joined a new Institute in which he worked with computers to solve various economic problems. When he was 61 he retired completely from his profession.

He has always been very active. He considers himself a serious player in life, whether the game is chess, cards, economics, infrastructure planning, or business. He likes to test himself with challenges. Another interest has been collecting mushrooms for medicinal purposes. A friend of his was collecting and processing specific mushrooms for this purpose. He was approached by the KGB who told him, 'Leave the country or go to Siberia'. (Only the State, not private individuals, were allowed to be involved in medical research.) He left Latvia for New York. Now that such activity is finally legal in Latvia, Pavel is pursuing it as a business venture.

Jerry sees this time as a turning point. He is 62 years old. He says he has been having more inward experiences, and no longer has so much interest in the outer activities he had been pursuing for the last fifteen years. 'I suddenly feel something is dead for me. I won't invest any emotional or intellectual energy in something which a week ago was interesting. I will resign from the presidency of the two clubs I organized. The finger of providence is pointing to me, saying "Do something else. Do intensive inner work".

'I feel I have fulfilled the task life gave me. I collaborated with all my heart. Now I must concentrate on my own inner life, in harmony. Now I am looking for the possibility of publishing some books I have written. These are four books from the period 1959-84. I am writing about a subject which has always fascinated me – evil.'

At times Jerry does reach a low point and suffer from depression. At those times he feels 'We are prisoners in this evil and stupid world. We live in a nightmare.' In a more reflective tone he says, 'The only thing that has sense is the awakening in the holy other, in the highest and good God. I live in eastern Europe. We always have the luciferic impulse from the east as Dostoyevsky shows in his book *The Brothers Karamazov,* in the scene with Ivan and the devil, and in the tales of children suffering.'

Recently a young artist from Crakow came to paint a serious portrait of Jerry. He said he was painting people who had successfully mastered 'self-realization' processes. Jerry asked the painter how he knew this about him. The artist replied, 'Well, I've read a lot of things you wrote'.

'In this period in my life', he says, 'I have an opportunity to look back and to judge my life. Now the question is, what is the future? I have no definite answer. I have a friend who has prophetic powers. He came here and looked at me. Sometimes he's able to tell when a person will die, and it makes things not so happy. But I like to know it. I'm not afraid. I could plan better if I knew it. If what he says is true, I have some time ahead of me as long as I preserve a healthy mind. I have plans. I would like to write a series of things. I want to write about the Cathars and about the question of evil. There is so much that I'm interested in.'

Rosalind worked in the school for the next ten years. 'I saw myself being on a track, going back and forth between the city and our country house. At the school a new generation was taking over. The younger people needed to be in charge. I realized I needed to make a change but I wasn't adventurous. I thought I would just move and have only one home. It isn't great to grow old in Chicago. I wanted to experience living all year round in the country, and my children and grandchildren were living there. It wasn't only family reasons that drew me. However, it is true that my children often asked, "When are you going to leave the city?"

'I was realistic about the situation. There was no job waiting for me there. I figured I'd find some kind of job, maybe as a salesclerk in a store. I thought with the house free and clear I wouldn't need much money. I was 59. I told myself, "I'll make it". I was not afraid of having no money. But I wanted a year off to digest everything. Right around this time my old friend and mentor came for a visit. We had a long talk. 'Maybe you've really done what you could do for the school' he said. He didn't advise me. He just made an observation. No one ever told me what to do. They always made me decide for myself.

'During this time when I was considering my next step, I was at a meeting one day. A specially fine music school was asking for an experienced teacher to come and advise them. A friend said, 'Rosalind can do it'. Could I? So I became a consultant to that school. Never in my dreams did I think of this. It was the beginning of a new life in so many ways. I had never travelled. Now this was like a free ticket to travel. It is amazing what happened. I spent a month at that school. Through word of mouth I was invited to other music schools. A new career began. This demanded new aspects of me, there was nothing to hide behind. I had to do public speaking although I was shy. I had dormant capacities and now they were called on. 'Do I know what I'm talking about?' I asked myself. The work I had done for so many years in the school helped me. I never looked at it leading to this back then.

'The first time I was terrified of making all the arrangements, of taking the airplane. But I came into the modern world. I came with a friend at first, then by myself. I began to get to know myself. A friend of mine has someone make all her arrangements when she travels. I have never had someone else to take care of everything. This person doesn't really exist. So I told myself, "Why wish for that? This is another illusion."'

Patrick

Patrick's sources of satisfaction continued to come from his family and his work as a deacon. He reflected that some people in the ministry are not happy, but for him the spiritual life was the basis for everything else. His wife's continued interest and involvement in the Church provided a strong common foundation for their relationship.

'When I was sixty the doctors discovered a tumor on my brain. I had to have surgery and radiation. When we knew we had to have the operation, my attitude was, "Let's go do this". I preferred radiation to chemotherapy. After I had my head shaved, Martha and I went out and bought a wig. I went to work and then to the hospital. The doctor asked me to talk to another patient because he thought I had a good attitude. This man was proud. He couldn't face losing his hair. I told him I was getting used to the wig. I said, "You really owe it to your children. You've been helping them all your life. Let them help you. Give them the opportunity."

'I felt graced to help others. Personal witness is the best prayer. I speak frankly and say where I'm coming from. My attitude is, "Let's do what we have to do and get it over with and maybe help someone else along the way." When I was on the operating table the nurse asked me about my ring (which has symbols of the Father, Son, and Holy Spirit). I explained it to her. Two weeks later I was giving communion and there she was. I believe if you have had God with you in the early days of your life you are more at peace later on. I've heard the saying: "It is hard to live as a Catholic, but easy to die one".'

Jack changed jobs and went to work as a teacher in the Youth Authority. Here he taught young people who were incarcerated for having committed dreadful crimes. They had had no guidance in their lives. Jack taught business management, cultural awareness, and employment skills.

As Jack looks back over his life he sees that the most difficult challenges were being away from his family in wartime and having his son pass away. 'You think your kids will outlive you. Other than those difficult times, there have been down times, but always someone picked me up. One of the most instrumental things has been that my former wife and I have a good relationship. We all get together regularly, and we are still like a family without getting in each other's way. She always supported me as Dad. There were never limits or formal visitations. Family was the center of our lives. Three out of my four children went to college.

'The strength of my life was the church. I still go to church every Sunday. I work with children to have a drug-free society. We men in the church work together. My focal point is to help the youth. There are a lot of lost youth who need male role models. We cannot expect athletes to be their role models, we have to be that ourselves. If we want to have a drug-free society, the adults have to react and show better things to do. Kids have too much idle time. They need more programs. We have to spend more, to invest in them. The community is the mainstay of society. It is also the catalyst. When I look at what has happened, I just don't know. People have become complacent. I don't think the advances have been used to the fullest. We need education and moral faculties. If you live in an immoral society, you will grow up that way. Parents are the key.

'When I grew up I didn't have everything, but I had food and clothes. If we got a bag of oranges or apples at Christmas, we were grateful. We shared what we had with our neighbors. We were not self-serving but looked for what we could do for each other.

'Have I changed? To some extent. I have grown more than I've changed. I rationalize more than I did as a youngster. I constantly strive to understand people. My mother used to say, "You give more of yourself to everybody else and neglect yourself". If I didn't do that I would hate myself. My personal ethic is I do what I enjoy as long as it doesn't hurt anyone else. People don't have to like me, just respect me.

'I'd rather put a smile on my face than a frown. I like to meet people at the crossroads and go the same direction, sharing our thoughts. I find myself always trying to be a piece of the puzzle with the people I meet. I love nature. If it rains and I'm getting wet, it isn't a problem. It's beautiful. Someone above me created it.

'My outlook is to be able to walk down any street in any town in any country and say hello. That's why I came. I like to communicate the feeling that I care. I have never been disappointed by this attitude. I have met interesting people, and I haven't been offended. I go places others wouldn't go, and I always find someone with whom to share. I hope to live a long time and be able to tell some of my stories to my grandchildren.

'What's most important to me is to make an impact on youth, to guide them. We have to set an example for kids to follow. If I could save one kid from being lost, it's worth all the effort.

'I've always worked with youth, even when I was in the service. My son does that now. When I began working with incarcerated youth, that was a new challenge. There are many gang members there, and at any moment they can clash. Kids join gangs for security. Gangs let kids know 'If you'll be one of us, we'll protect you'. At the Youth Authority the young people have a good place to sleep and three meals a day. This is better than being on the streets. Some don't want to return to the streets.

'Last summer I returned to Mississippi for a bi-annual reunion of my hometown. Twenty-five hundred people showed up. We asked ourselves, "How did we survive?" Kids today don't feel they'll live past twenty-five. Today the town is integrated; the mayor and chief of police are black.

'But we can't live in the past. We have to put old things away and go forward. Southern cities are integrated today, there are many black businesses.

'What happened? Everyone's rushing. There's pressure to dress a particular way. Everybody wants to belong, not to be an individual. What's it going to take to change things? Will it take a war? I don't know if we know too much or we don't know enough. When I was young, no one would laugh at you if you helped an old lady across the street. Today they rob old ladies. A good upbringing is the main thing. But what recourse does a parent have? We got whippings. But today that's considered child abuse. My uncle would have been put in jail. The legal system has to look at itself.'

Jack finished our interview by telling me he met his step-sisters and step-mother last summer for the first time. His father died in 1965. One of his brothers is a preacher, the other a farmer.

It was a special privilege to speak with these friends at this phase of life. I was deeply moved by their commitment, their clarity of what is essential in life, and their courage.

Natasha had a continuing connection with her husband through her dreams. She turned to spiritual life to strengthen the relationship. She went to church to light candles for him and nourished a personal relationship to God. She continues to work teaching singing at the Academy of Music, and is devoted to her students.

Claudia had a very difficult time as the relationship with Arne ended in a painful way. She feels sadness and loneliness as she tries to find a balance between being alone and being with people. She feels joy in her freedom, but also wants to feel needed. She has retired from her medical career, but continues to do part-time work so she has the financial means to help her children and afford traveling.

Nigel and Anne had been devoted to their aged parents who have all died during this phase, and to their children's adolescent years. Now they are free to go wherever they wish. They accept age and enjoy the prospect of growing older together. But they feel they still have much to offer, and look for their next place of service. They work on giving each other space and respect in their relationship as each has special interests and needs.

Evita accepts her age and the physical changes that have occurred. She is retired from her job and has decided that the central issue in her life is politics. With husband Herbert's support, she devotes herself to revealing the evil doings of the KGB and to helping Lithuania maintain its freedom. She and Herbert enjoy the preciousness of life and bring enthusiasm to it.

Pavel has retired and now devotes himself to many interests, including collecting mushrooms for medicinal purposes. He is active and interested in life.

Jerry has decided that after fifteen years of being very active outwardly, it is now time to turn inward again. He feels he has completed the tasks he came to do and is now free to work on his inner life, on writing, on contemplating the big questions of life.

Rosalind felt a change was coming. After a significant talk with her old mentor and friend, she took the risk of giving up her job without knowing where the next dollar would come from, moved out to her country house, and waited. Soon the answer came, and a new career unfolded – that of consultant. This challenge has made her develop new aspects of herself. She has learned to travel independently and meet many different people. She is devoted to her work and to the human relationships that have developed. She has a wide circle of dear friends as well as close relationships with her family.

Patrick has experienced the challenge of brain cancer and had to face the possibility of death. His spiritual life sustained him and he felt the preciousness of life even more strongly after recuperating and being able to help others.

Jack is devoted to strengthening the community in which he lives. He is active in church, is devoted to helping young people, treasures the closeness of family, and enjoys the beauty of life, of nature, and of the goodness of human beings.

8
Looking Back, a Different Perspective: Beyond 63

Old Age is not an illness, it is timeless ascent,
As power diminishes, we grow towards more light.

In *After the Stroke*,[1] May Sarton writes:

> When I was ill I resented that I had some years ago called old
> age an 'ascension' (see quote above) in an essay which
> appeared on the Op Ed page in the Times. It did seem too
> ironic for words, but I believe there is some truth in it as I go
> back to it now. The ascension is possible when all that has to
> be given up can be *gladly* given up – because other things have
> become more important. I panted halfway up the stairs, but I
> also was able to sit and watch light change in the porch for an
> hour and be truly attentive to it, not plagued by what I 'ought'
> to be doing.'

Some people experience a sense of liberation during these years. We
let go of the demands life has made on us until now, and allow
something new to come about. But that does not mean, of course,
that we have no pain or suffering. Most of us experience unpleasant
aspects of ageing, but we *can* find a source of help and healing in
this phase of our lives if we consciously prepare for it.

> What I feel I have come to understand is really simply this:
> none of us has any choice when it comes to getting old. It's
> above all else a fact of life. There are surely some pleasures left,
> but also plenty of tough challenges, often coming at a time
> when we feel least equipped to face them. Old age is about
> courage; it is about making the choice as to whether or not to

be defeated by ageing or to live out one's remaining years with style. Looking back, I guess my whole life and certainly my work have been devoted to the idea that human beings have incredible and thrilling potential and that the goal of our lives ought to be to come as close as possible to fulfilling what is so unique and remarkable about each of us. [2]

The years after 63 are often called 'the golden years'. We are no longer hounded by ambitions, possessions, or personal desires. We know what is important to us and we can appreciate the special times when they come. As one 68 year-old woman said, 'Every day there is one good moment. That is enough for me.' It becomes more important to be needed than to need. Many qualities that arise during the previous period (56-63), also hold true for the years after 63. In some ways we are now freer than we have ever been. We have a wealth of experience and a life-time to look back on, which can provide us with new understanding and gratitude. The following is the sort of train of thought which may help us to move forward in a positive direction:

You are now on the point of entering a period during which strange things will be happening to you. Perhaps you may feel that everything in your life is drawing to a close, and because the present does not succeed in satisfying you, you may feel the urge to return to your past. You will be inclined to cling to memory pictures that have remained within you from the past, and these may now well up in you with more force than ever. Many past things will take on a golden hue. But you must not allow yourself to be depressed by the gentle sadness of self-pity because of what you have lost and is now no more. This would be of no help to you, and would indeed hinder you from achieving a worth-while old age. You ought indeed to examine your past carefully, but only for the purpose of understanding the true reason for events. Do not lose yourself in sentimental reveries. This would not lend you support any more than indulging in regrets for what you have lost. Only complete sincerity in your self-examination can help you. [3]

This is a time when we can review and evaluate our lives, recognize moments of truth or moments when we avoided the truth, moments of courage and moments of cowardice, and so come to know and understand who we are. We can appreciate the people who benefitted us, who affected our lives and helped us along. We can also look at our enemies in a new way, perhaps seeing what led us into conflict, or to a change we made in our lives because of it. Perhaps we can go further and forgive our enemies, even love them.

There are things we can do that will help us face the challenges of these years. We have to let go of our attachment to our physical bodies, to our image of ourselves in the prime of physical life. The wrinkles are there as are the changes in skin and in muscle tone, the changes in physical balance and in our capacities to hear and see. Fear of growing older only causes us to put off working with the ageing process and using it in a positive way to develop inwardly. We may try frantically to stay young with creams and magic potions, but sooner or later we must face the inevitability of these changes.

Transformation of our senses

As we age the nervous system becomes less flexible, the walls of the arteries harden, causing the brain to receive less blood. Both soul and body have a tendency to grow stiff and rigid. If, however, we have continually been developing higher qualities of patience, interest, love, devotion, and equanimity, we can draw on these treasures in our later years. According to Rudolf Steiner we do not perceive the world merely through five senses alone. He speaks of twelve, and we could well add a thirteenth – a sense of humor. The twelve senses are windows on our inner and outer world.

In childhood our senses develop gradually through what they receive from the environment. Slowly they become capacities. In old age the sense organs weaken and lose their vitality, so that we have to replace outer stimulus with inner activity. As we cultivate higher soul and spiritual qualities, we not only replace what has been lost through the ageing process, but also open up new paths and possibilities for ourselves.

We know how important the *sense of touch* is for the child. Those who are held are healthier than those who are not – as has been found in orphanages and AIDS hospitals. In one hospital arrangements have been made with people working close by to come in during their lunch hour to hold and rock the babies. These babies are calmer than the others. The sense of touch invigorates, stimulates a response, a relationship. The physical act of touching goes beyond evoking a physical response, activating life-forces and calling forth a response in the soul.

The sense of touch is also life-giving for old people. Even though their movements may be clumsy, it is valuable for them to engage in craft-work or music – to knit, crochet, spin, sew, sand wood, or play an instrument. If an old person can stroke a beloved dog or cat, this works wonders in their feeling of contact with the world, with being needed, with participating in life rather than withdrawing from it. The transformation of the sense of touch is a *feeling of reverence* for what is around us.

We become aware of our **sense of life** when we feel nauseous, congested, fatigued, or just not right. It communicates to us that something is out of balance in our physical body. Old people have the tendency to become over-sensitive to every ache and pain, to focus on themselves so that everything revolves around how they feel. The more they indulge in this, the more they feel the brittleness of their bones and the sagging of their tissues. When they can become selfless, *making or doing something for someone else,* they are freed from the prison of their own body and can achieve calmness and equanimity in their soul lives.

We develop the **sense of movement** as children: we slowly master our limbs, first crawling then standing upright, then learning to run, skip and jump. Overcoming the pull of gravity allows us to feel *free* to accomplish deeds in the world. As we age, however, and bones and muscles deteriorate, our movements become weaker, and we lose some control over our limbs. It may become frustrating to walk down the street to mail a letter because our legs ache so much. We walk slowly and hesitantly, and this makes us feel restricted, less free. One person said to me: 'If I can't hike up the mountain, life isn't worth living'. Another found not being able to drive a car brought a feeling of great loss. It is important for old people to keep their sense of movement active as long as possible, despite the difficulties. Going for a short walk, dancing, eurythmy, exercise, all help to retain mobility of body as well as soul.

We are all eventually faced by limitations in our sense of movement, but we have a choice of attitudes towards this loss. We can be bitter and resentful, or we can strengthen our experience of inner freedom. When he spoke to the Harvard graduating class of 1978, the great Russian writer Alexander Solzhenitzyn suggested that some people interned in Soviet prison camps are spiritually freer than many people who are at liberty to move around our cities and towns. Such prisoners often manage to develop a sense of inner freedom even though they are deprived of communication, mobility, and material possessions. Developing our sense of *inner freedom* calls on us *to nurture our inner life*. If old people manage this, they can bear their infirmities without feeling cut off from the world.

When, as young children, we stand upright and look around at the world, we experience the **sense of balance** or **equilibrium**, which enables us to feel 'I am I'. We become aware of the individual spirit within us. This leads to a sense of *security* – of being in control of our bodies, of taking hold, of experiencing a degree of *independence* we did not have previously. The modern consumer mentality tends to encourage people to achieve security by surrounding themselves with things. But true security comes when we can let go of outer crutches. Old people who feel a *sense of inner balance* do not need to surround themselves with lots of possessions. They are *centered* within and no longer expect very much from the physical world.

The **sense of smell** informs us what is happening outside ourselves. When we pass a coffee factory or a bakery, the aroma enters our whole being and evokes a soul-response of pleasure, even awakening memories from earlier years. If the smell is unpleasant we want to recoil from it as if being attacked. Through the sense of smell *we are strongly attached to ourselves*. Can we transform this gesture so that instead of only having the world penetrate us, we can also enter into the world? *Compassion* can accomplish this in the soul realm, reaching out to meet people with love and understanding. As we age, our sense of smell grows weaker. We tend to withdraw into ourselves and become more anti-social. If we have developed a sense of compassion in earlier years, though, we will be less likely to take refuge within our shells, or strike out at those who try to come near.

When children develop the **sense of taste,** they enter into an even more intimate connection with the world, bringing what is outside right inside their physical bodies. The sense of taste often has a connection with the particular chemistry of a person's body. If someone is lacking in a particular mineral or vitamin, the body will crave a food that is rich in it, so as to restore the chemical balance between the substances of the outside and the inside world. Is the food too strong, too spicy, too bland? Here, too, as with the sense of smell, the transformation lies in reversing the direction of the process. Instead of just taking outside substance into ourselves, we need to strengthen our soul forces so that we move towards the outer world in a healing way. How do we improve the way we affect other people's lives? Are we too direct, too strong, too weak? Do we lack tact? The person who has developed *humility* and who shows interest in other people is transforming the sense of taste, and compensating for its loss. This transformation will serve us well in our later years.

Through the **sense of sight** the child absorbs his environment and learns to form judgements about it – people's actions, the flight of birds or the rustling leaves, the warm smile of his mother's face, all become inner experience. The eye is always trying to bring balance to what is seen, to complete what is incomplete. Even if a circle has part of its circumference missing, we will usually fill in the missing portion with our imagination. The eye adjusts to bright light, dim light and darkness. The soul-level equivalent of this activity is when we seek fulfillment through satisfaction and contentment. When we are satisfied with our lives, when as old people we can look back and *feel gratitude* for what our life has been, then we can be filled with *peace*. This is the transformation of the sense of sight.

The young child experiences temperature changes through the **sense of warmth.** Babies and young children are not able to hold warmth for very long and so get cold easily. They are much more sensitive to cold draughts and heat than adults and need protection from extremes of temperature. As old age approaches the body's ability to maintain warmth diminishes once more, and we may often see an older person putting on a sweater while those around are feeling quite comfortable. The immune system also becomes less resistant to microbes in the environment: old people are more susceptible to joint and back pains, stiff neck, bronchitis, and pneumonia. A warm blanket on their knees, a shawl or scarf around the neck and on the shoulders, and a hat, all help an older person retain warmth.

The body's sense of warmth and cold reflects and expresses a person's soul-state: we may either be too 'cold' to what is happening around us – in which case we have difficulty experiencing our own inner spirit, and are too separate from things; or too 'hot' – when we do not, perhaps, have enough of an outlet for our emotions, so they build up in the body and cause irritability and even violent reactions. There is then too little objectivity or distance from things. If the soul develops the right balance, neither too separate from nor too enthralled by the body, we can develop a harmonious sense of our inner self. The 'I' or higher ego actually penetrates and works through this sense of warmth, awakening a *wide range of feelings in our soul life.* When the 'I' penetrates our activity and experience, we begin to see our behavior from a more conscious perspective. Our *conscience* is awakened, so that we feel remorse and try to make up for our failings. Becoming conscious of the effects of our behavior enables us to take responsibility for it. But we also need to develop patience with ourselves and take a long view of our development through a whole lifetime. As we grow older, we can transform our diminishing sense of outer warmth by developing and practising a *warmth of heart,* which over many years can lead to qualities of *wisdom and reflection.*

Our **sense of hearing** allows us to receive information from outside through sounds, words and music; but to really *listen* we have to cultivate inner quiet as well. Do we really know how to listen or do we just fill every silence with our own thoughts? Can we hear the question occupying our friend's mind? Sound imposes itself on our consciousness and goes deep inside us – we cannot shut our ears, as we can our eyes, so in some ways we are at the mercy of the sounds we hear. How often are we distracted from concentrating or meditating because lines of a song, phrases of a conversation, or a melody keep streaming in? But we can practise resisting what impinges upon us in this way, by developing powers of focused concentration.

Children are very responsive to what they hear. Too much noise and harsh sounds can make a child nervous and irritable, frightened and jumpy. Soothing sounds, on the other hand, can calm a child, bring a feeling of peace, safety, and relaxation. As we age our hearing weakens on the one hand, and we feel cut off from the world. On the other, we become more sensitive to the sounds we do hear, and they affect our mood more strongly. As well as resisting intrusive sounds, old people can become very stubborn in their responses to what reaches them from the outer world. They feel more and more isolated and focused on themselves. Yet as we get older we can transform the sense of hearing, compensating for its gradual loss by trying to give full attention to what meets us, instead of resisting and shutting out the world. *Openness of mind* allows us to receive what is coming towards us.

The **sense for perceiving ideas (sense of thought)** allows us to go beyond outer hearing and grasp the meaning of things. We allow an idea to penetrate us and we become illumined by it. As we age, we tend to be less interested in new ideas, and feel more comfortable with those that are familiar. Our ability to grasp a new thought is weakened because our minds are less flexible than they previously were. We tend to live in the past, recalling the way things were in our youth or middle years. It is helpful for the elderly to be involved in artistic experience to keep their thinking mobile: painting with water colors, for example, so that colors flow freely into one another, helps to break down some of the hardening and rigidity. Joy at seeing colors blend and new forms arise, re-awakens our flexibility.

We transform the sense of thought by redirecting our soul forces: instead of trying to go outwards into the world around us to grasp ideas, we try to create *soul-silence* within. Then the world can speak and reveal itself to us. Out of this soul-silence we can develop new capacities of self-discipline, and interest in new ideas and people.

The **sense of ego** has to do with perceiving another's higher self. Can I *really* understand that my friends, family members and others are worthwhile individuals with their own goals, ideals, and values? Can I try to reach them on that level? Or do I only see their weaknesses, failings, problems? People in middle age usually enjoy meeting new people and getting to know them well. But as we grow older we often prefer the company of old friends and acquaintances. It is difficult to start making friends. Outside people are suspect: it can be surprising to hear the harsh way some old people speak about others. They don't seem to realize the hurt this can cause, and how much it can isolate them. But if old people express sincere interest in other people, they forget themselves for a time, and instead radiate warmth which attracts others to them. Old people like this seem able to bestow *blessing* on those around them, and are able to forgive those who may have injured them. In this act of *forgiveness* love streams from them, healing and nourishing those around them. Conscious development of the sense of ego creates forces for the future, whether in our present lives or after we cross the threshold to the spiritual world. It is wonderful to experience such people. When I have brought teenagers to help in retirement homes, I have seen how the warmth and generosity of some of the elderly evoked in them feelings of tenderness and caring, rather than the disdain or disregard which is nowadays often shown by young people towards those near death's door.

As we transform the twelve senses into new capacities we can prepare the way for a meaningful and blessed last stage of life.

Needs of old age

As we age we leave behind many of the superficialities of life and turn to the essentials. One woman said, 'I don't try to understand some of the things that I see in front of me. I just marvel at them. As the years pass, I read the statistics insurance companies publish about survival ages and rates. I think about the fact that I am now older than the average age for women to die. I wonder if I should spend my afternoon cleaning out my closet, writing my memoirs, or smelling a rose.'

We slow down and develop devotion to the small things in life. We notice the beauty of the opening flower, the song of a bird, the dew on the grass. At times the preciousness of such small things can be overwhelming.

We cherish our close friends, the quiet times of just being together. We share memories of adventures, of risks we took, of embarrassing moments. Our friends and family furnish us with lifelines to our own history as well as to what is going on in the world – which we are less and less actively involved in. We are different from our grandchildren's generation. Much of what they do seems strange. Yet the fact that the world has changed challenges us to be flexible and openminded. As Eda LeShan puts it so well, 'I have decided to go on growing until my last breath'.

In many ways, getting older is like returning to some of the insecurities of early adolescence. We no longer have control over our bodies. Things just don't work the way they used to. Remember when we stared in the mirror and felt helpless as we looked at the pimples breaking out on our face, or as we experienced our voices changing? This sense of helplessness comes back in our later years as we bump into tables, lose our balance or fall down the stairs. We used to be so sure-footed. Now we need to pay closer attention to the shoes we wear. The clothes that used to make us feel chic are now too constricting. We opt for something more comfortable, something that hides the bulges or flabbiness. Remember when we hid in sweatshirts or our fathers' long sleeved shirt to cover up our changing bodies! Here we are again, hiding our changes!

We need to know who we are. There isn't time to put this off for another decade or two. What is the landscape of our lives? Have we succeeded in living according to our values? Are we at peace? Every day becomes another opportunity to take stock and make changes. Life is precious.

I enjoy watching an older friend of ours when he and his buddy of over forty years return from taking their boat out on the Bay. Their eyes sparkle, their tanned faces beam. They seem like two boys after a wild adventure. But they're not boys. They're mature, wise and knowing men who have faced life-threatening illness, difficult family situations, and career successes and disappointments. In this case their great strength is their religious life, their devotion to their church and their devotion to their families.

Another friend, in his late seventies, continues to be active in his field of law, but what is most important to him is 'getting together with the boys' and giving advice to a friend or a friend's friend who is in difficulty.

One evening I had dinner in a café in San Francisco. Behind me in the next booth were three men in their late seventies. Their conversation was fascinating. I could hear certain patterns that seemed well-formed, phrases that were repeated over and over. It was clear these men were old friends. Their energetic conversation was in marked contrast to the effort it took them to put on their jackets and coats, scarves and hats. Their minds were vital and young, their bodies rigid and worn. The strength of their friendship was a solid bond.

A friend and I joke about one day sitting in rocking chairs, on the porch of a retirement home, continuing our discussions, observations and arguments. She and I giggle when we imagine being barely able to walk, yet still interrupting each other and stubbornly clinging to our own points of view.

Closely related to this issue of friendship is that of loneliness. By the time we have grown old, a spouse may have passed on, our children are likely to be busy with their own lives. We don't know when we are a burden and when we are welcome. We may not have a strong interest to keep us busy, and it's hard to develop one now. Perhaps we moved house so as to be closer to our children, but we don't have our old friends there. One active woman in her late sixties delivered 'meals on wheels' to people who were 'shut-ins', worked with delinquents in the local youth authority, and was always ready to do the book-keeping for our school fair. She was always busy knitting or crocheting something for her grandchildren, or to be given away. In her fifties and early sixties she had been an adventurous woman, but now she enjoyed quieter activities – especially being included in family and friends' get-togethers, where she would sit and listen to what was going on. She didn't comment as much as she used to. She was just grateful for being there. These years brought a softening to her otherwise assertive personality.

It is so easy to forget old people, especially if they have no family around them. They just seem to fade into the background. And that is exactly what is happening: they are fading out of life. Inviting them to our homes for a gathering, for tea, for a drive, can mean so much to them, especially if they have no family or close friends. To see the sparkle in their eyes makes the effort so worth while.

This problem was brought home to me on a visit to Ibiza, Spain. Because of its mild climate and beautiful scenery, people from the United Kingdom and northern Europe have chosen to retire there: many of them sold their homes in England to buy a house or apartment, leaving family and old friends behind. They adjusted to the new life, made new friends, enjoyed the fresh air and sunshine; and as long as both husband and wife were alive they seemed to cope. But when one partner dies, the other often goes into deep depression and cannot manage alone.

At a Symposium on *British Older People Residing in Spain,* held at Alicante, Spain, October 1992, representatives from many different non-profit groups working with the elderly, as well as those from the Spanish and British Social Services System, discussed the problems they were dealing with in the expatriate community. One of their concerns was funding for the care of the elderly. Most of those needing care had paid contributions to their country throughout their working life, but when they applied for help they were often just shunted from one agency or authority to another, and no one wanted to take responsibility.

Many of the organizations represented at this conference have developed useful programs to help the elderly; a Home Help program, for example, to prevent or delay admission to residential care by supporting the family unit. Day Care Centers have also been very helpful: the elderly can come for the day, have a substantial lunch, be given any help they need – whether practical or psychological – and have the opportunity to communicate and interact with other people.

'Tele-Help' is a telephone program to protect elderly who live on their own or are in some way incapacitated. It includes a check by phone every seven days and a volunteer's personal visit every other week.

In some programs, placing university students in the homes of elderly people has been successful. The older person and the student are often mutually supportive to one another.

In spite of such very helpful programs, which are now in operation all round the globe, a time often comes when older people are no longer able to live on their own, and there is no close family to take them in. It then becomes necessary to find them a place in one of the residential care facilities – which vary a great deal from place to place.

One of the difficulties in growing older is dealing with finances. People who have worked hard during their lives feel their pride and dignity injured by admitting they have insufficient money and can no longer cope. The high cost of residential homes leaves many elderly people and their families facing great financial difficulty.

62 to 65 is a common age for retirement. It is not a time to retire from life, though, but an opportunity to choose our activities freely, to explore and develop new interests and hobbies, preparing for this already in our late fifties and early sixties rather than waiting until retirement is upon us. People who are vital and alive in their sixties, seventies, and eighties are those for whom the retirement years are an opportunity for something new, for growth, for responding, for exploring, for enjoying the simple things in life. In these older years we are better at stepping back and observing what is needed in a situation. We may actually find that our skills are more in demand and that we are busier than we were before retirement.

Retirement is a wonderful time to do volunteer work in an area that has always interested us. We can choose how many hours to give, and do as much or as little as we like. It may be that by being freed from the pressure and daily schedule of a job, we can actually turn our attention to our life's real work. One friend retired when he was 65. Now he is busier than ever because he has a new kind of strength when he speaks. He has continued to grow, to change his mind about things he thought he had decided years ago; his matured perceptions have given a new power to whatever he does or says.

> People grow old only by deserting their ideals. Years may wrinkle the skin, but to give up interest wrinkles the soul... You are as young as your faith, as old as your doubt; as young as your self-confidence, as old as your fear; as young as your hope, as old as your despair. In the central place of every heart there is a recording chamber; so long as it receives messages of beauty, hope, cheer, and courage, so long are you young. When... your heart is covered with the snows of pessimism and the ice of cynicism, then and only then are you grown old – and then, indeed, as the ballad says, you just fade away.' 4

I know a number of elderly people who are doing very creative work in their 70s – writing, speaking, teaching. They have a lifetime of experience, insights and intuitions to share, yet no pressure of ambition.

When does old age begin?

What's the best way for us to still be needed, to be part of a living community and not spend our last years sitting in a waiting room hoping a visitor will arrive? There are as many possibilities as there are people. One eighty year-old mother has an apartment downstairs in her daughter's home. They have their separate spaces, their own lives, their own place for their friends and belongings. Yet from time to time 'Oma' can wander upstairs and have a cup of coffee with her daughter or grandchildren. Her memory isn't very good anymore, and in the evening we visited her she told us about the cable car in the Ruhr Valley more than a dozen times. But her shining face and sparkling eyes showed that she belonged. She had some tasks she did for the family, and she did them willingly and well.

Another elderly woman lived in a room off the kitchen in an apartment she shared with her daughter and granddaughter. It wasn't possible for her to live separately – few apartments were available and she needed some help getting around. Although she was a grumpy lady some of the time (and she had plenty of reason to be bitter), she too had a place where she belonged. She enjoyed the love of her teenage granddaughter, she sometimes ate her meals alone and other times she joined the family. But she had a home and a place in the world. Life was difficult, but the family worked through the problems together.

Being connected with people who mean something to them keeps older people active. Once the connection is broken, and conversation becomes 'visitor's talk', the whole relationship changes. Elderly people who are no longer really needed lose the strength to cope, enter upon a downward spiral of self-pity. Of course, there are many situations in which an older person needs to live away from home, in a facility where there is proper attention, 24-hour care and medical supervision. Someone I know tried to keep her beloved old uncle with her as long as possible. But when he had Alzheimer's disease and repeatedly got lost while she was out at work, she had to admit she could no longer have him at home. For a while she tried to hire someone to be in the house with him, but the cost was prohibitive. It was with a great feeling of loss that she had to take him to a special home. He died within a year. But his death freed her to move into the next stage of her own life. She had given her uncle, and her father whom she had also cared for in old age, a great gift of love and devotion. Now her children were at college and her elderly folk had passed over the threshold of death, she could pay attention to her own next step: she made a major career-change and moved her location as well.

It is all too easy when we look at a very old person to be misled by the wrinkled face, discolored hands and feet, and hunched body. We often see only their age instead of their perspective and wisdom, their humor and curiosity. I spent several days in a farmhouse in Latvia with 90 year-old 'Vecamamma' (grandmother of my friend). She was active and alert, up at 6 a.m. feeding her three piglets. About eight months of the year she lives in the farmhouse, but when winter closes in, she moves into town to the family apartment. Her daughter, who is herself retired, lives with her.

One morning Vecamamma walked down the lane, an old woman leaning on her cane, wisps of white hair showing beneath her kerchief. 'Where is Vecamamma going?' I asked. The answer was, 'She's going to the next farm to watch the Mexican soap opera, "Maria"'. Three times a week she ventures out of her old home, which she shared for decades with her husband, away from the wood stove she keeps so wonderfully warm, away from her piglets, her chickens, her garden, to interest herself in the adventures of a young woman eight or nine thousand miles away. When she returned she told us all about the latest episode of 'Maria'. I asked why she wanted to watch it, and she replied that it was interesting to experience someone else's problems:

'She was a simple girl with much sorrow. And she made herself successful and rich.' Vecamamma's eyes twinkled. Then she got back to the important work that had to be done.

Older people have so much to offer. Behind the grey or white hair, the bifocals, the limp, or the 'nodding off', is a world of wisdom and experience. How will we respond to the great tests of this phase? Our physical bodies test us, our minds test us, life is going on fast all around us and we've slowed down. Patience! But how wonderful it feels when someone says to us, 'Tell me about the way it was when...'

A man gave up his forty-year career as a minister to become a teacher for boys with discipline problems. He did that for seven or eight years; then after his wife died, he began traveling around the world. His perceptions were broadened by his experiences: his interest in the people he met, and his optimism about life were inspiring. He was trying to see what his next step in life would be. I came to know him because at the age of eighty he enrolled in a course I was teaching on Russian literature, since he was planning to visit Russia. Having him in the class was a refreshing and memorable experience – we all benefited from his insights into human behavior, his gentlemanly quality, his patience with the twenty year-olds, and his wisdom.

When I interviewed women in Europe I found that those who had been children or young adults during the Second World War had a different perspective from those who were born later. 'We were focusing our energies on survival. We didn't have the luxury of choosing goals or realizing our dreams. We just wanted to live and have something to eat.' They tended to expect less of each other and to have more appreciation for the small things of life.

Of course there are exceptions. There are men and women who have survived the Depression, war and other calamities, but who are bitter about their lives. They have difficulty accepting 'what life has dealt them'. A woman of seventy in Czechoslovakia said to me:

'What has my life been? First there were the Nazis, then the war, then the Communists. I know life is supposed to be better and freer now, but I'll never know it.'

This was in sharp contrast to the words of one of her contemporaries in Russia: 'I know my life has been hard. We have suffered terribly through the Second World War and the communist years. But I am so happy my daughter will have a chance for a different life. When I encouraged her to study English, it did not seem she would ever have had a chance to use it. But I had a feeling. Now she is able to teach and translate. She is meeting all kinds of people. Her life is filled with new possibilities.'

As we get older, many people who were important to us die. Our teachers, those who inspired us in our youth, our parents, uncles and aunts – all cross the threshold. As we find our own contemporaries leaving us – spouses, cousins, friends, sometimes our own children, we begin to carry them with us in thought, in prayer. Our relationship to the spiritual world changes. Sometimes we may feel the boundary between the living and dead becoming more transparent, and may have spiritual experiences connected with a close friend or family member who has died.

Sometimes it's even hard to remember who has died and who's still living. After a while it all becomes interwoven. One old woman would say in a loud voice, almost a shriek, 'Is that old Mabel still alive or is she dead?' She wasn't being disrespectful, but really didn't remember.

At this stage of life, then, we are looking back yet also looking forward. The pace seems slower, and there is more time for reflection. If we are vital and alive, interested in life, we continue to grow and stimulate those around us. But if we have not faced earlier crises, we get locked into certain recurring behaviour patterns, and can continue to harbour cynicism and bitterness about our unresolved hopes and dreams.

The grandparent years

In the following two passages – one poetry, the other prose – George Kane describes the death of his grandmother, bringing to life her interests, and the quality of his connection with her.

Elegy
for my Grandmother

The word gone out
points east and north,
a call from coast
to coast, and now
we gather a generation
poorer
for the last word.

A letter opened
too late and by the wrong
nails, or returned
to sender.

Your envelope given
over to other
hands, the words of your life spilled
onto the table, the ink
still stains our fingers.

George S. Kane [5]

As long as my Grandmother was alive, so were the things she kept around her. Out of a love for objects she had been a collector her whole life: stamps, postcards, coins, buttons from political campaigns, buttons for sewing, dolls, little porcelain mugs in the shape of faces, spoons, boxes of all kinds, plants. With the exception of the latter, everything she collected was inanimate, yet to her each was animate, each had a life of its own embodied in the story behind it – how it was found, in what musty little shop or obscure country auction it was bargained for, on what journey to what distant, exotic city.

All of us grandchildren had a special relationship to one or another of my grandmother's things. On the bottom shelf of the table in the living room was a glass candy dish whose lid we learned expertly to lift and set down without clinking. Somehow my grandmother's increasing deafness never seemed to impair her ability to hear that give-away sound of glass on glass.

At the table I would customarily sit so that I could look at the cabinet full of real Waterford crystal, porcelain cups and plates, a samovar, and various knick-knacks. Usually my eye would linger on an unusual-looking vase. It was a white hand, about eight inches tall, with the wrist serving as a base. Held delicately in the slender fingers (on two of which rings could be seen) was the actual vase – shaped like an egg, only slightly larger. I never saw flowers or anything else in the vase.

A few days after the stroke, my grandmother told my father, 'I want to go home. I want to be with my things'. A week later, just days before the end, she told him of her fear that her things would be scattered, dispersed, and the stories attaching them to her life would be lost as well. For her, that would mean the end of the lives of her things: instead of being mementoes of a journey, a person or a place, a time of her life, they would become, at best, like artifacts of a civilization dead because forgotten.

Keat's famous poem beginning, *This living hand, now warm and capable,* and ending, *I hold it towards you* does not describe the cool white physical fact of the vase I have taken with me, its hand reaching upward. But its coldness to the touch belies what I feel when I look upon those slim fingers, warmed and made capable by memory, just as memory is quickened by the form of the vase itself.

Its egg-shaped shell.
I have filled it with water.

George S. Kane [6]

When I became a grandmother I felt a joy rise up in me. Was it the thought that something of me would carry on into the future? Or the feeling that once again I would be connected with the shining eyes and trusting faces of little children? Or that without the day-in, day-out responsibility of being a parent, I could share the lives of little people who will be very special to me? Some of my friends feel old when they become grandparents. They picture grey-haired, bespectacled grandpa and grandma sitting in the living room reading the paper, lacking the strength or interest to be out in the world. But the grandparents of the Eighties and Nineties are a different breed. I look forward to going for walks, showing my grandchildren the beauties of nature, reading stories, baking cookies, going to museums, going camping, sitting quietly and watching ripples in a stream, laughing, playing with toy boats and trucks, knitting doll-clothes – all this and more. Does it interest me? It sure does. It's a wonderful balance to the fast-paced schedule of my work.

Becoming a grandparent brings images of my own grandparents and my children's grandparents. I spent many Sundays afternoons at my grandmother's house, with my family crowded around the kitchen table, eating smoked fish and sliced tomatoes, listening to the talk of the grownups, having special moments of conversation. My grandparents were divorced, so my times with my grandfather and his wife were quite different. He had moved to Florida and was constructing apartment houses. I was a teenager then, and enjoyed the conversations I had with him. He was a link to Europe, to another way of life as well as to an earlier time.

My own children did not have grandfathers, since both had died before they were born. But they had grandmothers, at least for a time. My mother lived with us for several years before she died, helping me with the children, cooking dinner when I had faculty meetings. We were able to provide a home for her, offer her support and companionship, and enrich our family life. Of course, this arrangement was not wholly trouble-free: there were misunderstandings and moments when I felt it was a burden to have her with us, but in retrospect I would not choose to have had it any other way.

There are many young people today, in my experience, who have little patience with family dynamics, who lack understanding for the fact that human relationships are complex, and who want only pleasure and personal reward. Relations with grandparents can counter this by helping us feel we are part of a chain of life, can enable our children to experience and express love and patience. Grandparents offer their grandchildren a special kind of love, one that thrives without strings attached.

There are many stories about the special relationships of grandparents and grandchildren – you can probably add your own. It can be one of the most significant relationships in a young person's life, offering stability in an uncertain world, especially when parents' relationships are foundering, or when other factors threaten, such as unemployment and drug-problems. So many grandparents have found themselves nurturing and raising their grandchildren that grandparent support-groups have sprung up all over America. I have experienced the strength and love of such grandparents in 'parent' conferences for children I have taught. A grandparent was often the rock, the solid ground upon which a child could depend. These grandparents had very likely imagined spending their later years in a quite different way, and were making a special sacrifice of love at a time when they would at last have had time to pursue other interests.

Old people and children – a special connection

Old age is related to earlier periods of life. The way we experienced our childhood has a bearing on how we live our older years. An expression I have heard quoted many times is 'The child who learns to pray in childhood learns to bless in old age'. I take this to mean that a child who experiences reverence towards the world, who is sensitive to the beautiful, the good, the true, who looks at the whole world of nature with thankfulness, who is moved in gratitude for the daily gifts of the earth, for peaceful sleep under the starry sky, for the feeling of protection and care, will carry deep moral forces into adulthood. Strength and beauty will radiate from the soul of such a person in old age, bestowing blessings on all around.

Mistakes made in childhood also resurface in old age. Physical disabilities and health problems may have their root in dietary deficiencies or habits imposed by parents in early years. Forced potty-training or making a child walk too early may have effects which go underground for decades, emerging as illness only in the late sixties or seventies.

Old people share with young children an interest in food, which is an expression of the way the soul connects with the body, with the earthly world. Children are fussy about their meals, interested in the textures and tastes of their food. Old people also like to talk about food, also become fussy and have particular likes and dislikes. When physical forces are diminishing in old age, food is a way we can maintain a connection to the body. It may seem that old people are just being difficult when they complain about the mashed potatoes being too lumpy or salty, or the green beans not being as tender as the ones they grew in their garden forty years ago. But this sensitivity to food can keep them connected to earthly life.

Being around children can help old people re-experience their own childhood years. Both young and old are closer to the spiritual world than people of other ages. The child is 'trailing clouds of glory from God who is our home' (Wordsworth), while the old person is once more moving closer to that same world beyond the physical. Neither young nor old are intensely involved with the cares and daily business of this earthly world; both are a little removed, carried by other forces than ambition and aims.

As an old person's immediate memory begins to weaken, the past comes closer. For old people, as for little children, a sequential sense of time starts to be replaced by a dreamlike collage of images. Old people who still have control over their thought-pictures can tell stories from their lives that have a fairytale quality. 'Once upon a time' or 'Long ago when I was young, before there were television sets or jet planes...' Children love hearing these stories over and over again, and are very lucky if they have grandparents who can tell such tales.

Some old people have strong memories of their adolescent experiences, and are often sensitive to the dreams of young people, recalling their own early loves or crushes. They may feel an urge to write their memoirs, reliving the idealism and adventures of their adolescent years. They can also sympathize with an adolescent's feelings of loneliness, since they, too, may be feeling the pain of loneliness, rejection, and misunderstanding. Like some teenagers they may withdraw into a safe place in order to protect themselves from pain. The withdrawal of old people is often a precursor to, and preparation for death. But old people, equally, may use their freedom from past responsibilities to devote themselves more intensely to life, to interests and challenges they have not previously had time for. Here again there is a similarity to the phase of adolescence, when teenagers can seek adventure without yet being burdened by responsibility and commitment. Both teenager and old person are moving into uncharted territory, the former filled with strength, exuberance, and life forces while the latter loses them. The teenager is coming down to the earth while the old person is being released from its hold. Both are open to the spirit in a way that is very hard to achieve in the intervening years, when we are more deeply involved in the business of life and its demands.

How couples face these years

Retirement alters the relationship of married couples. We are together more, probably, than we have ever been in our lives. Are we really prepared for it? So much depends now on a woman's ability to deal with having her husband around all day long. If they have had a traditional kind of arrangement in the past, he may now bring his 'expertise' from the business world into the house and start reorganizing her closets or kitchen. This can irritate her. It's much better if he has a workshop or study to organize. But at the same time he can't help noticing things he hasn't noticed before. So the couple has to work this out. It's not a big problem, but it can still cause some rough moments.

It's important for both partners to have their own interests, get out of the house alone for a while, as well as doing things together. New arrangements have to be made at home. How will the chores be divided now? Does he expect her to make him lunch every day? Is that her expectation as well?

As husband and wife are spending more time together in retirement they come to rely on each other much more. This may well be more of a change for the husband, if he has been active outside the home all these years. He comes to rely more on his wife's comments and advice than previously. Often the man becomes softer and milder during his time, but if he has not worked on transforming any negative feelings from the past, he may become a bitter old man instead.

Women also age in different ways. Some become very self-pitying, concerned only with their own aches and pains. Others are bitter about life. They nag at their husbands. Nothing is ever right. It takes patience on the husband's part to keep his sense of humor and balance. Sometimes you can see old couples who are very sharp and sarcastic towards each other, so that it seems surprising that they can stay together at all; but behind the apparent mutual irritation lies mutual need and a long history of tenderness and support as well as criticism and anger. Other women develop gentleness and quiet strength as they age, and are a beacon of light to their families and friends.

The dual autobiography of Will and Ariel Durant contains many wonderful reflections on their long marriage and working relationship. After forty years of marriage Will wrote,

> Everything here is conducive to quiet composition, but I find that your absence leads me to sit and mope for minutes at a time; I would be less distracted by your gossipy talks over the phone... Come as soon as you can.

> Today, October 31, 1970 is the fifty-seventh anniversary of our marriage. On November 5 I shall be eighty-five, not old enough to be a sage, but ready to finish this book and my life. I speak only for myself. Ariel is still in full vigor and spirit... My greatest blessing now is her continued presence. The sound of her slippered feet moving swiftly about the house is a comforting obligate assuring constancy. When she sits down to work or talk with me she is a bubbling fount of inspiration and insight... All in all I have had a happy life; I am grateful for it, and would be glad to live it again. [7]

Nena O'Neil was amazed and touched at the difference in old-fashioned marriage values from what seems to be a more recent experience. She reflected on a situation where her mother's health had held her father back from a trip he had been looking forward to for a long time:

> She doesn't have to say that she is sorry for holding him back. She expects his devotion and he gives it, not out of guilt, not out of duty, but out of love. She cared for him and devoted her life to the family through all their lean years, scrubbing and cooking and ironing in the normal way, now it is his turn to care for her. They have cared for and taken care of each other throughout their married lives, and now it is no different. This is simply what marriage is for them. The things done for one another, the love, are not accounts to be balanced daily; caring and love and obligations are evened out over the long years of a lifetime. [8]

My husband and I decided not to wait until retirement to realize our dreams of traveling around Europe for a year. We borrowed money, bought a camper van, and had a wonderful time. We mixed some business with pleasure, but mostly we were on our own, following our whims, enjoying the days without pressure of deadline and agenda. This year turned out to be a dress rehearsal for our future retirement. We learned what it was like for two very busy adults, whose days are normally packed with contacts with other people, to just spend time together day after day in a small space. We learned many new things about each other: areas where we irritated each other and needed more space, but also how much we enjoyed each other's presence.

One of the hardest aspects of the older years is how to cope with each other's failing health. In our forties already, my friends and I started to exchange stories of back problems, weakening eyesight, and sore muscles. In our fifties our bodies became even more regular topics of conversation. As people move into the sixties and seventies their health is a major concern. More and more as I imagine our life together in later years, I wonder who will take care of whom? How will illness and infirmity color that phase of life?

The long journey

This book has traced a path and journey through different phases of life and relationship. During our young adulthood we were dreamers spinning our dreams, wrapped in sentimentality and optimism. The shock of waking up rinsed the dream-dust from our eyes and prodded us into doubt and thoughtfulness. With some warning the path gradually descended into the valley of the shadow of death: we plumbed the abyss – some of us head-first, others reluctantly, fighting all the way. Once we hit the bottom – the place where the gravity of life and its demands exerted most pull upon us – we started to glimpse a spark of light shining out once more from the distance. Some of us were quick to see it and begin working our way towards it, while others stayed in the abyss a long time. Once we have emerged from the depths, we experience our lives in a different way, as richer, deeper, more precious than we realized. We recognize that we ourselves have to some extent caused our own and others' unhappiness; and, even more important, we begin to take the first steps towards changing things. We begin a pilgrimage to the essence of life, to the other, to the self. If we can learn to offer ourselves in communion with life, to partake in a true marriage of spirit, to renew our vow of marriage and fidelity to another person, we make our relationships real and joyous. We learn to accept both the scars and the laugh-lines, for we have helped create them. Our relationship then becomes a free gift and the ripening fruit of the harvest of our lives.

Faith in the other person is a reflection of faith in ourselves, through which we can acknowledge and grasp the key of our own development. Each step in our metamorphosis – as in all nature, in all the universe – is the bud of our new beginning, the step towards transcendence. Being emerges on a new level; love and growth become one. We have been weaving the tapestry, filling in the weft with color and texture. As we look back we can see its design and begin to understand the meaning of our sojourn here on earth.

Natasha feels the most important thing at this time is to have someone to live for. Being a mother and having a child is what has brought her through. Now the family all live together.

'What is most important is that I am needed. If I weren't needed I would feel my life has no purpose. I couldn't live without my family. I also realized I can't live without my work even though it is exhausting.' Natasha still gives private lessons at the Academy and in her home. She has trained a whole generation of opera singers.

'I myself need so little. I think I have everything. A good job. I feel free and confident in my work. I have a good family. I love them all. I am ready to give everything and help in whatever way they need me. I still feel life is going up. I feel more and more confident every day.' With a mischievous smile, Natasha says, 'The most "terrible" thing is that I don't feel I am almost 69. That is probably very bad.'

Claudia has been experiencing terrible loneliness during this time. Sometimes she bubbles over with the excitement of her travels, her children, her grandchildren. But other times she says she does not see any prospect in life.

'People don't realize how lonely I am. I give an impression of being happy and contented. Sometimes I go for weeks without speaking to people.' Lately, though, there has been a change. Claudia started to find and get in contact with old friends who were of special importance to her in high school and university, during her years in the United States and in her early training years in the hospital. This has proved to be very rewarding. She says, 'There is a mutual special caring and no holding back of emotion, an understanding of one's needs and thoughts. Even though the contact is mostly by telephone, or by sharing a sudden thought via fax, it is the awareness of a friend's existence that gives me the great feeling of not being alone at all!'

Claudia feels very grateful for the strong guidance in life she received from her parents. They raised their children to take responsibility, to know how to behave in all kinds of situations. 'It was out of the question not to do our work properly.' But her parents were different from many other people of their generation, allowing their children to discuss things, to have differing opinions, to feel confident about meeting people of all kinds. 'The warmth and love given to me by my parents have embraced me all my life.' Her parents were very cultured people who enjoyed music, art, literature, drama. Their home was filled with warmth and wisdom. 'I have never been seriously involved with religion. After the war for a while I went to church. I think I am a Christian person in my profession and out of it, but not through a church. I'm down to earth. There's not much of philosophy in me.'

Being needed is still very important to Claudia. She can give time to her daughters now, and is happy to help them through any difficulties.

'Because my profession was very important to me, there should never be the question that I didn't care for my children. I cared for them from my heart. I hope they never had the feeling "Mama is not here". They always knew where I was. But now I want very much to be included in their lives. But I almost never call on my children. I mostly wait till they call on me. They are so absorbed with their work and family. If Bianca would be nearer I would see more of her than any of the others. Today she likes to have me around. Marius and Leon are counting on their "mamma-grandma" to be part of their lives, and little Laura smiles at my touch.

'Now that I have the time I would like to go to the theater again. When I studied journalism and literature in my youth, every week I went to the movies, theater, and concerts. I would like to travel again, but it would be nicer to do this with another person.

'I would, for instance, like to help at a restaurant. I would like to volunteer there so I would be in contact with people. It's not that I need to occupy my time. I'm still working, but it is at home. Every week dozens of files arrive by special post for me to evaluate medically for insurance companies. I've got plenty to do, and this is how I pay for traveling and for this apartment. But I am by myself much of the time. If I'm old and can't travel, I hope to keep this apartment so I don't have to move. Yet I would like to move near one of the children and grandchildren. I have a nice income but it is being eaten up by this apartment which is so pleasant, airy, and quiet. I can do all kinds of secretarial work. I can give speeches, write them. I have tried several times to approach people for a job, but they say I'm over-qualified. I said, "That's my problem, not yours". Well, let's see what happens when the French restaurant opens up nearby. I might try again. What I really dream of is to open a café or a garden center with my son-in-law. That I would like very much.

'When I look at the younger generation I can only tell men and women to really learn something to occupy themselves and keep them when difficulties and sickness come. They should also have something to be themselves. The women always should be free of the support of men. Marriage is not a necessity. Something could change in their relationships and they need to be able to take care of themselves. But I would also like to tell young women they should adjust more to men. If I mention this to young women today, they say, "Why should I do this? I don't think so. He can do the same". This is so interesting. I have been raised in a patriarchal surrounding. I have never felt anything against patriarchy, but Fritz and Rolf took too much advantage of it. They would never pack a suitcase or pick up their underwear. Ridiculous! But I feel men have to adjust to women today more than is necessary. Women should be careful. What is happening is not the right way. At least this is so in Germany. I think woman should be equal to men, but they should still be women. I always did better than many men in my profession, but I always stayed a woman. This is why I got this far. I never wanted to show them up. I would like to have a relationship with a man – but I don't like it that a man, at least here in Germany in older days, wants me to be his property. I do not want that. I just want to be myself. I can very easily adjust, of course I can. I like to belong to someone, but I don't want a person close to me to tell me what I have to do, in his opinion. I cannot stand this. Young Arne was the one and only man in my life who even backed me up with this and let me change the words, "I must" to "I want".

'My love for my profession has brought me over all the difficulties in my life. This has been the most important thing. When people ask me what I would have done if I had had to choose between work and family, I always say it would have been my work. But I was very fortunate to have both. Through this I could overcome difficulties and was prepared to care for my children without help.'

Pavel looks back on his life from the vantage point of 69 years of age. He says he is always searching.

'What am I searching for? I am looking for the way how to live better. This is not only for financial betterment, but to be active and involved in life. I have not a single moment of regret about getting older. I am very happy that as I am getting older, I am also getting wiser, smarter, and more mature. I have more understanding for problems. Do you think I'm old? I'm not. What drives me? I have always had a feeling I need to be involved at the center of activity. The biggest satisfaction is when I see my daughter thinking things through and making decisions. Then I realize I would have done it that way also.

'A relationship with a woman is very special. You create your own criteria for what you really need and want in a woman. You decide whom you should connect your life to, and then you must work it out yourself. No one can give you advice about who is the right woman for you. I've had the opportunity to meet smart women during my life. Some women have a beautiful outer appearance, but inside there is nothing. I'm sorry to say it in this way, but I hate foolish women.

'Of course, I've made mistakes in my life. Each person is a personality, and a personality is not simple, but complex.' Considering that 98 per cent of the men born in 1924 in the former Soviet Union were killed in the war, Pavel is grateful for his life and his experiences.

Rosalind reflects on the changes that came about through her new career in consulting.

'In old age you gain more confidence because you see you are really able to do things. I didn't carry my dummy image into my consulting work, but my intelligence was of a different kind. I had an intelligence others didn't have. All kinds of capacities are needed in a situation. I found an area in which I could work.'

Rosalind will be 70 this year. She wavers between staying home and continuing her extensive traveling. 'The work is important... is it really important? I don't think one ever feels totally secure. But you don't make progress unless you use your will and make things happen. I do everything. I can take care of myself, that I know.

'I've been remarkably healthy all my life. I get tired. The doctor said I used up so much of my life force caring for Jeff. I get tense sometimes and that affects my digestion. I had a bout of skin cancer. But in general I feel strong. I had to overlook much in my health because I was needed to take care of Jeff. I also think my good upbringing, healthy food, strong rhythm helped me. The Puritan work ethic also drove me. My ideals of becoming a singer when I was younger fed me, it kept me younger than my friends, it fulfilled so much. I believe all these things helped.

'My health is good. My father died of a heart attack, my mother of a cerebral hemorrhage. It's important to study your illnesses as you get older. We lose faith in doctors because we think they are gods. We have to guard against giving up because we think we're going to die. You have to make peace with dying. My mother helped us so much with this. She said, "Don't mourn when I die. Go on with your lives. Wear bright colors". I don't see death as an incredible separation. Yet we're all susceptible to last-minute clinging.

'When I say all these things consciously I sound brave, but I know a person can really slip in moments.

'What's becoming more important as you get older? I'm concerned about people. People talk to me. I don't know if I'm helping or not. I feel the only way to meet old age is to study it and learn some tricks. It is like worrying what to do with teenagers – there are troublesome teenagers and troublesome old people. How can I not be that way?

'I'm not anxious to live to an old age. I don't think there's good luck in outliving all your contemporaries. It's important to keep connected with the new generation. I'm so fortunate with my children and grandchildren, even though I know the time will come when they won't have time for me.

'I love being a grandmother. I'm an educator and I'm so interested in seeing my grandchildren going through the stages. Now I can see so much more than when I was a teacher.

'I want to help. I want to save the world. By teaching teachers I am helping children so things can get better. It's really an ideal you just don't stop having.

'I don't bear resentment towards people. I see so many people who aren't needed. I'm grateful people seem to need me and value me.

'My older sister and I joke a lot about old age. You recognize things happen and you have to accept things. I tend to avoid the doctor. It's alright to get older, but it takes me longer to do things. A lot of things don't get done around the house, in the garden. However, I just can't put the concentration into getting it done.

'At home I like to wake up early, study, preserve these morning hours before I am interrupted. My life is full. I feel grateful.'

Patrick reflects on these years.

'As I approach the end of my life, I ask myself, "What means a great deal to me now? What have I done that gratifies me?" It is the closeness of my family, the love for one another and for the spiritual life. This pleases me. I'm not a millionaire, I'm rather an insignificant person. I hope I'm doing good as a deacon. I feel God graced Martha and me with five children. We've had our ups and downs with them, but I do feel proud about our family, their spiritual sensitivity, their values, the way they teach their children spiritual values, but most of all the love between the family members

I cry easily. Goodness affects me. It chokes me up. I hope I can continue to do good in my life with my family, and in business. Since I retired I have been working part-time. I have a different attitude now than when I was a young man making a buck. I feel good if I can help people, give them good service and get the lowest price for them. I've had my low points. I've had bosses I didn't like working with. I knew I didn't have the intestinal drive that goes with theater.

When I am around people who do not have a spiritual life I can only try to give a good example. Young people come here to our house, sit and talk, and we have been there for them. I was told during my deacon's training, "You grow where you're planted". I have many family and business connections. The best I can offer is attention, listening, and responding. Hopefully that will be a helpful response. I think I have a talent for public speaking, and I love to preach. It is a responsibility to preach the word of the Lord. It gives me satisfaction. I keep on learning and I admire others and am open to them. The door doesn't close. It just keeps opening.'

Only five of the twelve friends we have been following are over 63.

For Natasha, what is most important is to have someone to live for, to be needed, to feel life has purpose.

For Claudia, it is most important to be needed. She looks back at her life with gratitude for her profession and her family. She has gained a sense of joy and connection by rediscovering friends from many years ago. This link to other people through sharing feelings and thoughts has relieved her of the loneliness she had previously felt.

Pavel is always searching for ways of living better. He is happy about getting older, and is still growing and maturing. He is grateful for family and for the gift of life itself.

Rosalind realizes that the gifts age brings can be helpful to others. She still wants to change the world and serve other people. She loves children and especially her grandchildren. She still sees herself as an educator and is interested in the development of children and in how life is changing for them. She feels the fullness of life and hopes she can grow old gracefully. She is grateful for her life and has made peace with dying.

Patrick is grateful for the closeness of his family, for their love for one another, and for the spiritual life. He is touched by goodness and the grace of God. He is glad he can use his life to serve people, to be an example, and to be there in times of need.

This chapter can close with Patrick's words, 'The door keeps opening.'

9

The Threshold of Death

Let me not pray to be sheltered from
dangers but to be fearless in facing
them.
Let me not beg for the stilling of
my pain but for the heart to conquer it.
Let me not look for allies in life's
battlefield but to my own strength.
Let me not crave in anxious fear to
be saved but hope for the patience to
win my freedom.
Grant me that I may not be a
coward, feeling your mercy in my
success alone; but let me find the grasp
of your hand in my failure.

Rabindranath Tagore [1]

Facing our own death is the most intimate and individual experience; different people develop different relationships to it: 'I want to die quickly', 'I hope I will have time to say goodbye to my loved ones', 'I want to die painlessly', 'I want to die at home with my family and with as clear a consciousness as possible'. As much as we may think about and speak about our own death, we cannot anticipate how we will actually feel about it when the time comes. Our society has been unwilling to face the issue of death – we don't grow up seeing it as part of the natural cycle of life, but as something to be feared, ignored, whispered about or denied.

When my older brother was killed in a car accident, I was five years old. The adults did not pay attention to me – no one tried to explain or help me understand where Joey was. So I was left to my own dramatic imagination. I was not included in the funeral, and was not helped to say goodbye to him in any way. From then on, into adulthood, death was a very frightening subject. As I grew older I experienced the deaths of my grandparents and then my parents. The first time I realized death did not have to be 'brushed under the carpet' was when I attended the funeral of a child who had died of leukemia. This was a very sad and painful death, but the family had kept the child at home, surrounding him with love right up to the end. I had never before had a chance to look at a dead body. At this funeral the casket was open and I did look, though I was scared. Friends of the family played music; they read poetry, and spoke about the child's life. Some of the anxiety I had carried with me for many years was healed through this experience.

When my mother died, I felt she gave me a great gift. In the five days of her dying, she passed through clear stages, from complete consciousness to unconsciousness. I experienced her gradual departure – leaving her body behind, but somehow remaining with me. I began to experience the reality of something I had previously only thought intellectually: that there is more to death than dying. The 'I' goes on, in a different form. We are not *only* our bodies. Our spirits prevail. From the time of her passing I carried special gratitude for that experience.

My friend and colleague Nancy Poer has enriched my life through the work she has done with dying people. Nancy has called attention to the two thresholds of birth and death, in both of which our relationship to the spiritual world is altered. She has cared for many people during their last weeks, and taught others of us to do so as well, giving members of our community the opportunity to experience the phases of the dying process, and to support the dying person with dignity and respect. She has also alerted us to subtle changes that take place after death as the spirit leaves the body, and how we can assist that process through playing music or reading to someone who has died.

Since then I have experienced the death of a number of friends, have sat in the room with the dead body, have read favorite passages to the person whose body was lying there surrounded with flowers. I have also made peace with several people whose untimely death came before we had resolved difficulties in our relationship. In my twenties I would have thought these experiences strange, grotesque, even bizarre. Because of my own fears, the idea of being alone in the room with a dead person was pretty threatening. But as I learned to think about the dead person in a loving, supportive way, my emotions passed from fear to respect and love.

In the past year I have experienced a number of deaths of friends. Each experience is unique and calls forth a different response. The recent death of Ben was one of the most beautiful examples a dying person can give to others. His death was completely unexpected. He was diagnosed with cancer on Thanksgiving Day and died on Christmas Eve. When he realized the seriousness of his situation he spoke plainly to his wife and two daughters: 'Tell me how you feel. Tell me what you are afraid of. I'm not afraid.' They talked throughout the night, sharing their deepest feelings and fears, and reaffirming their love for each other. When a psychologist came to the hospital to see how Ben was doing, Ben's strength and courage helped this man, who was himself facing some uncertain and potentially frightening health problems. Through tears the psychologist said: 'I came to help you, but you are helping me.' Ben's funeral was a celebration of a life that was filled with love, with interest in people, with joy. All his friends and family will miss him greatly, yet we can feel he will be present with us.

The death of a teenage friend, Kirsten, was a different experience. She had no time to say goodbye. She and her closest friend were killed when their car hit ice and angled into a large trailer truck. Her mother, Linda, who was in the car, miraculously escaped death although she was very seriously injured. She also could not say goodbye, for while the funeral was going on she was in a critical condition – her skull and pelvis broken, her eyes destroyed beyond repair, and other very serious injuries. But her daughter's classmates came to the hospital and sang to her. Friends became her 'eyes' and described to her all that had happened at the funeral.

I have been amazed at Linda's strength. Only two years ago she experienced the death of her husband, Paul, and now she has lost her only child. She recently told me, 'I need to find out why I am living. I know I have work to do.' Deaths like those of Kirsten and her friend, Nina, leave us with many questions and mysteries. Why now? What is the meaning of it?

Dr. Elisabeth Kübler-Ross made a major contribution to our understanding of the human being through her work with the dying[2]. She felt that trying to protect people from knowledge of their imminent death was just stripping them of their integrity. As she worked with terminally ill patients, she discovered specific stages in the process of acknowledging and coming to terms with death, which dying people both need and want to work through. These stages are also present in those who grieve over the death of someone else. The stages she observed are: Disbelief, Denial, Bargaining, Anger, Depression, Acceptance, and Moving On.

Many counsellors have since modified these steps in the light of their own experience, but I see them as still relevant and insightful. Let us examine these stages:

1. Disbelief
2. Denial
3. Making bargains
4. Anger
5. Despair and depression
6. Resignation and acceptance
7. Moving on.

Facing death

1. Disbelief – when we are told we are dying we first react with shock and disbelief: it cannot be true, we are only imagining it. We become numb and cannot really fathom that this is happening to *us*. It is as though we do not really take in the words.

2. Denial. We try to convince ourselves that this is not happening, to pretend it is only a dream, a hallucination. We act hopeful, as if we had never heard the news.

3. Bargaining. We don't yet take in the finality of the situation. Instead we attempt to regain control in a situation where we feel helpless. We may say (to God, to the doctor, to anyone): 'If you would only... give me six more months, then I'll accept my death. I just want to see my grandchild born.' Or '...see another sunrise, another spring day, another Christmas, finish the project I'm working on...' Each of us has our own list. 'If you let me have what I want, then I'll give you what you want.' We try to make a deal.

4. Anger. Now our emotions become active, and we are furious. The pain is intense. We can lash out at the people we most love, at the doctors, at God. This is unfair. Why me?

5. Depression, withdrawal, emptiness, and isolation. Once we realize the bargain isn't going to work, we withdraw and want nothing to do with other people. Now we feel helpless, at the edge of a big black hole, alone in the world, filled with self-pity. Our behavior becomes erratic and at times we are unreachable.

6. Acceptance of reality. Gradually we begin to feel differently. Now we want to understand what is happening to us. We need to discuss it. It is a time to set things straight, to heal relationships that need healing, and say goodbye. Equanimity is the mood of this stage.

7. Moving on. Here we develop the courage to face whatever comes. We give ourselves over to a greater reality. Peace, love and happiness often shine from the eyes of someone who has reached this stage.

> Those who have the strength and the love to sit with a dying patient in the silence that goes beyond words will know that this moment is neither frightening nor painful, but a peaceful cessation of the functioning of the body. Watching the peaceful death of a human being reminds us of a falling star; one of the million lights in a vast sky that flares up for a brief moment only to disappear into the endless night forever. To be a therapist to a dying patient makes us aware of the uniqueness of each individual in this vast sea of humanity. It makes us aware of our finiteness, our limited lifespan. Few of us live beyond our three score and ten years and yet in that brief time most of us create and live a unique biography and weave ourselves into the fabric of human history.[3]

The loss of a beloved

When we lose a person very close to us, we go through the same stages as in facing our own death. If the dying person can go through the process described above, this also helps close friends and relatives. Often the courage and peace of a dying person gives comfort to those left behind. If the death is sudden, however, those who were close to the person who has died go through the stages afterwards.

1. Disbelief. 'This is isn't happening. It's a dream. It can't really be happening'. Maria's husband suddenly died. It was so unexpected one could almost believe it hadn't happened. But she couldn't escape the reality. She went through the preparations for the funeral with very varied moods, from hysterical sobbing to euphoria, as the family worked out how to acknowledge their father's passing. She kept herself together in an amazing way. The funeral, although very painful, also had a celebratory aspect to it – a celebration of his life, a celebration of the gift of life itself. She smiled through the tears and faced the hundreds of friends who came to bid their farewell to this man who had been their friend or supervisor. It was only after her children and everyone else had gone home, and the bills had been paid, that she fell apart.

2. Denial. 'This person has not really died'. We wake up in the night convinced it cannot have happened. Then this changes into guilt. 'Why couldn't I have helped more while he or she was alive?' We search for answers by blaming ourselves. This is a state of intense anxiety.

In this state we mourn for our loss while at the same time denying what has happened. Rosemary Clooney, an American singer, describes this experience: 4 She had campaigned tirelessly for Robert Kennedy in his bid for the presidency in 1968. She was with him the night he was assassinated, and afterwards was seized by the delusion that he wasn't really dead. This experience, compounded by a recent divorce, culminated in an emotional state that led her to hospitalization and eight years of analysis and group therapy before being able to start her life again.

3. Bargaining. In facing the death of a loved one, we feel a loss of control. We then begin to try to bargain our way out of the situation. 'Just let papa live until his daughter's wedding.' 'Let little Freddie live till Christmas.' 'If you let this person live, I'll do such and such.'

Our desperation gets more intense as the loved-one gets sicker and sicker. A parent watching a child facing death may try to bargain his/her own life in exchange for the child's.

4. Anger. Why was my sweet child taken away? Why has my husband/wife left me? Why is *my* child ill? Why am I the one singled out? Why did he drive on that slippery road? This anger can be directed at other people who have nothing to do with us, but have not suffered such loss. Why are they spared? Why can't the doctors do more? I hate everyone.

5. Depression. This is a dangerous stage: people trying to face the loss of a partner or child may harm themselves. The day-in day-out support of a few trusted friends is essential. The more a regular routine can be followed – a regular rhythm, if possible, of eating, sleeping, going to work – the better chance there is of working through depression. Time is the greatest healer. At such periods, though, we should not try to make any major life decisions.

6. Acceptance. The feeling of total helplessness can become the ground for acceptance. Once we realize fully that there is no way out, something new begins to happen. One day we wake up and feel we are on the other side of a chasm. The sunrise is beautiful. The day is lovely. And for the first time in a long time, we look forward to what the day will bring. We have been shut out of life for a long time, and now we rejoin the human community. Gradually we begin to see friends again, go out for an evening, accept dinner invitations. There is nothing we can do to alter what has happened, so we make the best of it.

7. Moving on. This is a time of re-evaluation and rebuilding. We step back out into the world, often with an increased capacity for making decisions. We feel as though we are getting renewed strength from somewhere beyond ourselves. Our personal experiences show us new possibilities of helping other people.

When I was in Vilnius, Lithuania, I discussed ageing and death with some friends. Here are some excerpts from that conversation.

'In October my father died. I had very little contact for the past five or six years. I had very bad memories of him and his terrible times with alcoholism. He came to me in my dreams and asked me to pray for him. He asked me to put a figure of Christ on the cross on his grave. During this year I have felt terrible loneliness after his death. I never realized what a great loss his death would be.'

'After my husband's father's death twelve days ago, I had a strong experience. The day before, on May 12, I participated in a funeral of a child killed in a politically motivated explosion. As I sat in the funeral of my father-in-law, I felt such strong emotions. I wished I could give everything to have one moment together with the person who had died. I want to forget all my complaining now about difficulties. There are many more serious things than that. I knew these things earlier but I only came to know this when these terrible things happened.'

'I lost my mother a few weeks ago. It was a terrible blow. Who am I sorry for? My mother? Myself? Most of all I miss her warmth. She was the one who waited for me, cherished me.'

'It makes you think what bad things you might have done to the person. You tell yourself to do only good things from now on.'

'After my mother's death I realized I had the moral obligation to help someone else. Now I can express the right words to a person in need. Earlier such words were only a formality.'

'I feel wiser after my mother's death. My husband's native village is 70 kilometers from Vilnius. My native village is 100 kilometers away. My parents lived with my brother; my sister was nearby. Vidis' mother was a widow and lived alone. Now I am thinking, was I wise and clever to spend all weekends and summers with Vidis' mother instead of my own? I was always thinking my mother would understand and would forgive me. Now I am thinking, was I right? My mother cried whenever I came. She was so glad to see me.'

'The relationship between parents and children goes deep in the heart. They are very close. Something is broken now.'

'Our parents spoil us. They help us. My mother cleaned floors in the evening to earn money so she could afford to stay home during the day and take care of my children. The aim of one's life is to help one's children. This is not a matter of sacrifice. This is what life is all about. Mothers for us are like God.'

'I returned from the hospital yesterday after a week's stay for an operation. I realized as my mother wept when she said goodbye to me when I was wheeled away for the operation, that the tears of mothers are diamonds.'

After this conversation I wondered whether similar things would have been said in New York, Chicago or Sacramento. Perhaps we would have had similar feelings but expressed them differently.

Whichever society we live in, we still have to readjust our lives after the death of a beloved. But death also helps us plumb the depths of life.

Epilogue

So each of us has gathered the particular threads of our family, our gender, our nationality, our birth-order and our relationships over time. Our 'I' has much to work with as it transforms what has been given, to create a tapestry that truly reflects what lives beyond space and time.

There is more to the tapestry – there are the threads of temperament, soul attitude, and ways of seeing, points of view – but those will have to wait for another book...

I celebrate the tapestry of life: the colors, textures, the loom on which it is woven, the ideas that create the design, and the one who weaves. The tapestry of our own life interweaves with many other tapestries to form a great, grand fabric of actions, feelings, thoughts, relationships and being.

As I pull together the threads of this book, I wish to especially celebrate the lives of two friends who died during the time this book was in the process of being published. Kirsten Bergh died at age 17 in a car accident in Harlemville, New York. She was a poet, an artist, an enthusiastic student of life, and she had capacities of insight and understanding far beyond her years. Nurtured by her loving parents, Linda and Paul, Kirsten was a wholesome young woman who would have contributed positively and selflessly to society. When I last saw Kirsten, a year before the fatal accident, we discussed her feelings about her father's untimely death. The poem she wrote for him could now stand for her too.

For you, Papa

I thought I heard your footsteps
running towards me
disturbing the stones.
But when I opened my eyes,
I saw it was only the waves,
Pulling and swirling like hands.
I thought I felt your smile,
Warm and loving upon my face.
But when I opened my eyes,
I saw it was only the sun,
Beaming at me from across the water.

I thought I heard you
Whisper my name.
But when I opened my eyes,
I realized it was only the wind
Playing in my hair.

I thought I felt you
softly kiss my cheek.
But when I opened my eyes,
I saw it was only a leaf
Caressing me with gentle strokes.

And then I felt your love
In and all around me.
Powerful yet gentle like the waves,
Warm and shining like the sun,
soft yet strong like the wind,
Tender and alive like the leaves.
And I didn't even have
to open my eyes.
I knew you were there.

Kirsten Bergh

Ben Skonieczny's life was longer. He died at age 57 after living a full and rich life of spiritual devotion, human warmth and humor. Ben died on Christmas Eve just before many friends arrived to sing carols around his bedside. He was very much 'out there' in the world – as a priest who left the priesthood to marry Kay, as a loving father, a fundraiser, a public relations director, a long-range planner and an avid sports fan. He was a man who was not embarrassed to cry when he spoke about his love for his family and for God. I knew Ben as a very active parent and Board member when I taught his daughters at the Sacramento Waldorf School, and I knew him as a friend. When Ben made the decision to leave his job at Kaiser Permanente Medical Association, he wrote his own 'mission statement' as part of preparing for the next step in his professional life. He kept it in his daily planner. When he wrote it he had no sense death would come so soon:

> Happy am I that my spirit is centered in a healthy and strong body. I have been chosen by the Lord but my choosing comes from within. I respond to my choices freely and with courage. I look for the Lord at all times on my journey. I am not afraid to ask, seek and even knock. I believe that my prayers are always answered for my own good.

> I treasure Kay, my lifelong companion, above all others. I love Amy and Molly unconditionally without expectation. Those whom I love I hold in my heart, and no one or no thing can wrestle them away from me.

> I am positive, filled with humor-walking, with a smile and a twinkle in my eyes, without fear because I have seen the Lord.

> I am convinced that all things are working together for my good. For this I am forever thankful.

Ben Skonieczny
31 October 1994

An epilogue closes the curtain on a drama. The audience rise out of their seats and leave the theater, to ruminate on the play and ponder whether it sheds any light on their own lives. I hope, dear reader, that you have found much to reflect on, and that this book will have helped awaken new insights and understanding. As parting words, please join me in the Jewish toast to life: *Le Chaim.*

Notes

Dedication

1. Kane, George Stuart, by permission.

Prologue

1. Song of the Sky Loom (Tewa) Native American; in Padilla, Stan: *Chants and Prayers. A Native American Circle of Beauty*, The Book Publishing Co., Summertown, TN, 1995, p.72.
2. *An Interrupted Life; The Diaries of Ettie Hillesum, 1941-43*. Ettie Hillesum, Washington Square Press, N.Y. 1981, pp.247-8

SECTION I: TIME, GROWTH, AND HUMAN RELATIONSHIPS

Chapter I: The Human Being in the World of Matter, Soul, and Spirit

1. E.E. Cummings, 'i thank you God for most this amazing day.' *E. E. Cummings, Complete Poems, 1904-1962*, Ed. George Firmage, Liveright, NY, 1991. p.663
2. Steiner, Rudolf; *Occult Science;* Rudolf Steiner Pub. Co., London, 1949. p.46
3. O'Neil, George and Gisela; *The Human Life*, Mercury Press, New York, 1984.

Chapter II: The Alchemy of Relationships

1. Gibran, Kahlil; *The Prophet;* Alfred A. Knopf, New York, 1991; pp.18-19.
2. Kane, George, 'April', given to me by G. Kane from his private collection.
3. Pritzker, Linda: *In Answer to My Daughter's Questions,* from Bar Mitzvah prayer book assembled by Rosemary Pritzker, 1997.
4. Pritzker, Rosemary: *My Mother,* from Bar Mitzvah prayer book, assembled by Rosemary Pritzker, 1997.

5. Bellah, Robert, *Habits of the Heart, Individualism and Commitment in American Life,* Harper & Row, New York, 1985.
6. Buonadonna, Paola, 'The European' newspaper, 21-24, January, 1993, p.10.
7. Schwartz, Judith; *The Mother Puzzle, A New Generation Reckons with Motherhood;* Simon & Schuster, New York, 1993, p.21.
8. König, Karl, *Brothers and Sisters,* Rudolf Steiner Pub., Blauvelt, N.Y., 1991, p.87.
9. Ibid, p.38.
10. Ibid, p.39.
11. Ibid, p.64.
12. Ibid, p.76.
13. Ibid, p.86.
14. Gibran, K. *The Prophet,* pp.64-65.
15. Badinter, Elizabeth, *A French Perspective On War of the Sexes,* reviewed by Mary Blume, International Herald Tribune, Feb. 15, 1993. p.14.
16. Gilligan, Carol, *In a Different Voice, Psychological Theory and Women's Development,* Harvard University Press, Cambridge, Mass, 1982.
17. Trives, Eleanor, *The Open Door,* Arts et Métiers Graphiques, France, 1967, p.81.
18. Steiner, Rudolf, *Karmic Relationships, Vol. 1-VIII.,* Rudolf Steiner Press, London. 1977.
19. May, Rollo, *Man's Search for Himself,* The New American Library Inc., New York, 1967, p.206.
20. Steiner, Rudolf, *The Spiritual Beings in the Heavenly Bodies and in the Kingdoms of Nature,* R. Steiner Publishing, London, 1951, pp.51-52.
21. St. Paul, Corinthians,
22. Baumer, Franklin L., *Modern European Thought, Continuity and Change in Ideas, 1600-1950.,* Macmillan Publishing, New York, 1977, p.20.
23. Easton, Stewart, *Rudolf Steiner, Herald of a New Epoch,* Anthroposophic Press, Spring Valley, N.Y., 1980. p.105.

Chapter III. Life Cycles and Human Rhythms

1. 'Ecclesiastes', The Pocket Bible, Washington Square Press, New York, 1970, p.278.
2. Erikson, Erik quoted by Sheehy, Gail, *Passages, from Predictable Crises of Adult Life*, A Bantam Book, E.P. Dutton, Pub., New York, 1977. p.20.
3. Ibid, p.21.
4. Ibid, p.22.
5. Trives, p.29

SECTION II. THE PHASES OF LIFE

Introduction

1. Jung, C.J., Letter of 1947, Vol. 1 483 quoted in *Word and Image*, Edited by Aniela Jaffe. Bollingen Series XCVII: 2, Princeton University Press, 1979, p.213.
2. Sheehy, G., *Passages*, p.30.

Chapter 1: Life is Ahead of Us: 21-28

1. Lindbergh, Anne Morrow, *Gift from the Sea*, Pantheon Books Inc., 1955, pp.46-7.
2. Brothers, Dr. Joyce, *The Brothers System for Liberated Love and Marriage*, P.H. Weyden, 1972, pp.253-256.
3. Ibid, p.253.
4. Ibid, pp.255-6.
5. Levinson, Daniel, *The Seasons of a Man's Life*, Knopf, New York, 1978.
6. Goldberg, Herb, *The Hazards of Being Male, Surviving the Myth of Masculine Privilege*, A Signet Book, New American LIbrary, New York, 1977.
7. Schwartz, pp.32-33.

Chapter 2: Trying to Organize Our Lives: 28-35

1. Levinson, p. 57.
2. Jung, C. J., *Word and Image*, Ed. Jaffe, p. 56.
3. Brothers, Chapter 5.

4. Audre Lourde, *Interview With the Muse*, Broadside Press, Detroit 1977, p.79

Chapter 3: Plumbing the Depths: 35-42
1. Sheehy, G. *Passages,* p.350.
2. Sheehy, G. *New Passages, Mapping Your Life Across Time,* Ballantine Books, New York. 1995.
3. Brothers, p.66.
4. Ibid, p.63.
5. Hauser, Hephzibah Menuhin, *Interview with the Muse, Remarkable Women Speak on Creativity and Power,* Moon Books, Ca., distributed by Random House.
6. Treichler, Rudolf, *Soulways,* Hawthorn Press, Stroud, England, 1989, pp.57-58.

Chapter 4: Making our Mark on Life: 42-49
1. Edwards, Anne, Sonya, *The Life of Countess Tolstoy,* Simon & Schuster, New York, 1981, p. 216.
2. Ibid, p.217.

Chapter 5: The Menopausal Years: A new beginning
1. Krames, 'Hormone Replacement Therapy,' communication, p.4
2. Struben, Dr. Friedhelm, 'Die Wechseljahre im Leben der Frau, Ein körperlicher and seelischer Wendepunkt', Südwest (orally translated for me by Renate Bastian, Bielefeld, Germany.)
3. Krames, p.8.
4. Sheehy, *The Silent Passage, Menopause,* Pocket Books, Simon & Schuster, 1993, New York. p.222.
5. Ibid, p. 95.
6. Ibid, p. 237.

Chapter 6: Reassessing Our Priorities: 49-56
1. Brothers, Dr. J., *What Every Woman Ought to Know about Love and Marriage,* p.74.
2. Ibid, p.74
3. Ibid, p.57, citing Mead.

Chapter 8: Looking Back, a Different Perspective, Beyond 63
1. Sarton, May, *After the Stroke, A Journal*, W. W. Norton & Co., New York, p.124/125)
2. LeShan, Eda, *Oh To Be 50 Again! On Being Too Old for a Life Crisis*, Pocket Books, Simon & Schuster, New York, 1986) p.xiii-xiv.
3. Glas, Norbert, *Fulfillment of Old Age*, Anthroposophic Press, N.Y., 1970, p.14.
4. Manchester, William, *American Caesar, Douglas MacArthur*, 1880 -1964, Little, Brown, & C., Boston, 1978, p.702.
5. Kane, George, 'Elegy for my Grandmother' from manuscript.
6. Kane, George, from manuscript.
7. Durant, Will and Ariel, *A Dual Autobiography*, Simon & Schuster, New York, 1977, p.305.
8. Nena O' Neil, *The Marriage Premise*, personal recollections.

Chapter 9: The Threshold of Death
1. Tagore, Rabindranath, 'Fruit-Gathering' quoted in Kübler-Ross, Elisabeth, *On Death and Dying*, Macmillan, New York, 1969. p.1. She quotes from *Collected Poems and Plays of Rabindranath Tagore*, MacMillan, New York, 1944.
2. Kübler-Ross, Elisabeth, *On Death and Dying*, Macmillan, New York, 1969.
3. Ibid, p.276.
4. Winer, Deborah Grace, 'Rosemary Clooney, A Happy Singer Again', International Herald Tribune, p.18, Feb. 6-7, 1993.

Epilogue
'For You, Papa', Kirsten Bergh (private collection)
'Mission Statement' by Benedict Skonieczny

Bibliography

Tapestries

Badinter, Elizabeth, *A French Perspective On War of the Sexes,* reviewed by Mary Blume, International Herald Tribune, Feb. 15, 1993.

Bateson, Mary Catherine, *Composing a Life, Life as a work in progress,* Plume, Penguin, 1990.

Baumer, Franklin L., *Modern European Thought, Continuity and Change in Ideas,* 1600-1950., Macmillan Publishing, New York, 1977

Bellah, Robert, et al, *Habits of the Heart, Individualism and Commitment in American Life,* Harper & Row, New York, 1985.

Brothers, Dr. Joyce, *The Brothers System for Liberated Love and Marriage,* P.H. Weyden, 1972

Brothers, Dr. Joyce, *What Every Woman Ought to Know about Love & Marriage,* Ballantine, 1985.

Buonadonna, Paola, The European newspaper, 21-24, January, 1993.

Cummings, E.E., 'i thank you God for most this amazing day.' *E. E. Cummings, Complete Poems, 1904-1962,* Ed. George Firmage, Liveright, N.Y., 1991, p. 663.

Durant, Will and Ariel, *A Dual Autobiography,* Simon & Schuster, New York, 1977

Easton, Stewart, *Rudolf Steiner, Herald of a New Epoch,* Anthroposophic Press, Spring Valley, N.Y, 1980.

'Ecclesiastes', The Pocket Bible, Washington Square Press, New York, 1970.

Edwards, Anne, Sonya, *The Life of Countess Tolstoy,* Simon & Schuster, New York, 1981

Erikson, Erik H., *Identity and the Life Cycle,* W.W. Norton, New York, 1980.

Frankl, Victor, *Man's Search for Meaning*, Washington Square Press, New York, 1963.

Freud, Sigmund, *Civilization and its Discontents*, Doubleday, 1958.

Gibran, Kahlil, *The Prophet;* Alfred A. Knopf, New York, 1991;

Gilligan, Carol, *In a Different Voice, Psychological Theory and Women's Development*, Harvard University Press, Cambridge, Mass, 1982.

Glas, Norbert, *Fulfilment of Old Age*, Anthroposophic Press, N.Y., 1970.

Goldberg, Herb, T*he Hazards of Being Male, Surviving the Myth of Masculine Privilege*, A Signet Book, New American Library, New York, 1977.

Hauser, Hephzibah Menuhin, *Interview with the Muse, Remarkable Women Speak on Creativity and Power*, Moon Books, Ca., distributed by Random House.

Jaffe, Aniela, ed. *Word and Image*, Bollingen Series XCVII: 2, Princeton University Press, 1979.

Kane, George Stuart, 'Elegy for my Grandmother' from manuscript.

Kane, George Stuart, 'April'.

Kane, George Stuart, 'Lullaby for Benjamin'.

Koenig, Karl, *Brothers and Sisters*, a study in child psychology, Rudolf Steiner Publications, Blauvelt, New York, 1991.

Krames, Hormone Replacement Therapy, communication

Kübler-Ross, Elisabeth, *On Death and Dying*, Macmillan, New York, 1969

LeHaye, Tim, *Understanding the Male Temperament*, Revell Co., N.J., 1977.

Leman, Dr Kevin, *The Birth Order Book, Growing up First Born*, A Dell Book, 1989

LeShan, Eda, O*h To Be 50 Again! On Being Too Old for a Life Crisis*, Pocket Books, Simon & Schuster, New York, 1986.

Levinson, Daniel, *The Seasons of a Man's Life*, Knopf, N.Y., 1978.

Lindbergh, Anne Morrow, *Gift from the Sea*, Pantheon Books Inc., 1955.

Manchester, William, *American Caesar, Douglas MacArthur, 1880 - 1964*, Little, Brown, Boston, 1978.

Matthews, M., Schaefer, S., and Staley, B., *Ariadne's Awakening, Taking up the threads of consciousness,* Hawthorn Press, Stroud, England, 1986.

May, Rollo, *Man's Search for Himself,* The New American Library Inc., New York, 1967.

Nelsen, Jane, *Understanding, Eliminating Stress and Finding Serenity in Life and Relationships,* Prima Publishing, Rocklin, Ca., 1988.

New Testament, St. Paul, Corintheans,

O'Neil, George and Gisela; *The Human Life;* Mercury Press, N.Y., 1994.

O' Neil, Nena, T*he Marriage Premise,* personal recollections.

Ornstein, Robert E., *The Psychology of Consciousness,* Penguin, New York, 1975.

Progoff, Ira, *Depth Psychology and Modern Man,* McGraw Hill, New York, 1959.

Rochlin, Gregory, *The Masculine Dilemma,* Little, Brown & Co., Boston, 1980.

Roosevelt, R. and Lofas, J., *Living in Step,* McGraw Hill, New York, 1977.

Schwartz, Judith; *The Mother Puzzle, A New Generation Reckons with Motherhood;* Simon & Schuster, New York, 1993.

Sheehy, Gail, *Passages, Predictable Crises of Adult Life,* A Bantam Book, E.P. Dutton, Pub., New York, 1977.

Sheehy, Gail, *The Silent Passage, Menopause,* Pocket Books, Simon & Schuster, New York, 1993.

Song of the Sky Loom (Tewa) Native American; in Bartlett, John, Bartlett's Familiar Quotations; Little,Brown & Co., Boston, 1980.

Staley, Betty, *Between Form and Freedom, A practical guide to the teenage years,* Hawthorn Press, Stroud, England, 1988.

Steiner, Rudolf, *Karmic Relationships,Vol. 1-VIII.,* Rudolf Steiner Press, London, 1977.

Steiner, Rudolf, *Occult Science;* Rudolf Steiner Pub. Co., London, 1949.

Steiner, Rudolf, *The Spiritual Beings in the Heavenly Bodies and in the Kingdoms of Nature,* R. Steiner Publishing, London, 1951.

Struben, Dr. Friedhelm, Die Wechseljahre im Leben der Frau, Ein Körperlicher and seelischer Wendepunkt, Südwest (orally translated for me by Renate Bastian, Bielefeld, Germany.)

Tanner, Ira J., The *Gift of Grief, Healing the Pain of Everyday Loss,* Hawthorn Books, New York, 1976,

Treichler, Rudolf; *Soulways,* Hawthorn Press, Stroud, England, 1989.

Trives, Eleanor, T*he Open Door,* Arts et Métiers Graphiques, France, 1967.

Tapestries, Weaving Life's Journey

Batdorf, Carol, *Spirit Quest, The Initiation of an Indian Boy,* Hancock House, Surrey, B.C., 1990.

Baumer, Franklin L. ed., *Main Currents of Western Thought,* 4th ed. Yale University Press, New Haven, 1978.

Bittleston, Adam, *Meditative Prayers for Today,* Floris, Edinburgh, 1993

Carson, Rachel, *The Sense of Wonder,* Harper & Row, New York, 1956.

Easton, Stewart, *Herald of a New Epoch,* Anthroposophic Press, New York, 1980.

Elliot, George, McFarland, Philip, Granite, Harvey, and Peckham, Morse, ed. *Themes in World Literature,* Houghton Mifflin, Boston, 1970.

Emerson, Ralph Waldo, 'Nature' in Nature, Addresses and Lectures, A.L. Burt Co.

Hiebel, Frederick, *The Gospel of Hellas, The Mission of Ancient Greece and the Advent of Christ,* Anthroposophic Press, New York, 1949.

Kübler-Ross, Elisabeth, *On Death and Dying,* Macmillan, New York, 1969.

Lievegoed, Bernard, *The Battle for the Soul,* Hawthorn Press, Stroud, England, 1993.

Lievegoed, Bernard, *Man on the Threshold, The challenge of inner development,* Hawthorn Press, Stroud, England, 1985.

Lund, Knud Asbjorn, *Understanding Our Fellow Men,* privately printed, date given, out of print.

Moore, Robert, *The Warrior Within, Accessing the Knight in the Male Psyche,* Avon Books, New York, 1992.

Morrow, Honore Willsie, *The Father of Little Women,* Little, Brown & Co., Boston, 1927.

Pearson, Carol S., *Awakening the Heroes Within, Twelve archetypes to help us find ourselves and transform our world,* Harper, San Francisco, 1991.

Pearson, Carol S., *The Hero Within, Six Archetypes We Live By*

Pelikan, Wilhelm, *The Secrets of Metals,* Anthroposophic Press, Spring Valley, New York, 1973.

Progoff, Ira, *Depth Psychology and Modern Man,* McGraw Hill, New York, 1959.

Shakespeare, William, *The complete works of,* Clark &Wright, ed., Doubleday, New York, Vol. II

Smart, Ninian, *The Religious Experience of Mankind,* Charles Scribner's, New York, 1960

Steiner, Rudolf, *Human and Cosmic Thought,* Rudolf Steiner Press, Great Britain, 1991.

Steiner, Rudolf, *Occult Science;* Rudolf Steiner Pub. Co., London, 1949.

Steiner, *Intuitive Thinking as a Spiritual Path,* Anthroposophical Press, New York, 1995.

Stibbe, Max, *Seven Soul Types,* Hawthorn Press, Stroud, 1992.

Tolstoy, Leo, *the Works of,* Walter J. Black, Inc., New York, 1928.

Wieland, Friedemann, *The Journey of the Hero,* Prism, Great Britain, 1991.

Other books from Hawthorn Press

Soulmaking
How the four temperaments, the seven soul types and twelve points of view help personal growth

Betty Staley

Our lives unfold in complex patterns. Our relationships, unique personalities, the time and place in which we are born, all contribute to our life's design. In *Tapestries,* the threads of developing relationships, life phases, passages, gender, family birth order and nationality are charted. *Soulmaking* goes further.

Here, you are invited to explore the many aspects that make up our personalities. The four temperaments, the seven soul types and the twelve points of view are the raw materials for soulmaking, for spiritual development.

The four temperaments unlock the secrets of living in time. The opportunities to transform our temperaments in adult life are described. Understanding and integrating the seven soul types helps deepen life's journey. Exploring the twelve points of view leads to a greater understanding of other people. The development through the life phases of the temperaments, soul types and points of view is outlined.

Finally, the quest for spiritual development is addressed: facing and making changes; paths of transformation, living in balance and the stages of the development of love.

This accessible companion book to *Tapestries* is a unique guide to the ways of the human soul.

Publication: Spring 1998

Lifeways series

Between Form and Freedom
A practical Guide to the Teenage Years
Betty Staley

Betty Staley offers a wealth of insights about teenagers, providing a compassionate, intelligent and intuitive look into the minds of children and adolescents. She explores the nature of adolescence and looks at teenagers' needs in relation to family, friends, schools, love and the arts. Issues concerning stress, depression, drug and alcohol abuse and eating disorders are included.

210 x 135mm; 288pp; sewn limp binding; illustrations; ISBN 1 869 890 08 6.

To a Different Drumbeat
A Practical Guide to parenting Children with Special Needs
Patricia Clarke, Holly Kofsky, Jenni Lauruol

This is a book which aims to enhance the process of caring for children who have special needs. Based on personal experience, it is about growing, about loving and about help in this specific area of parenting.

248 x 190mm; 240pp; sewn limp binding; ISBN 1 869 890 09 4.

The Incarnating Child
Joan Salter

'Our birth is but a sleep and a forgetting.' Joan Salter picks up Wordsworth's theme and follows the soul life of tiny babies into childhood and adolescence. A specialist in maternal and child care, she addresses physical, spiritual and psychological development as well as environmental factors.

210 x 135mm; 224pp; sewn limp binding; ISBN 1 869 890 04 3.

Parenting for a Healthy Future
Dotty T. Coplen

Here is a commonsense approach to parenting. Dotty Coplen helps parents gain a deeper understanding of parenting children from both a practical and holistic, spiritual perspective.

216 x 138mm; 126pp; ISBN 1 869 890 53 1.

More Lifeways
Sharing Parenting and Family Paths
Edited by Patti Smith and Signe Schaefer

Foreword by Gudrun Davy and Bons Voors

Fired by continuing Lifeways workshops over the last fourteen years, *More Lifeways* offers parents further space for support and encouragement. Signe Schaefer and Patti Smith invite you to a conversation about things to question, areas to explore and things to agree with.

215 x 138mm; 352pp; paperback; photos; ISBN 1 869 890 86 8.

Raising a Son
Parents and the Making of a Healthy Man
Don Elium and Jeanne Elium

Many parents feel frustrated and confused by the behaviour of their sons and are in need of some practical guidance. *Raising a Son* offers just that: advice on firm but fair discipline that will encourage the awakening of your son's healthy soul.

216 x 138mm; 256pp; sewn limp binding; ISBN 1 869 890 76 0.

Thresholds
Near Life Experiences
Gabriel Bradford Millar

People returning to life from serious accidents sometimes describe their near-death experiences. This book gathers together accounts and revelations experienced in the midst of temporal life.

216 x 138mm; 192pp; paperback; photographs; ISBN 1 869 890 68 X.

Voyage through Childhood into the Adult World
A Guide to Child Development
Eva A. Frommer

A deep concern for the uniqueness of each individual child permeates this book which offers practical solutions to the challenges of raising a child at each stage of his or her development.

216 x 138mm; 152pp; paperback; ISBN 1 869 890 59 0.

Social Ecology Series

Battle for the Soul
The Working together of Three Great Leaders of Humanity
Bernard Lievegoed

Bernard Lievegoed died in 1992. He considered this work to be his final testament. The book was dictated to Jelle van der Meulen, who says of Lievegoed: 'I believe he saw the spiritual battlefield on which in the near future the great spiritual battle will be fought between the powers of materialism and those of esoteric Christianity. For that is what the book is about: the things which are to come.'
238 x 135mm; 144pp; ISBN 1 869 890 64 7.

Enterprise of the Future
Moral Intuition in Leadership and Organisational Development
Friedrich Glasl

Friedrich Glasl describes the future of the modern organisation as a unique challenge for personal development. Every organisation, whether a business, a school, a hospital or a voluntary organisation, will have to develop closer relationships with the key stakeholders in its environment – its suppliers, customers, investors and local communities. Our consciousness as managers needs to expand beyond the boundaries of the organisation to work associatively with the community of enterprises with whom we 'share a destiny'.
216 x 138mm; 160pp; paperback; ISBN 1 869 890 79 5.

Eye of the Needle
His Life and Working encounter with Anthroposophy
Bernard Lievegoed

An exploration of Lievegoed's personal life, and his wide-ranging interests.
216 x 138mm; 112pp; paperback; ISBN 1 869 890 50 7.

How to Transform Thinking Feeling and Willing
Jorgen Smit

This book aims to enable readers to follow a meditative path leading to deepening insight and awareness of themselves and the world around them. Includes practical exercises.
210 x 135mm; 64pp; sewn limp binding; ISBN 1 869 890 17 5.

In Place of the Self
How Drugs Work
Ron Dunselman

Why are heroin, alcohol, hashish, ecstasy, LSD and tobacco attractive substances for so many people? Why are unusual, visionary and 'high' experiences so important to users? These and other questions about drugs and drug use are answered comprehensively in this book.

216 x 138mm; 304pp; hardback; ISBN 1 869 890 72 8.

Man on the Threshold
Bernard Lievegoed

Concerned with inner training and development, this book takes an anthroposophical approach to its theme.

210 x 135mm; 224pp; paperback; ISBN 0 950 706 26 4.

More Precious than Light
How Dialogue can Transform Relationships and Build Community
Margeet van den Brink

Introduction by Russell Evans

Profound changes are taking place as people awaken to the experience of the Christ in themselves, and in significant human encounter. As tradition fades, individual and social paths of growth emerge. These are helped by building relationships through helping conversations, through dialogue, through exploring heartfelt questions which can lead to liberating personal insights.

216 x 138mm; 160pp; paperback; colour cover; ISBN 1 869 890 83 3.

New Eyes for Plants
A Workbook for Observing and Drawing Plants
Margaret Colquhoun and Axel Ewald

Here are fresh ways of seeing and understanding nature with a vivid journey through the seasons. Detailed facts are interwoven with artistic insights, showing how science can be practiced as an art, and how art can help science through using the holistic approach of Goethe. Readers are helped by simple observation exercises, by inspiring illustrations which make a companion guide to plant growth around the year. A wide variety of common plants are beautifully drawn, from seed and bud to flower and fruit.

270 x 210mm; 208pp; colour cover; fully illustrated; ISBN 1 869 890 85 X

Rudolf Steiner
An Introduction
Rudi Lissau

This portrait of Steiner's life and work aims to point out the relevance of his activities to contemporary social and human concerns.

210 x 135mm; 192pp; sewn limp binding; ISBN 1 869 890 06 8

Seven Soul Types
Max Stibbe

A description of the seven soul types of man, indicating the most significant inner and outer characteristics of each. Recognition of soul types can be invaluable in communicating with others in social, educational or therapeutic situations.

216 x 138mm; 128pp; sewn limp binding; ISBN 1 869 890 44 2.

Soulways
Development, Crises and Illnesses of the Soul
Rudolf Treichler

Soulways offers insights into personal growth through the phases and turning points of human life. A profound picture of child and adult development is given, including the developmental needs, potentials and questions of each stage. Drawing on his work as a psychiatrist, Treichler also explores the developmental disorders of soul life – addictions, neuroses, hysteria, anorexia and schizophrenia.

210 x 135mm; 320pp; paperback; ISBN 1 869 890 13 2.

Vision in Action
Working with Soul and Spirit in Small Organisations
Christopher Schaefer, Tÿno Voors

This second edition has been thoroughly revised and updated for the 1990's. *Vision in Action* is a workbook for those involved in social creation – in collaborative deeds that can influence the social environment in which we live and where our ideas and actions can matter. This is a user-friendly, hands-on guide for developing healthy small organizations – organizations with soul and spirit.

235 x 152mm; 256pp; paperback; ISBN 1 869 890 88 4.

The Twelve Senses
Albert Soesman

The author provides a lively look at the senses – not merely the normal five senses, but twelve: touch, life, self-movement, balance, smell, taste, vision, temperature, hearing, language, the conceptual and the ego senses.

210 x 135mm; 176pp; perfect limp bound; ISBN 1 869 890 22 1.

Biography and self-development series

Springboard
Women's Development Workbook
Liz Willis and Jenny Daisley

Winner for the BBC of the 1989 Lady Platt Award for Innovative Equal Opportunities Training and the 1993 National Training Award.

A practical self-development workbook, designed for women to work through themselves or in a training group, *Springboard's* reputation continues to grow. Packed with exercises and real-life examples, it is down-to-earth, positive and practical. The workbook is used by many large companies in their training schemes for women, and has sold over 90,000 copies to date.

297 x 210mm; 288pp; sewn limp binding; illustrations, cartoons; UK 3rd edition; ISBN 1 869 890 69 8.

Workways: Seven Stars to steer by
Biography Workbook for Building a more Enterprising Life
Kees Locher and Jos van der Brug

This biography workbook helps you consider your working life, and make more conscious choices, at a time of great change in our 'workways'. Background readings, thirty seven exercises and creative activities are carefully structured for individuals or self-help groups.

297 x 210mm; 352pp approx; sewn limp binding; ISBN 1 869 890 89 2.

Orders

If you have difficulties ordering from a bookshop, you can order direct from:

Hawthorn Press
1 Lansdown Lane
Stroud
Gloucestershire
GL5 1BJ
United Kingdom

Fax: (01453) 751138   Tel: (01453) 757040

All Hawthorn Press titles are available in North America from:

Anthroposophic Press
3390 Route 9
Hudson
NY 12534

Fax: (518) 851 2047   Tel: (518) 851 2054

Lifeways Conferences take place every summer at Emerson College. If you are interested in a summer week with workshops, activities, music and adventure for men, women and children, contact:

Summer Course Secretary
Emerson College
Forest Row
E. Sussex
RH18 5JX